WE WILL
END THE CONFLICT
NOW

VICTORY OVER PORNOGRAPHY
FROM THE PERSPECTIVE OF
A RECOVERED ADDICT AND HIS WIFE

WE WILL
END THE CONFLICT
NOW

WILLIAM A. AND MAE DONNE

PLAIN SIGHT PUBLISHING
AN IMPRINT OF CEDAR FORT, INC.
SPRINGVILLE, UTAH

ISBN 13: 978-1-4621-1214-2

Published by Plain Sight Publishing, an imprint of Cedar Fort, Inc.,
2373 W. 700 S., Springville, UT 84663
Distributed by Cedar Fort, Inc., www.cedarfort.com

LIBRARY OF CONGRESS CATALOGING-IN-PUBLICATION DATA

Donne, William A., 1979-, author.
 We will end the conflict now : victory over pornography from the perspective of a recovered addict and his wife / William A. and Mae Donn.
   pages cm
 Includes bibliographical references and index.
  ISBN 978-1-4621-1214-2 (alk. paper)
 1. Pornography--Religious aspects--Christianity. 2. Sex addiction--Religious aspects--Christianity.
I. Donne, Mae, author. II. Title.

  BV4597.6.D66 2013
  241'.667--dc23

            2013003273

Cover design by Angela D. Olsen
Cover design © 2013 by Lyle Mortimer
Edited by Whitney Lindsley, Melissa Caldwell, and Katrina Corbridge
Typeset by Whitney Lindsley

Printed in the United States of America

10 9 8 7 6 5 4 3 2 1

To those seeking and celebrating victories

Praise for

WE WILL END
THE CONFLICT NOW

"Your book . . . has helped me make positive changes in my life. . . . Whenever I find myself stressing over old issues I turn to your book and it helps me remember perspective. Thank you so much."

—*Michael B.*

"This book . . . was another extremely effective tool in overcoming the hurt and pain that is brought on with pornography addictions. Not only did William help myself, a spouse of a recovering addict, [but he] also had a tremendous impact on my husband. I know this is a battle that is not easily overcome and needs a special type of focus and attention. Most people look at this subject as too taboo to discuss. But William helped make this something comfortable to talk about and also gave us the tools we need to start beating this addiction."

—*Barbara H.*

"Without this book, I can say I don't know if my wife and I would be where we are today. Thank you!"

—*Aaron L.*

"I am not trying to discount our time with a counselor, but we . . . did not make nearly as much headway as we did with this book and in talking with both of you. It was so helpful to hear from someone who actually knows what we have been through"

—*Kelly P.*

"As I read . . . *We Will End the Conflict Now*, I found myself continually nodding my head in agreement with each principle and story I read. It was the perfect tool I needed as I began my road to recovery. The way William defines addiction and how to overcome it . . . is absolutely inspiring. Reading about his personal experiences and the techniques he used to help overcome his addiction has given me the hope and courage to do the same."

—*Rick D.*

"At times I wonder if it will ever stop feeling so overwhelming to live in this world. But you give us hope! Thanks again."

—*Brendan R.*

"I am finding the book to be very helpful in my journey of recovery. Thank you so much. It has brought me closer with the twelve-year-old girl I had left behind—me. It has also helped me with my husband. You and your wife are definitely heaven sent."

—*Trista C.*

"Thanks so much for all your help! My fiancé finally went to his first meeting this morning! I am so proud of him!"

—*Allyson M.*

CONTENTS

Authors' Notes . . . . *xiii*

Introduction *1*

Preface: Road Map to Recovery *5*

Part 1: What Is Addiction?

  1. Defining Addiction 11

  2. Self-Reliance and Self-Mastery 17

  3. On Defining Pornography 21

  4. Is Pornography Adulterous? 25

  5. Where Do You Draw the Line? 29

  6. On Masturbation 43

  7. On the Role of Curiosity 47

  8. The Real Cause of Addiction 51

  9. On Love and Reversing the Trend 59

  10. On Our Initial Reaction 65

  11. On Communication 73

  12. When Desire Is Lacking 77

  13. On Marriage and Divorce 83

  14. Signs of the Times in Theory 89

  15. On Evil and Hate 99

Part 2: Ending the Conflict

  16. Threshold of Victory 107

  17. How Long Will It Take? 111

18. Building a Foundation:
*The Four Corners of
Accountability and Recovery* 119

19. An Analogy on Complete Repentance 135

20. Tell the Whole Truth. 139

21. It's the Little Things That Count 147

22. On Sacrifice 153

23. U-Turn Sacrifices 157

24. Filling the Voids. 163

25. Control Your Surroundings. 167

26. Ever Watchful 175

27. Building for Championships 181

28. Protecting Your Victory, an Analogy 183

29. Is the Conflict Over?. 185

30. Purpose in Suffering. 187

31. Preface to My Wife's Section: On Healing 191

Part 3: From Wife to Wife

32. You Are Not Alone 197

33. The Toll of Addiction 201

34. Seven Steps of Grieving 211

35. Mourning a Loss 215

36. Moving Forward 231

37. Hope and Healing. 241

38. The End Is Just the Beginning:
A Final Word from Husband and Wife. 251

A Final Note to Parents and Leaders. 255

Notes. 259

About the Authors 267

"UNDER HIS PILLOW LAY THE NEW TESTAMENT. HE took it up mechanically. The book belonged to Sonia; it was the one from which she had read the raising of Lazarus to him. At first he was afraid that she would worry him about religion, would talk about the gospel and pester him with books. But to his great surprise she had not once approached the subject and had not even offered him the Testament. He had asked her for it himself not long before his illness and she brought him the book without a word. Till now he had not opened it.

"He did not open it now, but one thought passed through his mind: 'Can her convictions not be mine now? Her feelings, her aspirations at least. . . .

"She too had been greatly agitated that day, and at night she was taken ill again. But she was so happy—and so unexpectedly happy—that she was almost frightened of her happiness. Seven years, *only* seven years! At the beginning of their happiness at some moments they were both ready to look on those seven years as though they were seven days. He did not know that the new life would not be given him for nothing, that he would have to pay dearly for it, that it would cost him great striving, great suffering.

"But that is the beginning of a new story—the story of the gradual renewal of a man, the story of his gradual regeneration, of his passing from one world into another, of his initiation into a new unknown life."[1]

AUTHORS' NOTES

THIS IS A BOOK ABOUT YOU . . . AND YOU, TOGETHER. Yes, it is divided up into halves, one about overcoming pornography addiction for the man, and the other about healing for the woman. But this is not a "his or her" book, nor should your journey toward recovery and healing be delineated as such. We understand that you, man or woman, husband or wife, may be dealing with this addiction on your own. For whatever reason, you have picked up this book, hoping to find within its pages a measure of understanding and comfort. I promise you will find what you seek, but only if you read this book in its entirety, in humility, and with a desire to change—both of you. Men, read your section and the section on healing for wives. Women, read the man's section in addition to your own. There are components within each for both of you. And if you are in a position to do so, read the book together—however you want to make that work. We wrote this book with the hope that it would initiate dialogue among the two of you and that through that dialogue you would find your way along the path to redemption. This is our intent, our hope, and our prayer for you . . . and you.

Is this book for Christians? Yes. Is it specifically for Christians? No. It is for everyone—no matter his or her religion. If you've ever attended an Alcoholics Anonymous meeting, you might believe, as I do, that it is an inspired program. It has helped millions of people worldwide. And yet, without shame, it recognizes a higher power and the need for reliance on that power to achieve recovery. For many, that power is God as the Western world defines him. However, even with God as a recurring motif at those meetings, it has not stopped thousands upon thousands of non-Christians from attending their meetings and gleaning from them the principles necessary for change, forgiveness, and the strength to endure to the end.

Do we use in this book references specific to our Christian faith? Absolutely! Because that is who we are, and that is what we know. But we also use references from other religions, people, and cultures all over the globe. Why? Because they teach truth. In the end, it is no secret: I believe every single one of us can turn to God and find understanding and peace. I believe he has the power to help change our hearts and minds, *if* we seek after and work like heck for those changes to come about. But if you do not believe in God or are not religious at all, that is also fine. I respect your decision on the matter and simply ask that you also respect mine. Be forewarned, there will be times when my wife and I reference strength we received because of our faith in God. When you get to those paragraphs or sections, you may feel as if you cannot relate. If this is so, do not despair; do not give up. Read them, analyze them, and apply them if and as you will. I promise that if you continue, in spite of religious barriers, you will uncover principles that can help you.

Now, we have been told that some people will refuse to read this book because it quotes leaders of various faiths and dispositions. Let me say this: if someone were to ignore a book because of the race of its author, we would cry "foul!" With religion, it must be no different. Furthermore, if you need help and you close this book prematurely because you disagree with a religion's tenants or a culture's traditions mentioned herein, you are not ready to be free from addiction anyway, so move on. To overcome something that is selfish in nature, one must be willing to give up anything and everything selfish, including pride, hatred, prejudice, and so forth.

Truth is truth no matter the package in which it is wrapped. Personally, I see no logical reason to disregard true principles simply because they are part of a different way of life than my own. In fact, if those principles hold keys to victory in any degree, I want to know them and live them and share them.

Sir William Drummond once said, "He, who will not reason, is a bigot; he, who cannot, is a fool; and he, who dares not, is a slave."[1] I have been a slave much of my life to the snares of pornography. I do not dare be one again, and I hope I am not so much a fool that I would overlook the wisdom of a man or woman out of spite for their affiliations. This is a book for anyone who has ever struggled with pornography in any degree—any degree! And by that, I mean this is a book for everyone.

The problem of pornography encircles the globe. It runs rampant through our communities, among our schools, and within our homes. It knows no bounds. It cares nothing for whether you vote Democrat or Republican. It does not care where you call home: Africa, the Americas, Europe, Asia, Australia, and so on. Nor does it look first to see whether you live your life according to Catholicism or Lutheranism; Mormonism or Judaism; Buddhism, Daoism, Hinduism; or any other –ism out there. It's tied only to totalitarianism. It seeks to control the whole by undermining the individual.

Because of its relentlessness, we must be willing to put aside personal opinions, political platforms, and religious differences for a common cause. We must be willing to glean what truths and principles we can from one another in order to help each other overcome life's struggles and strengthen the community around us. We believe in what we have written here. You will notice some principles repeated. There are two reasons for this: one, you are getting two different perspectives, and two, there is great value in repetition. The principles behind the words, stories, examples, and references hold the keys to recovery and healing.

To you beginning this journey, whoever you are, wherever you are, whatever you believe: we stand by you. Let nothing stand in your way and "the truth shall make you free" (John 8:32).

—*William A. and Mae Donne*

INTRODUCTION

"You do not just treat pornography addiction; you conquer it."[1]

I, WILLIAM, WAS BORN IN 1979. I WAS NAMED AFTER MY grandfathers, both of whom were soldiers in World War II. My paternal grandpa was a paratrooper. To me, one of his greatest accomplishments in life was coming home from the war to the bride he had married at the outbreak of war, having never compromised his standards nor his commitment to fidelity. My maternal grandfather fought in the Ardennes Counteroffensive, more commonly known as the Battle of the Bulge. In what many have called the largest and "bloodiest battle" of the war, some 610,000 Americans participated with nearly 90,000 casualties.[2] Among the injured was my grandpa, who later received the Purple Heart in thankful recognition for wounds sustained in the cause of freedom. But of more lasting importance to me is the fact that he, like my other grandpa, escaped death, and sometimes only by miraculous means. Clearly, they had things to accomplish still, and by their future families they strived to make the world better. They were great men. In many ways, their legacy lives on, as does the freedom we now enjoy because of the *collective* fight in which they took part. And when I think back on them, as well as the many other soldiers who have fought, are fighting, or will yet fight to retain or regain freedom, I am humbly reminded that injuries come but they also heal; that some scars last—gentle reminders of the fight—but the poignancy of memory fades; and, above all, the joy that comes with victory will forever outlive the pain of the fight.

Today, in so many ways, the fight for freedom continues. We may not have asked for the battle, but it is here, we are engaged in it, and it is *ours* to finish and win.

1

I was six when I first remember kids at school talking openly about sex. I was about nine when one of them showed me a pornographic magazine during recess. He handed me a page from it. Startled and curious, I took it home and hid it under my bed. I was scared. I sensed it was not appropriate for me to look at, so I finally worked up enough courage to get rid of it. I ripped it into shreds, then took it out back and burned it. I thought doing so would erase all traces of the provocative image. But it did not. The image had been burned into my brain, and its effects, like the smell of smoke on clothes, lingered long. To this day, I can see that image in my mind—if I try to recall it. I simply do not.

By the time I turned twelve I had developed an addiction to pornography. I was just a kid.

Sixteen years later, shortly after I turned twenty-eight and after a long, lonely, and silent struggle with pornography, I gained control over my addiction. Why did it take so long to overcome? In short, I tried to do it on my own. I was ignorant as to the severity of the problem. I was ashamed and embarrassed to talk to anyone about it. I was also selfish and stubborn. I wanted to defeat it by myself. But ultimately, I didn't know how, nor did I know where or to whom to turn for help.

Do I share these facts to garner sympathy? No, but rather to show you just how innocent I was when this terrible vice took control of my life, and to remind you, at this crucial time in your own lives, just how innocent we all are. Even in our old age, we are much like children, trying to love and feel loved in return. In our oft-times misguided search, we turn to sources that promise fulfillment but only succeed in hindering it. This is common, but it must not be.

As we work together to overcome our addictions and our feelings of hurt, we must not lose faith in the innate goodness of humankind. It is easy, I know, to feel guilt, anger, and even hatred toward yourself, someone who has hurt you, or something that you believe caused your spouse to hurt you. But contention in any form is, in the purest sense of the word, damning. It will only prolong the day of promised deliverance. "Quarrel not at all," Abraham Lincoln warned in a letter written during the Civil War. "No man resolved to make the most of himself can spare time for personal contention. Still less can he afford to take all the consequences, including the vitiating of his temper and the loss of self-control."[3]

For each of us to succeed in this undertaking—or help a spouse, child, or friend to succeed, or help ourselves to heal from the hurt caused by an addicted loved one—we must find a way to look beyond what we see as a disgusting habit and find instead a common struggle similar in form to any other struggle known to humankind throughout history. We must find a way to look beyond what we deem a perverted sinner and see instead the innocent child within. We would not abandon a helpless infant in need; then let us not abandon that child now, no matter his or her age.

No one sets out determined to hurt him- or herself. I certainly did not wake up one morning and decide to ruin my life for a time. And while there were indeed times in my life when I clearly chose the path of suffering, I never once intended to hurt anyone else, especially not my parents, siblings, or, as it proved later, my wife and children. And yet that's what I did. In fact, unable to reverse the past and with my problem still a dark secret known only to me, that's what had to happen so that ultimate healing could take place. In the end, by making my past known to them, I had to hurt for a small moment the ones I loved, so I could help forever the one I did not—me.

Now, you may ask what authority my wife and I have to write a book about overcoming pornography and healing after the betrayal it causes. The answer is simple: none. We are not psychologists or therapists or doctors. We hold no advanced degrees that prove we understand addictions or the complicated workings of the mind more than the next couple. We have never had a scientific article on the subject published. In short, we do not know nor do we pretend to know everything there is to know about pornography and overcoming addictions. But we *do* understand addictions. I *am* a recovered addict. We have *both* found healing. And, above all, we *know* there is a way to beat this thing.

Within this book are our experiences and insights; they are true, and they hold key principles to help you overcome your own struggles regardless their origin. In our lifetime, as short as it has been, we have learned that it is not so much an understanding of how the brain works that helps us conquer addiction, but an understanding of how the Spirit works—an understanding of how certain basic, universal principles can release "those which are bound with chains" (Psalm 68:6).

That is all we can promise you: that over the subsequent chapters, where facts and psychological test-cases may be lacking or even fail, the principles will not. And neither will you—if you ponder, discuss, and apply these principles with an open mind and heart. The study and application of principles can improve behavior faster than any clinical expertise on the subject. I believe that.

Our personal story is different than yours, but the outcome can be the same. This is your time! The victory is yours for the taking. And take it you must!

Preface

ROAD MAP
TO RECOVERY

*"'This burden that is upon my back will sink me lower
than the grave. . . .'"*

*"'If this be thy condition, why standest thou still?' He answered,
'Because I know not wither to go.'"*[1]

FAR TOO OFTEN, WITH AN ERRAND TO RUN, I HOP IN
the car with only a general idea of my destination, trusting that certain landmarks will jog my memory, and that I will know it when I see it. Going forward in this manner has always led to two things: getting turned around and getting frustrated. Because of this, I need to know where I am going ahead of time.

As you begin down this road of behavioral change, you too need to know where you are headed. For this reason, I have included a general map, or outline, of the steps for recovery. But this is NOT a step-by-step book. It is a book of principles. The principles herein have the power to act as a kind of catalyst for recovery. Wives, we will touch more specifically upon healing in a separate section, but that does not mean there are not truths that can and, indeed, need to be gleaned from these chapters about the addict. Many principles in them will apply to you as well, as you struggle to find peace and healing in the wake of discovering a loved one's addiction.

But perhaps more important than a clear idea of the destination, you need to make sure you have enough fuel in the tank to get there. You need to make sure you have what it takes to see this process to the end. "For which of you," Jesus Christ taught, "intending to build a tower, sitteth not down first, and counteth the cost, whether he have sufficient to finish it?" (Luke 14:28).

You are not building a simple tower. You are building for the first time or *re*building a home, and the cost will be high. But it will be worth it.

"Or what king," Jesus continues, "going to make war against another king, sitteth not down first, and consulteth whether he be able with ten thousand to meet him that cometh against him with twenty thousand?" (Luke 14:31).

We are at war against an immoral, even an amoral, enemy. Thus far the cost has been steep, and it will continue to exact from the accounts of your heart and mind even more than previously invested. But the victory is yours. "Fear not: for they that be with us are more than they that be with them" (2 Kings 6:16). I am in your corner. My wife is in your corner. I trust that you have family or friends who are available to help you. And if you believe in God, certainly he too is with you.

If you are reading this book, you have, to some degree, passed through the first step: *Denial*. From here we learn to *Be Honest* and *Accept* our mistakes and nurture a desire to change. Propelled forward by an increasing desire, we take responsibility for our mistakes and Prepare to change them. With preparation in place, we then take *Action*, working with loved ones to attain our goals. And finally, for the rest of our lives, we must *Maintain and Defend* what we have accomplished by the grace of God, family, and friends. But these steps are too vague to be of any good as they are. Suddenly being honest might be a giant leap for someone dealing with a backlog of personal dishonesties. Most likely, you have many instances of dishonesty in your life, and you will not be able to recall them all at the snap of a finger or at the demand of a loved one.

Therefore, this book is about taking small steps to achieve the same distance covered by the giant leap. It will dissect and analyze many individual components that, in turn, make up the generic steps noted above. By these small and simple steps, you will facilitate recovery and healing. In general, they include but are not limited to the following:

1. Defining addiction: what is it and how do we control it?

2. Defining pornography: what is it and where do we draw the line?

3. Drawing lines: discern what causes you to fall and what you need to avoid.

4. Understanding the real cause of addiction.

5. Controlling reactions.

6. Learning to communicate.

7. Setting realistic expectations for recovery and healing. Learning what heals and how you can be in control.

8. Establishing the four corners of recovery and accountability:

    a. Tell your spouse and family

    b. Tell your closest friend(s)

    c. Tell your employer/coworker(s)

    d. Tell your church and/or professional leader(s)

9. Being completely honest and repenting completely: no secrets!

10. Analyzing your life and pulling out the little things that lead to temptation and relapse.

11. Being willing to sacrifice as needed: get rid of anything that *might* lead you back to pornography.

12. Filling the voids: find positive things with which you can fill your life in the place of pornography; escape to God.

13. Controlling your surroundings: set up rules and protective boundaries for your life and home.

14. Being watchful: avoid danger areas and be on the lookout for yourself and others.

15. Protecting your victory: maintain life patterns thus far established.

16. Looking for and accepting purpose in suffering and sin: become a teacher and testifier of deliverance.

The principles behind each of these steps will apply to the addict seeking recovery and his wife seeking healing. But let me say again what I have said already: this is not a step-by-step book. It has been my experience that men fail to overcome pornography because they do not first understand the principles behind the steps. This book is also not really of the self-help variety, because it has been my experience that it most often takes a "family" (define that as you wish) to overcome the selfish, alienating addiction to pornography.

As you go forward, may you continually remember that "whatever your present environment may be, you will fall, remain, or rise with your thoughts. . . . You will become as small as your controlling desire; as great as your dominant aspiration." 6 It is my promise that you can overcome this addiction, and that you can learn to forgive, heal, love again, and feel loved in return.

PART 1:
WHAT IS ADDICTION?

by William A. Donne

1

DEFINING ADDICTION

*"All depends on the way unexpected movements of the enemy—
that cannot be foreseen—are met, and on how and by whom the
whole matter is handled."*[1]

WHAT IS AN ADDICTION REALLY? AND HOW DO YOU know if you are addicted to something?

I struggled to answer these questions for many years. In fact, on several occasions I justified that my problem was not an addiction, but rather a series of one-time occurrences, which is why, in part, it continued as long as it did. This justification is easy to make because a one-time occurrence is precisely how any addiction starts. At a certain point in my life, I looked at pornography for the first time. As mentioned, that moment came in the form of a magazine handed to me by a classmate. It was a one-time occurrence.

It doesn't matter if we see a pornographic image as a result of our curiosity, or because somebody shows it to us, or because we stumble across it—it can happen to anyone, anywhere, and at any time. To say nothing of its accessibility on the Internet, I have stumbled into pornography in magazines, in clothing catalogs, on ads stuffed inside the newspaper, and on television screens while channel-surfing at home. I have been handed trading cards with overtly sexual images on them from friends in junior high. I have seen it on the coffee tables or counters of friends' houses. I have found it lying on the street on my way home from sports practice. I have discovered it in the stalls and in the trash cans of public rest rooms. I once even found it on the gym floor of a church, when all I wanted to do was play basketball. For all of us struggling with addiction, no matter how we came across pornography the first time, it was a "one-time occurrence."

On the heels of that moment, we took our first step toward dealing with the situation. In hindsight, however, it was a wobbly step, and we failed. The first mistake I made when my friend showed me the magazine was taking it home and hiding it to look at later. The second mistake I made was keeping this occurrence a secret. No doubt, regardless of the confusion or guilt you may have experienced, you too, in one form or another, looked back at the pornography and kept its existence hidden from others. You justified, as I did, that it was no big deal because you didn't *really* seek it out or because you didn't *really* look at it or because you didn't *really* want to look at it. You told yourself it would not happen again. For the most part, these justifications allowed you to feel guilt-free. But it also made it easier to similarly dismiss the moments when you saw and looked at pornography a second time, then a third, and so on.

Speaking now to everyone, when we are confronted with temptation, the first step to deal with it is simply to look away, turn off the TV, leave the website, walk out of the store, and so on. We will touch on this in greater detail later, but if any one-time occurrence is to remain just that, then we must not go back to that picture—ever! Nor can we go somewhere else seeking something similar.

As soon as any of us return our eyes or thoughts to a particular object, image, or idea, it ceases to be a one-time occurrence and becomes an addiction on one level or another.

Example: You see an immodestly dressed lady jogging down the street and, almost instinctively, you return your gaze—in whole or part, in the open or secret—to look again. Are you addicted? Yes.

The same goes for advertisements in magazines, in newspapers, and on store windows. The same goes for websites, characters in movies or on TV shows, cartoons, soap operas, music videos, video games, comic books, romance novels, and even critically acclaimed stories that treat and describe sensuality and sexuality in a way that entices and brings to the mind images that are often more vivid than pictures. The same goes for people we pass on the street, at swimming pools, at gyms, or at work. The list can go on and on; it is as diverse as the people and situations around us.

"C'mon, that's a little extreme," you might say. Well, yes, you're right—it is. But we must take extreme measures to overcome extreme struggles. In this case, I am calling it an addiction because, quite simply, the fact we returned our gaze signifies we were unable to completely control ourselves. And that lack of self-control is the very root of addiction. When we cannot control ourselves but rather find our actions or thoughts controlled by something or someone else, we are addicted to that very thing.

The dictionary concurs in its definition, defining *addiction* as "the state of being enslaved."[2] It does not say how often you have to be enslaved or for how long, just that, at some point, you are enslaved, bound and pulled as if by chains, to look again.

Taking into consideration the denotation of the term *addiction* as we have now defined it, we learn that for someone to be addicted to something does not mean he necessarily accesses it or thinks about it every day. In fact, during the sixteen years of my addiction, there were days, weeks, months, and even years when I did not turn to pornography. But I did return.

My uncle, whom I loved and looked up to, was a prime example of this. While his personal struggles revolved around drugs, the principles are the same. He fought his addiction off and on for several years, sometimes coming clean for months, even years at a time. He made changes in his life, moved closer to family, and began the long rebuilding process. He came to my high school graduation. On my dresser, I have a picture from that occasion of me with him and his wife. He was clean. He was as happy as he had been in a long time. It was the last time I saw him. A couple months later, I left to serve a mission for my church. Before a year had passed, I received the tragic news from home. My uncle had passed away. The cause? Drugs. *Does it really matter how much time there was between these series of one-time occurrences?* No. He could not give drugs up completely, and so they took everything from him, as addictive substances always will if they are not controlled and the appetite for them is not conquered.

"But then how," you might ask, "do I know if it is really behind me?" Or "how do I trust it will not come back into the life of my spouse or child?" We will talk about this later, but for now let me leave it at this: the moment you turn away from pornography or anything that is addictive in nature, it is behind you. This is important to remember. If you just looked at pornography this morning, but are now reading this book in an attempt to gain control, then there you go. Congratulations! It is behind you, and I couldn't care less whether it's been behind you a few hours, a few days, or years.

To leave it there—where it belongs—is a choice you will have to make separately. The great task of life, then, becomes to proactively live your life in such a way that prevents your pornography addiction from coming back. Doing so takes work—hard, conscientious work—and it is required of everyone daily. For many, it will be required on the hour, every hour. But you can do it!

For those of you struggling to forgive and forget, this same principle of leaving it behind you will be integral to your healing as well. At some point on your own, you too will have to make the hard decision to leave your spouse's past—which has so violently entangled you without warning—in the past. You don't have to look back and you can trust again. This may be the hardest thing you will ever do.

I remember the many times my wife wondered aloud how she too could know pornography was behind me for good. Eventually we came to the conclusion that we could not say with absolute surety that it was. After all, it is everywhere, so it seemed just a matter of time before some variation presented itself when we least expected it. But we could say with one hundred percent confidence that if we abided by certain rules, we would always keep its destructive effects at bay.

In essence, a key to successful recovery and healing lies in trusting the tools you have to block the inroads of pornography from *going forward*, and not in succumbing to a fear of an unknown future or the depression that comes from dwelling on things we cannot change in the past. This type of fear is debilitating. It must not be allowed to consume our faith in humanity or our hope for better days to come, thus robbing us of the progress we seek.

Referencing Lot's wife in an address given to college students, Jeffrey Holland stated that, "To yearn to go back to a world that cannot be lived in now; to be perennially dissatisfied with present circumstances and have only dismal views of the future; to miss the here-and-now-and-tomorrow because we are so trapped in the there-and-then-and-yesterday—these are some of the sins, if we may call them that, of . . . Lot's wife."[3]

As a reminder to you addicts, even though it is your spouse's ultimate decision to forgive and trust again, that process starts with you. You must earn back their trust by keeping your eyes shut, your heart locked, your hands clean, and your mind pure.

Ralph Waldo Emerson once wrote in his essay "On Self-Reliance," "Nothing at last is sacred but the integrity of our own mind."[4]

This is true. Our mind, like the soft skull of a newborn, is fragile. We must protect it at all costs—all costs! The way we do this is by learning to control everything we think, say, and do.

2

SELF-RELIANCE
AND SELF-MASTERY

"I am too high-born to be propertied."[1]

HENRY DAVID THOREAU PENNED THE FOLLOWING IN his essay "Civil Disobedience": "I think that we should be men first, and subjects afterward."[2]

Not so coincidentally, Thoreau's inspired essay speaks to the need and, more important, the moral obligation of the individual to rise up and oppose government when it is unjust. It calls for the individual to take control of his own future, not by abolishing government altogether but by working together as a team of individuals for a common purpose—to make government better. While I am neither promoting nor discouraging civil disobedience in regards to the political structure of our God-given country, I am calling for civil disobedience when it comes to the govern-*mental* state that currently controls our thoughts, words, and actions.

Addressing the influence "Civil Disobedience" had on his life, Martin Luther King Jr. remarked, "I became convinced that noncooperation with evil is as much a moral obligation as is cooperation with good."[3]

Herein we learn that we need not be subjects to a hierarchy of inappropriate thoughts or images force-fed before our eyes by the waning moral structure of our society. We do not have to cooperate with inappropriate thoughts and images. We can seize control of our situations now. With wise discernment, we can rise up against the unjust and amoral dictatorship of our minds, and bring freedom and peace of mind to the people—ourselves, our friends, and our families—both present and future.

"Man," wrote James Allen, the author of *As a Man Thinketh*, "is always the master, even in his weakest and most abandoned state."[4] We can be in control of our thoughts and thus our destiny.

Allen later describes this relationship between thought and circumstance. "Let a man radically alter his thoughts, and he will be astonished at the rapid transformation it will effect in the material conditions of his life. Men can imagine that thought can be kept secret, but it cannot; it rapidly crystallizes into habit, and habit solidifies into circumstance."[5]

This can go both ways: bad thoughts leading to bad habits and thus poor circumstance; or good thoughts, thoughts that edify, leading to good habits and thus prosperity in all its forms.

So how do we restore, or perhaps build for the first time, a mental landscape where purity and the resulting prosperity prevail? We must methodically employ self-mastery, temperance, and self-reliance.

Let me make something clear. Simply because the word *self* is at the forefront of these two terms, does not mean recovery should or even can happen on your own. A vast difference exists between relying on one's self and being self-reliant. The first means you think you can do it *all* on your own and do not require the help of others. You may even spurn it. The latter, however, alludes to a sense of responsibility and dependability, and, paradoxically, requires the opinions of others about how reliable or dependable they deem you to be, so that when you are on your own, you can be trusted to carry out each and every task required for the sustenance of life and happiness. They are labels we all must continually re-earn.

Right now, regardless of how strong or even invincible you may feel, you are most likely not reliable enough to be immediately free from a past that has plagued you for years. You will need to depend on others if you are to eventually enjoy the independence you seek—independence as in freedom from your mistakes and the accompanying consequences and pain, and *not* isolation from others.

My struggles spanned sixteen years of my life because I tried *by myself* to rely on *my* understanding, *my* strength, and *my* willpower instead of letting others help. Trust me when I say, there will be times, especially in the beginning, when having others involved will be the only thing that keeps you from returning to the flame. Rarely are we strong enough to completely overcome it on our own. Addiction is all about "me, me, me." To succeed spiritually, you must rely on God. And to overcome pornography addiction indefinitely, you will need the help of others too. That being said, change must start with you, with your choice to learn and apply the principle of temperance now.

By definition, temperance has its roots in moderation or restraint of action, thought, or feeling. It means we have complete control over self. No outside influences can make us do anything. We are men and women first, not subjects. John Newton—the former slave ship captain turned clergyman and who also wrote the hymn "Amazing Grace" about his conversion—said "the word 'temperance'. . . signifies self-possession. It is a disposition suitable to one who has a race to run and therefore will not load his pockets with lead."[6]

We can readily admit that if we were to run a race, no matter the length, we would not carry an extra burden, lead or otherwise, which might slow our pace and lessen our ability to finish.

From this analogy, two important questions arise. One: why then do we load our pockets with "lead"? Why do we purposefully choose to look at images or participate in activities that we know are weighing us down—physically, mentally, emotionally, and spiritually? And two: what do these lead objects look like that make them so desirable to stow away in spite of this knowledge?

Both will be addressed in due time. Answering the latter first, however, will shed light on the former.

3

ON DEFINING PORNOGRAPHY

"A man is but the product of his thoughts;
what he thinks, he becomes."[1]

IN 1964, JUSTICE POTTER STEWART, THEN OF THE US
Supreme Court, famously stated in the case *Jacobellis v. Ohio* that he could not intelligibly define pornography, "but I know it when I see it." His declaration, made in an attempt to protect the state's right to show obscene films, differed from the opinions of his fellow Justices. Eventually, at the end of a heated debate where few were in agreement, the US Supreme Court overturned the initial ruling and the obscene material was allowed screen time. As a result, a great divide remained among the Justices over the definition of pornography and the need for censorship.[2] This great divide exists today throughout our society. In fact, I am confident that it has never been as hotly disputed as it is now.

However, when it comes to the definition of pornography as it relates to us, to our friends, and to our families, we cannot afford to be as indecisive or divided. Thus, it is an absolute necessity that we define pornography as we know it and see it—but even more important as we have never known it nor seen it before. What do I mean by this? Simply put, it does little good to define what everyone recognizes as pornographic. If recovery were as simple as saying *this* is pornography, then all you'd have to do is stay away from *this*, and you'd be fine. But it's not that simple, and the fact that you are reading this book searching for a way to overcome what you have not yet been able to do on your own is proof enough.

Consider the following scenario. You are running along a path in the woods. Someone, coming from the opposite direction, kindly issues a warning as they run past you. "Hey, buddy, watch out for that rock ahead. Don't trip." As you continue along, your eyes scan the way for any number of giant rocks that might trip you, assuming, as seems only natural, that only a big rock would be dangerous enough to trip you up and warrant such a warning as received from the other runner. But then, when you least expect it, you step on the tiniest pebble; it rolls under your shoe, your feet fly out from under you, and you land on the ground. Dazed, you look back in awe and embarrassment at the small pebble that caused such a great fall. Most likely you take some comfort in the realization that no one was around to see you fall, as if that somehow negates the reality of the experience.

Now, what was the purpose of the fall? Well, that depends on how you treat it and what you do with its memory. Do you dismiss it as a fluke and keep running with an eye out for only large rocks? Or do you allow yourself to change and redefine your once-broad definition, so that the next time someone warns you to watch out for a rock in the path ahead, you will, with increased focus, look for rocks both large and small?

George Santayana, the early-twentieth century philosopher and essayist, wrote that progress "depends on retentiveness" and that "when experience is not retained, as among savages, infancy is perpetual. Those who cannot remember the past are condemned to repeat it."[3]

Addiction is all about perpetual infancy and the dependence that comes with such a phase. Because addicts are usually embarrassed or enraged by their failures, they often push a failure from their minds as fast as possible, eliminating the chance for progression, which can only come from retention, analysis, and refinement. And so pebble by pebble, they continue to fall, never aware of their surroundings and ever confused as to the cause.

As it concerns pornography, we likewise continually fall when we fail to filter—and by filter, I mean the act by which we hyper-define and then separate the smallest potential dangers from our lives. Regarding drug addicts you probably have heard the term "crash" used to describe the violent, depressive aftereffects of intense, prolonged drug use. This can be said of pornography addiction too. But the cause of this crash is not the hard-core pornography you were looking at last, nor the soft-core pornography that acted as a stepping-stone. Rather, the root cause was and is something else, something so small and so subtle that it has escaped your attention this long time.

To avoid, then, the outcome we have repeated a thousand times and are yet condemned to repeat if we do not change something, we must look back on our past and redefine what we have always thought pornography to be. The Supreme Court Justices failed to do so in 1964. We will not. Many others are afraid to define it and speak out against it in the name of decency and a high moral standard. We will not be.

In regard to virtuous living, Aristotle noted that "it is possible to fail in many ways."[4] That's a bit of an understatement, in my opinion, because I have failed so *many* times and at the hand of so *many* different types of pornography that I cannot even begin to tell you the *many* ways by which any one of us may fail. The facets of pornography that exist today are innumerable, and they will only increase. But that does not mean we must not try to define the term as strictly as necessary for the survival of ourselves and our families. And, above all, it does not mean that there are not equally as many, if not more, ways by which we can and will succeed.

4

IS PORNOGRAPHY
ADULTEROUS?

*"This I say then, Walk in the Spirit, and ye shall not
fulfil the lust of the flesh." (Galatians 5:16)*

OUT OF ALL THE SECTIONS IN THIS BOOK, I BELIEVE
this topic to be one of the hardest to address, and, likewise, it may
be one of the hardest to read and come to terms with. If you are like I
was, up until now you have somehow managed to lessen the reality of
your problem. As a defense mechanism and in order to lessen the pain
of your immorality, you have pulled a curtain across the window that
would, if you dared look, show you in all its horror the true reflection of
your misdeeds. In part, this has allowed you to address the problem in a
matter-of-fact way. However, the question posed in the title of this chapter, and the answer that must inevitably follow, is designed to tear that
curtain down. While my wife and I have written the other sections with
the hope of instigating dialogue, for this small moment, I simply want
you husbands and wives to listen to me and trust that in the end hope will
be instigated instead.

Adultery, in its strictest definition, is the act of sexual intercourse
between a married person and someone other than the spouse. On
this subject, God, through the prophet Moses, gave strict commandment. Written in stone, the mandate was clear: "Thou shalt not commit

adultery" (Exodus 20:14). Certainly not specific to Christianity, variations of this immutable law are found in the all the major cultures and religions of the world: Judaism, Islam, Hinduism, Buddhism, and so on. In some cases, the violation of this law was punishable by imprisonment, stoning, and even death.

It is in our nature, though, to see how close we can get to the edge of any boundary. Clearly, as time distanced the people of Israel from the giving and receiving of commandment, this became the case. Many began to justify that they could get "this close" to adultery without breaking the divine edict. In their thoughts and fantasies, they could get even closer. For this reason, it seems, Jesus Christ amended the law—but not in the manner we amend laws today to allow for something once outlawed in the name of rights and freedom. Rather, he made the commandment stricter, promising in consequence freedom from spiritual bondage. Referencing the original commandment, he then added: "But I say unto you, That whosoever looketh on a woman to lust after her hath committed adultery with her already in his heart" (Matthew 5:28).

Suddenly, there was no room to justify thoughts or actions of a sexual nature. From that moment forward, adultery was not an act as much as it was an intention. Mental or emotional infidelity to a spouse was finally recognized as being just as wrong and destructive to a marriage as physical adultery.

With little doubt in my mind, someone (your wife most likely) has likened your pornography addiction to an adulterous relationship with not just one, but hundreds, even thousands of women—after hours at the office, at the hotel room, on a business trip, even in your own home. Also with little doubt in my mind, you probably took offense at the insinuation. "I would never have an extramarital affair," you might have even retorted.

Let me say this about that line of reasoning: it is false. In your heart, you know you can't say that you would never commit physical adultery, especially if you continue to satisfy sexual desires by the bestial habit of looking at pornography. The danger of pornography is that when indulged in long enough, what once enticed becomes flat and the addict must constantly seek out greater degrees of it in order to achieve the same effect. Perhaps you are familiar with the old folk tale about the frog and water. The story warns that if you throw a frog in a boiling pot of water, it will immediately jump out; but if you let the frog swim in cold water and subtly raise the temperature by a few degrees, you will boil it alive. Pornography is no different. And in this manner, it can quickly lead to the physical act of adultery.

In his autobiography, *Out of the Depths*, John Newton adds to this theory, saying: "Satan will seldom come to a [person] with a gross temptation. A green log and a candle may be safely left together, but bring a few shavings, then some small sticks, and then larger, and you may soon bring the green log to ashes."[1] Indeed, pornography addiction results from the gradual process of flame to stick that, in the end, succeeds in burning forests and homes. Where pornography exists, the act of physical adultery is not far behind.

If there is still doubt in your mind as to the adulterous nature of pornography, let me share with you the term's etymology. It is eye-opening. The suffix *–graphy* you no doubt recognize as meaning a piece of writing or art, or a specific field of study: biography, geography, cartography, and the like. We rightly associate terms with education, as well as the human ideals derived from education, namely, intelligence and wisdom. So what exactly are we so astutely studying when we indulge in pornography? *Porno-*, from the ancient Greek *porne*, means "prostitute." Thus, pornography at its "purest" form is nothing more than the study of prostitutes and the artistic works in which they appear. In pornography then, you have spent your time, money, and energy on prostitutes.

Your wife is right. At the least, in your mind and heart you committed adultery. It is my sincere hope and prayer that your infidelity has gone no further than the computer screen or the television set. I am acquainted with wonderful men who could not gain control over their pornography problem before it moved them by swift and imperceptible degrees into the physical arms of another. Their responses have been very similar: they did not start out with the intention to cheat on their spouse. In their eyes, I have seen pain and remorse I would not wish on anyone. And in the pallid, lifeless countenances of their wives, the different but equally bitter pain is just as heartbreaking.

Regardless, hope and healing are real.

It is my belief that just as Jesus Christ said to the woman taken in adultery, so he says to you: "Neither do I condemn thee: go, and sin no more" (John 8:11).

No more! No more, no more, no more.

And wives, in the same manner that Paul and Silas were freed from prison, so I promise that you too can be freed from the imprisonment you feel. After much suffering, the Bible relates the prison doors that held them captive were miraculously opened before Paul and Silas, who had done no wrong; and the jailor, who had previously stood by and watched them whipped, then took them in his arms "the same hour of the night, and washed *their* stripes" (Acts 16:33). The stripes in your heart can be healed.

From this moment forward, I believe both of you can and will do what it takes to reverse the consequences of habit. The road ahead will be hard—the path is strict. Just as Jesus Christ gave the people of the New Testament a higher law, so must you formulate and keep a higher law. And you must remember it always. Boundaries must be established and new lines drawn. They, perhaps, will seem restrictive. But by their protective nature, you will be spared bondage. You can be set free.

5

WHERE DO YOU DRAW THE LINE?

"It is impossible to eradicate the passions; but we must strive to direct them to a noble aim, and it is therefore necessary that everyone should be able to satisfy his passions within the limits of virtue."[1]

IF THERE WERE A THOUSAND INAPPROPRIATE SCENES in a movie would you watch it? What if there were nine hundred ninety-nine? What if there were nine hundred ninety-eight? What if there were nine hundred ninety-seven . . . and so on? At what number does your *no* become a *yes*? At what point does sin suddenly become a virtue? In the face of the immorality that is, by imperceptible degrees, invading the forms of entertainment today, where do you draw the line?

Growing up, this was a common scenario and question posed by my dad under various circumstances. It became somewhat of a comedic catch-phrase in our family actually, yet it is a question of great significance. I pondered its application often as I sought to overcome my own struggles with pornography. And I ponder it still, as my wife and I now work together to maintain our victories and raise our boys in a world of rapid moral decline. In our discussion on the denotations and connotations of pornography, it is critical that we ask it again: where do we draw the line?

Like anything in life, there are degrees to pornography. The world often only recognizes two of them: soft core and hard core. However, there are rarely only two degrees to anything. Imagine if there were only two outside temperatures: 5 degrees and 120 degrees; or if our ovens could only bake at the same two marks; or if there were only two speeds at which cars could drive: 5 mph and 120 mph.

Under these perhaps comical situations, it would be virtually impossible to live comfortably or safely. The same goes for pornography. More than just two degrees, pornography is part of a spectrum that has thousands of levels between and beyond what is commonly referred to as soft- and hard-core pornography.

However, because we are trying to determine what to avoid and not whether we should wear shorts today or how long to cook the meat loaf, we do not need to define or explore all of the little degree marks *between* and *beyond* soft- and hard-core pornography. Rather, what we should be concerned with are the degrees *below* that which we refer to as soft-core pornography: the tiny, seemingly insignificant bread crumbs that lead us into the hotter temperatures for which we are not prepared.

Why? Because this is how addiction to pornography begins and continues. By defining the lowest, most subtle levels of pornography, we are then able to work together to keep our homes and lives entirely free from that lowest form of it and, naturally, anything beyond.

As it now stands, many of us expose ourselves, spouses, children, friends, and other family members to pornography every single week, and we don't even realize it.

"Not me!" you might argue. "I would never show pornography to my spouse or child!"

This is true, I understand, but only according to your own personal definitions of pornography. You see, everyone believes pornography is something other than what they are involved in. Sometimes this is done out of ignorance. Often, however, we justify viewing a certain level of pornography so we can continue to enjoy the entertainment we love.

If I were to define pornography as any sexual image of a man or woman without clothes on in a magazine or on a seedy website, there would, I assume, be no argument. If I were to define pornography as the graphic depiction of any sexual act in those same two mediums, there would still be no argument. And why? Because these qualify as soft- and hard-core pornography, respectively.

But what if that same sexual act, complete with nudity, was in a movie? Or what if the scene was still in a movie, but this time it did not contain any outright nudity? Or what if the scene just showed a woman in her underclothes? Or what if this same image was plastered on a store window or in a catalog? Or what if I were to take it a step further and say pornography can be a picture of a woman in a bathing suit? What would you say then? Are these types of pornography?

"It depends," I often hear. In the past, I have similarly replied. But what exactly do we think it depends on? Does it really make a difference if the suggestive images are in an overtly sexual magazine marketed to men compared to an advertisement on a store window, in a catalog, or on the television, if their purpose is to showcase sensuality and entice? Is there really any difference if such images or scenes are broadcast into our homes and minds by way of a movie scene as opposed to a computer screen or a magazine hidden under the bed?

Here, the arguments start. Here, the lines begin to blur. But if you are to overcome your addiction, or if you are to help your partner overcome his addiction, then you must determine where you need to draw the lines—and I emphasize the word *lines*. Because a thousand roads lead to pornography—not all of them easy to detect—and we must address them all.

The "Et Cetera" of Pornography

Perhaps further defining pornography will help us better determine what lines to draw and where. Pornography, as defined in *Webster's Dictionary*, is "writings, photographs, movies, etc., intended to arouse sexual excitement."[2]

Highlight this definition. Underline the term *et cetera*.

When I was a young married man, my dad gathered my siblings and me together and shared an influential experience he had at work one day. Though he had no direct knowledge of my problems at the time, he applied his experience to the destructive effects of pornography and gave us strict warnings concerning our participation in it. After our family meeting, he wrote down his thoughts and sent them to his kids and grandkids. With his permission, the following quote is taken from his letter. It is in regards to the definition of pornography as just defined.

"What [the definition] doesn't say speaks volumes. It does not say that a person must be unclothed or engaging in particular acts in order for it to be pornographic. It also uses the word '*etc.*' which means that *anything* intended to arouse sexual excitement is pornographic. In fact, I looked up some synonyms for the word pornography. They are eye opening: Immodesty, Crudity, Profanity, Obscenity, Indecency, Impurity. Reading these words, can any of us deny that a large amount of what we are watching on television, or in the movies, or reading, or listening to, is pornographic?"

Question: So where do you draw the line? Answer: Where you have never thought to draw it and perhaps where you have never been willing to draw it before. This takes courage and support. But it must be done.

Remember my uncle. I mentioned that his drug addiction came back, and that eventually it was the cause of his premature death. But why did it come back? That's the real question. Because he never really gave it up. He gave up hard drugs, yes. But the day of my high school graduation, he could not go but a few hours before excusing himself to secretly have a smoke. Alcohol was still a part of his life too. I guarantee you these "soft" drugs, which are not even considered by many to be drugs, were the small steps that led him back to the big drugs that took his life. He simply swapped hard for soft, small for big, but that did not mean he was any less addicted. The object of his addiction simply changed.

If we are to succeed 100 percent of the time, we cannot swap one addiction for another, one crutch for another, no matter how less severe it may seem. Doing so will always lead you back to something bigger—line upon line, degree by degree.

For the sake of guiding this discussion, let me offer some very specific examples that might help you better analyze where lines might need to be drawn in your own lives. Not that long ago, the movie *Titanic* smashed box-office records, luring many a romantic-at-heart into the theater to see it at least once, if not multiple times. It was praised as an amazing spectacle of storytelling, cinematography, and special effects. The fact that its story took place on the ill-fated *Titanic*, a historic ocean-liner touted as unsinkable, made it even more enticing to its potential audience.

The story followed a young man and woman and their cruise-line fling. It contained one scene involving nudity. This too was groundbreaking at the time, but because of the historic and artistic value audiences and critics assigned to it, the movie retained its PG-13 rating. A symbol of true love and sacrifice for many women and men, many justified going to see it. I personally never saw the movie. But I saw that one scene many times.

Ironically, many "unsinkable" men came out of that movie spiritually damaged by the looming iceberg of pornography expertly encapsulated within the movie's dangerously rough ocean waters. It continues to do damage today.

The same can be said of the effects caused by a more recent series of young adult books and their blockbuster silver screen-adaptations. In theme and by way of character development, they promoted virtue and abstinence. Yet, with every turn of the page or with every scene that faded into another one, there existed mounting, adolescent sexual tensions—tensions bestial in nature that eventually consummated before the impressionable eyes of many men, women, and children.

"But," you might very well begin to rebut this statement, "that was only a small part."

You and I both know this is not true. If we were to analyze the scripts, we would not only find that it was not *just* a small part, but that the stories were in fact built around those respective scenes. Still, even if it was just a random scene placed in the movie to guarantee a PG-13 rating, or a snippet of a much more graphic scene edited to avoid an R rating, would it not still be pornography?

Does it make a difference because it was part of a movie? What if I were to show it to your husband or son? Would you allow me, a stranger, to walk up to them and show them such an immodest scene out of the blue?

Your answer: "No, of course not." Then why do you show it to them or allow them to see it?

What if I took a screen print of that scene and stuck it on your wall? Or converted it into a JPEG and used it as the background of your desktop monitor?

"No," some will say, "because then it would be in my home constantly, whereas in the movie it was just a quick scene that came and went."

Thus we often make allowances for pornography based on the vehicle by which it is delivered into our homes and minds, assuming wrongly that by leaving the theater, the inappropriate images have left us.

In reply to such an idea, I give you my word (take it, please, from someone who has been there): no scene or image, no matter the length of screen time, just comes and goes. It matters not if it hangs on your wall or not. If you or your spouse or your child have seen it once, it will be seen again, nailed to the corridors of the mind where imagination can and often will turn it into something more enticing than it once was.

As mentioned before, if I allowed myself, I could still recall the image in the inappropriate magazine showed to me at recess twenty-something years ago. But I don't even try. I am in control. By virtue of my failures, I have learned to draw strict lines concerning all types of entertainment, situations, habits, *et cetera*. They are lines that I cannot afford to cross; lines which I cannot afford to approach—not even by the smallest of steps.

Reality Shows and Pornography?

As noted earlier, it is no secret that nudity and pornography often go hand in hand. It is a gross error, however, to assume that all of the roads to pornography start with nudity. In fact, I would be willing to wager that more often than not, it is something much more subtle that leads a man, step-by-step, to his computer to find pornography. What are these "much more subtle" catalysts? We have discussed some already and will discuss more later on, but let me add this reminder: an immodestly or seductively dressed woman—on TV or just walking down the street—can just as easily lead a man to pornography addiction as an explicit picture in a magazine. Sexual innuendo or tension in song or dialog, or the intonations of an off-screen sex scene are just as likely to affect a man as the highest degree of hard-core pornography we publicly shun. Perhaps even more so because of what they leave to the imagination and because of the desire they instill within the man for something more.

In light of this, let me offer yet other definitive examples of how subtly pornography can infiltrate our homes and lives. Some of the most popular television shows today are based on reality. Ironically—with participants chosen from a cache of beautiful bodies and controversial personalities, and with "plots" often steeped in infidelity, sensuality, and eroticism—these shows, which are more voyeuristic than entertaining, are anything but a reflection of real life. Yet we justify watching them because they are "real," or we find fascinating the emotional and psychological game of life played out on the screen, or for some other reason. In part, perhaps this is true. But I feel confident in saying that the draw to watch for men often comes from the thought or hope that we might see women in skimpy clothes or swimwear or in situations known only to secret, internal fantasies. Cloaked in reality and with our wives often beside us, we justify that what we are watching is not harmful. It is a way to look at something enticing without feeling guilty and without our spouse knowing—oblivious, as we think she is, to our roving eyes and thoughts focused on sexual story lines, seductive attire, and shapely forms flickering before us.

Also under the reality umbrella are several talent-type shows. I know many people who religiously tune in to watch celebrities compete against each other on the dance floor. Others I know watch similar shows but with amateurs dancing for a shot at fulfilling life-long dreams. In both cases, the talent of the contestants is undeniable. Yet some of the outfits and routines, designed and worn for the sole purpose of being provocative and alluring, clearly fall into the "et cetera" category of pornography.

This may be hard to hear. Personally, I used to love watching such shows. I love the arts. I appreciate dance and enjoy watching competitions, especially with my wife. Many of you are the same, I'm sure. Yet we would be foolish to believe that these programs have absolutely no effect on the men watching them. After honest introspection, many, I believe, will admit to noticing and perhaps even returning their gaze to the contestants' skimpy costumes or the body parts revealed by them, or perhaps even returning their thoughts to the suggestive routines.

While presenting this scenario to a group of boys, ages fourteen to eighteen, one immediately raised his hand. "Those shows," he said, "are tough for me." Just as quickly, every boy in that room concurred by raise of hand or verbal statement. They too found it hard to not look at the body of the dancer or be enticed by the suggestive routine. I told them to go home and discuss it with their parents, some of whom I knew were fans of such shows. If we do not discuss with others the instances that tempt us, those images or thoughts, even if they come by way of something as seemingly insignificant as a celebrity dance show, have the power to act as the subtle first steps that can lead a man to crave and seek out more. No doubt, I told the boys, your dads likewise struggle to not look at or be affected by the same outfits and routines—not because they're "bad" but because they're human, and because fighting these sexual urges is a common struggle for all of us, no matter our age.

I understand that this example may again seem extreme. Whenever I share this experience with men and women, I usually get two reactions in one: agreement of the principle but argument over the specifics. In the case of the latter, the initial reaction of the wife often goes something like this: "I love that show. It doesn't affect me. It shouldn't affect him. Why should I give up a show that I love simply because he cannot control his eyes and thoughts? It's not fair."

Just because a woman believes what she is watching does not bother her, does not mean it will not negatively influence the loved one sitting next to her, be it a spouse, boyfriend, or son. You give it up because you love him and respect what he is fighting for.

From men, I have heard similar frustrations vented: "I love that show. It doesn't affect me, so why should I give it up just because she thinks it affects me? It's not fair."

We can easily dismiss the first few scattered raindrops of a torrential downpour. But the first raindrops of that storm are no less responsible for the flooding that occurs afterward than those drops in the middle or at the end when the storm seems heaviest. In this sense, you only think it does not affect you. Having been there, I cannot buy this excuse. Nothing just comes and goes without effect. Heed my forecast and avoid the drops that foreshadow the coming tempest.

To both parties now, I agree—perhaps it is not fair. But is this really about being fair? Or is it about helping someone in need? If you find yourself entertaining similar frustrations or doubts, know that it is natural. But, as hard as it may be to hear, it is also selfish. While we will talk about sacrifice later on in this book, it is important to disclose now that blocking the inroads of pornography will require sacrifice daily—from both of you. Most likely you will be asked to or you will realize the need to part with books, movies, Internet habits, cable subscriptions, or the like, all of which you love or have grown accustomed to.

It will be hard. In all cases, however, you must ask yourself: as great as this item or show or habit is, is it really so important that I would risk falling back into old patterns of addiction over it? Is it really so vital to my existence that I would risk leading my spouse or child into addiction because of it? Of course the answer is no. But to turn the tide, it will take consistent effort, constant follow-up, humility, and sacrifice. How tragic it would be for any of us to learn that in some manner we provided the proverbial straw that broke the camel's back. We are responsible for those under the wings of our influence. We are indeed our "brother's keeper" (Genesis 4:9). With this our charge, we must be willing to analyze our own habits, among them our favorite shows and movies, and make any necessary sacrifices for the benefit of all involved.

Now, let me return for a moment to the subject of dancing less you think it is dancing I am preaching against. Through a character in one of his philosophical novels, Friedrich Nietzsche once wrote, "I would believe only in a God who knows how to dance."[3] Nietzsche's philosophies do not always align with my faith in God. But while dance is certainly not a criterion by which I extend or withdraw faith, I think I would have a hard time understanding and accepting God, the great creator of the universe, if he did not delight in the arts or approve of individual creative expression; and I think that is important to remember here. God does not want us to feel a sense of restriction in terms of what we don't watch, don't think about, or don't do. Rather, he wants us to feel a sense of conviction. He wants us to make decisions for ourselves because they are the right decisions to make, and because by making them we secure for ourselves and our families greater degrees of happiness and safety.

Dancing is not bad, neither is television or the Internet, for that matter. The examples I highlighted were a couple out of thousands I could have chosen instead. But I wanted to pick something that showed just how subtly pornography and its variations can enter our homes under our watchful eyes and steal away the hearts and minds of those we love. As C. S. Lewis famously wrote from the perspective of the head devil in *The Screwtape Letters*, "Do remember the only thing that matters is the extent to which you separate the man from [God]. It does not matter how small the sins are provided that their cumulative effect is to edge the man away from the Light and out into the Nothing. Murder is not better than cards if cards can do the trick. Indeed, the safest road to Hell is the gradual one—the gentle slope, soft under foot, without sudden turnings, without milestones without sign posts."[4]

This is not to say that watching such shows as those we've discussed will lead to an experiment or a fascination with pornography, but it might. And if it might, is it worth the risk? If this drink *might* have a very small dose of poison in it, do you take a drink? Do you let the man next to you take a sip? Do you hand it to your son? In such cases, common sense and wisdom prove sufficient to make the right decision without pre-set lines.

But in most other cases, lines must be drawn and boundaries must be both erected and respected. We must not allow ourselves to naively say about the types of entertainment we enjoy: "On with the dance! let joy be unconfined."[5] For it is when we ignore boundaries altogether and live the unconfined life that we are at our most vulnerable.

Who Draws the Line?

Before moving on, it is critical that we explore a variation of the original question with which we started this lengthy chapter: who decides where to draw the line?

Stereotypically, men are described as fixers. A woman shares concerns with her husband; she wants him to listen and understand her feelings, but he can't help but try to fix what he perceives the problem to be—or so the stereotype goes. In truth, it is always easier to solve a problem that is not our own when we are looking from the outside in. It is a much more difficult and subtle process, however, to help someone learn to solve his own problems. It takes humility, patience, and communication, among many other attributes.

Ironically, when a woman first discovers her loved one's problem with pornography, she too often goes into the fix-it mode ascribed to men. Overcome with a wave of emotions, she is wont to decide what rules are needed, how they will be enforced, and what punishments any violations will incur. This is a common occurrence and may not always be a bad thing. However, if such decisions are fueled by panic, anger, or the like, or made without any communication whatsoever, they run the risk of hindering the goal of recovery.

Ultimately, recovery is the addict's choice. As uneasy as it may be to hear, if a man is not of his own accord invested in the rules, his chances of recovery are slim—no matter how many rules or expectations are piled on top of him. It is no different with any of us, really. Think of your own childhood. How much more likely were you to obey rules and find strength and happiness in obeying those rules when you took part or at least felt like you took part in forming them? Where there is a wise investment, dividends follow with interest.

Provided the appropriate environment and timing, the addict, with the help of his partner, might recognize the need for such boundaries and commit to heeding them. But when blindsided by rules, or when rules are forced upon him without any say in the matter, the rules can lose their value, and so might the man. As noted before, a sense of personal conviction is the key to success, and not feelings of restriction. Restriction constricts progress while conviction propagates it.

My grandpa was often heard counseling his married children and grandchildren to "be united." With this in mind, the answer to the question of who draws the line is simple: both of you should draw it. This does not mean you end up with *his* and *her* boundaries, though. Rather, it means that through appropriate, tempered communication, in which you both take turns talking *and* listening, you establish rules that you *both* agree to keep. If a certain show is off-limits for the addict, then it should be off-limits for everyone else too.

Don't let your conversations turn into a "who's right or wrong" tug-of-war. If you allow them to become a "me versus him" or "me versus her" power struggle, success is unlikely. Power struggles have always been about losing—if you can get the other side to lose, you win. In your marriage, especially as you work together to establish boundaries and help each other keep them, there can be no losers. In the end, victory is best achieved by communication, compromise, commitment, and more communication.

This means that the woman will most likely need to work at letting her partner, who has thus far exhibited a serious lack of control, be a part of the decision-making process as it concerns boundaries. The addict must always give up control, but, paradoxically, it is important for him to feel he is in control and making changes of his own free will and choice. After all, the pride and joy of winning a sports competition is most keenly felt by those who played in the game and not always by those who sat on the bench.

However, in reality, men, your minutes on the court are currently limited, so to speak. You must realize that you have little ground to stand on, and for the next while you are in a sort of proving period. If your spouse feels strongly that something is inappropriate or that a certain rule needs to be put in place, then listen to her and submit to her desires. She is trying to keep you safe. The rules may not be necessary in your mind, but your humble observance of them will speak volumes about your commitment to overcome your addiction. It will likewise go a long ways to rebuilding the trust shattered by your pornography habits. At the same time, you too will begin to regain the ability to master your thoughts and actions. If you already feel you are in control, then prove it by setting rules with your spouse and obeying them—because you can!

To you wives, I understand that situations and personalities differ from couple to couple. Sadly, I have witnessed husbands spurn the opportunity to discuss rules designed to keep them safe. Moreover, I am aware of other men who continue to view inappropriate entertainment with little regard to the debilitating effects it has on marriage, family, and home. In such instances, continued obstinacy often forms rifts greater than those created by the initial discovery of pornography. Utterly alone in your efforts to help your husband, strengthen your marriage, and protect your home, you are left to make and enforce rules without conversation. Under this set of circumstances, it is your right to do so.

Having said that, I hope and trust this is not now the case. Men, I will assume that if you are reading this book with your wife, you are not the type of husband that has acted in so reckless and selfish a manner. And if you are, or rather if you have been, then I trust, from this moment forward, you will no longer be that man. Be honest with yourself; unite with your wife; and where you have no control, let her help you draw the lines necessary to your recovery.

Permit for a moment a personal example. After I began disclosing to my wife the heartbreaking depth of my addiction, virtually every night became occupied by discussion. These conversations often lasted into the early morning hours or took up time during the workday. On one occasion while I was at work, my wife called and suggested we move the computer to an open room. My first internal reaction was one of anger and embarrassment. I hated to admit that I needed this seemingly cliché step in order to regain control. At the same time, while I knew it was probably the right thing to do, I did not see how it was going to be feasible considering I worked from home. With limited time to discuss the matter fully, it was concluded that we would think it over and talk about it later. But upon entering the door of our home, a few hours after our discussion, I immediately noticed that my wife had moved the entirety of my office into an open area downstairs. It was clear that she must have started the laborious process minutes after the phone conversation in which we agreed to wait to decide together on a course of action.

This should not reflect poorly on my wife. She was scrambling to come to terms with an onslaught of information and concerns. In a sort of emergency panic mode, she felt the need to do something immediate to start fixing the problem now. Lack of trust aside, she went to great lengths to move everything downstairs because she wanted to help me. I did not see that then, though. Suffice it to say, I was hurt; I was angry at myself and I was angry at the situation, and all these things came out in a verbal outburst in which both our hurt and confusion were translated into words and tones we would gladly take back now. In my frustration, I kicked at a closet door, leaving a hole at its base. I was wrong to lose my temper. I cannot say it in any other way. The closet door has since been fixed, but the memory of that failure on my part, like a hole of regret in my mind and heart, remains with me still.

Yet from this experience, we patched things up and better communicated as a couple trying to keep our family alive, and not two individuals trying to live for ourselves alone. In the end, we learned the valuable but hard lesson I am now relating to you. Be patient. Be considerate. Be charitable. But above all, be united. If you do not have such feelings, then seek them. I personally believe in the power of prayer. Furthermore, I believe in a loving God who wants you to succeed—no matter the mistakes you have made or the hurt you have caused. In answer to prayer, he can and will grant these gifts to you, and through him you both can find the strength to solve the problems before you—together. Christ says, "For every one that asketh receiveth; and he that seeketh findeth; and to him that knocketh it shall be opened. Or what man is there of you, whom if his son ask bread, will he give him a stone? (Matthew 7:8–9). The answer, of course, is no. Where sustenance is needed, we would not rob our child. But if that same child rarely cried, would we as readily discern his need? Cry then; as often as you need sustenance, cry, and the help you request will come. Where impatience was, patience will be. Where apathy sat, empathy will rise. Where anger once consumed you, love—the great extinguisher of hate—will endure.

In the end, know this: the degree of success you experience together will not be determined so much by the number of lines you draw, or the number of shows you give up, or the number of times you compromise, but by the manner in which you draw the lines. If tempers are checked and cordial, honest communication continues, you will succeed—in spite of your differences. "Our ability to reach unity in diversity will be the beauty and the test of our civilization."[6] Our country's history is a powerful witness to this. It stands today on a foundation of freedom drafted by men of varying backgrounds, passions, and persuasions. Sacrificing individual desires and agendas, they came together for the greater good of the whole. In your marriage, you can too.

6

ON MASTURBATION

"We must not let our passions destroy our dreams." [1]

PERHAPS EVEN MORE TABOO THAN PORNOGRAPHY, the topic of masturbation can be an embarrassing subject to talk about. It can likewise be embarrassing for a person to admit they have turned to such behavior as the means of satisfying carnal lusts. But it too must be discussed and overcome. There can be no secrets.

With that introduction, I am not here to say whether masturbation is right or wrong. How you perceive it will likely depend on your religion, culture, or upbringing. But for the general discussion here, I want to say that whether it is okay or not, or in what circumstances it is okay, is up to you *and* your wife. The key part here, of course, being the latter—your wife. Masturbation is often done in secret. If this is so, and you have engaged in or are consistently engaging in it without the knowledge or consent of your wife, then by virtue of that, you are in the wrong.

If someone is struggling with masturbation, we must be sensitive to his struggle and try to avoid giving voice to our disgust or anger. It is important for wives, family members, and church leaders to realize that masturbation is equally addictive. I would wager that nine times out of ten, the act of masturbation coincides with the act of viewing pornography. They are virtually one and the same.

As early as fifth grade, I remember boys making the motions of masturbation with their hands as a joke or, sometimes, as an insult. I had no idea what they were talking about, so out of curiosity, I tried it. Doing so led a whole world of feelings I had never before experienced. It was exciting, it was confusing, it was addicting, and it soon led me to pornography. Having dealt with many men on the road to recovery, I have learned this is not such an uncommon scenario.

Years ago, I had an ecclesiastical leader who regularly interviewed the young and old men under his stewardship. He used to ask if they had looked at pornography or masturbated. But after discovering so many were struggling with it, he changed his question. "When," he instead asked, "was the last time you looked at pornography?" "When was the last time you participated in masturbation?"

The frequency with which his direct question was answered by an affirming reply, though frightening to many, simply confirms the overwhelming existence of this habit and the pervasive influence of pornography on our society. While there have been a few studies here and there, I have seen some statistics that predict as many as 90 percent of men masturbate and upward of 65 percent of women do.[2] Outside religious circles, this habit might be considered sexually healthy. Inside religious circles, the message is clearly one of moral warning. But it is inside the circle of marriage, which circle intersects both the religious and non-religious, that it becomes dangerous when used as a replacement for intercourse. Perhaps more dangerous are the effects to those boys or girls who begin experimenting with masturbation at an early age, and become addicted to the feelings of stimulation. How might this impatient habit hurt or diminish the beauty of intimacy they will enjoy later with their spouse?

> In modern society, it is far too common a tragedy for young people to cultivate a strong sexual appetite even before they begin to date. One cause of this serious problem can be the sin of masturbation. Children should be taught, at around the first signs of puberty, what masturbation is and why it is wrong. Parents who avoid guiding their children in this matter do them a disservice.[3]

Billy Graham, the well-known Christian evangelist, added his testimony to this when he touched upon why the misuse of our bodies is so destructive to the individual and God's plan for that individual and their family.

> The Bible celebrates sex and its proper use, presenting it as God-created, God-ordained, God-blessed. It makes plain that God himself

implanted the physical magnetism between the sexes for two reasons: for the propagation of the human race, and for the expression of that kind of love between man and wife that makes for true oneness. His command to the first man and woman to be "one flesh" was as important as his command to "be fruitful and multiply." The Bible makes plain that evil, when related to sex means not the use of something inherently corrupt but the misuse of something pure and good. It teaches clearly that sex can be a wonderful servant but a terrible master: that it can be a creative force more powerful than any other in the fostering of a love, companionship, happiness or can be the most destructive of all of life's forces.[4]

It is ironic that the term masturbation takes for its foundation a derivative of the word *master*, and that its definition cites self-gratification. In direct contradiction, like pornography, masturbation can and will quickly become addictive in nature, thus robbing us of the self-control and self-mastery erroneously indicated by this term.

By its nature, self-gratification increases the sex-drive outside marriage, anxiously promotes the need to fulfill that drive *now*, and destructively promulgates the sacred feelings and purposes associated with intimacy into realms void of any real person or edifying relationship.

For a spouse or parent, this realization might open up a new set of mixed emotions, confusion, disgust, and anger. It is understandable, because a habit that was limited to eyes and subsequent thought has now taken on physical action. It is physical action that we fear most because it opens a Pandora's box of potentially greater sins and greater heartache.

For your fear to subside, however, you must understand that because these two habits—pornography and masturbation—are often engaged in at the same time, and because they are rooted in selfish fulfillment, they can both be overcome at the same time by applying the same principles discussed throughout this book. Likewise, the steps to healing the hurt felt because of masturbation are also the same.

Above all, honest and open communication—now and forever—will tame curiosity, promote trust, pioneer healing, and prevent further heartache.

7

ON THE ROLE OF CURIOSITY

"The fox condemns the trap, not himself."[1]

YOU ARE PERHAPS FAMILIAR WITH THE PROVERB that says curiosity killed the cat. Curiosity is one of the great gifts innate in all living beings. Because of it, many discoveries have been made. Yet the seed of curiosity has just as often sprouted into dangerous and, yes, deadly habits. In the case of our addictions, curiosity first introduced us to the allurement of the medium we now shun. It was also curiosity that led us back to it time and time again. However, a great distinction exists between these two periods of curiosity. The first cannot be blamed; the second cannot be justified.

Curiosity springs from observation. As children grow, they naturally observe changes in the human body. For boys, differences between the adolescent girl sitting next to them in class and a fully matured woman are undeniable. There is no sin in noticing this biological fact, nor is there anything inherently evil in their piqued curiosity about the human body or in their desires and even bumbling attempts to find out more. It is, after all, in our nature to learn by experimentation. Take for instance the following quote from Mary Shelley's *Frankenstein* about the monster's first experience with fire.

One day, when I was oppressed by cold, I found a fire which had been
left by some wandering beggars, and was overcome with delight at the
warmth I experienced from it. In my joy I thrust my hand into the live
embers, but quickly drew it out again with a cry of pain. How strange,
I thought, that the same cause should produce such opposite effects![2]

For me, the parallels are clear. Like the monster, in the innocence of
childhood I came across something to be observed—the image from an
adult magazine. It was circumstance that placed it before my eyes, and
not by choice. I could have turned away, but out of curiosity I chose to
look at it. I simply wanted to know what the differences were that I had
begun to observe in the older women. When I looked at the photo, I felt
something new and strange, an exciting physical and emotional stimulation, and in it I recognized something beautiful.

"Beautiful?" I can hear some of you saying, shouting actually. I
understand your concern, I do. So let me explain it in this manner: I
feel it is important for us to recognize, especially if we have kids, that
even at young ages children are susceptible to experiencing sexual feelings
that, when controlled and used properly and at the right times, eventually propagate the human race. Extensive research shows this to be true.
Because of this, I find no reason to make a child feel ashamed for being
intrigued by the human body or feeling some level of attraction to the
opposite sex. To regard their initial innocent curiosity on the same level
as conscious adult intent can prove tragic. Rather than treat their feelings
and curiosity as black-and-white-bad, and scare them into not talking
about them again, we need to open the doors of communication—now
and in the future.

That aside, in my ignorance, I let my curiosity get the better of me.
I took the photo home. I stuck my hand in the warmth of the fire. Had
I then been able to see the future consequences of that act, how strange
it would have seemed to me that something so natural would end up
producing something so unnatural. As you know, I began to sense my
mistake and got rid of the image. Had I simply told someone, I think I
would have been okay. But I didn't, and years later I justified that I was
again satisfying a natural curiosity by looking at pornography anew. The
consequences of that fire, however, would stay with me for years to come.
Every time after that first innocent encounter, my curiosity was fueled by
a greedy, insatiable appetite that found sustenance in the secrecy of the
first experience. Out of curiosity, I looked behind virtual doors wondering

what could be there when, in reality, I already knew the answer. This, I know, goes for you too. No matter how you spin it, outside of that first time, circumstance and curiosity can no longer be blamed. The culprit that continually kills the cat was and always will be ourselves.

8

THE REAL CAUSE
OF ADDICTION

*"You are much more likely to make your man a
sound drunkard by pressing drink on him as an
anodyne when he is dull and weary."*[1]

WHEN PEOPLE FIND OUT I WAS ADDICTED TO POR-
nography, many—especially women—are immediately disgusted.
With distorted countenances, they've asked: "How can you look at that
stuff?" or "How come you don't just stop?" These are valid questions. The
answers to these questions, however, are not so simple. Actually, concerning the latter question, the answer might be simple if the decision to stop
looking at pornography was a matter of to look or not to look. Yes, eventually it does come down to that; in the end, we must decide not to look.
But more than that, to stop turning to pornography we must learn to
address and control the catalyst behind looking. Thus, rather than "how
can you" we might make more headway by asking "why do you": why are
we or they looking at pornography in the first place? The answer to this
question, I believe, will reveal the fertile soil in which our addictions take
root. Addictions of any kind cannot take root in themselves; they are the
result and not the cause. Therefore, it holds true that they are nourished
by something else, something bigger than the addiction itself.

Curiosity aside, addicts turn to pornography for many reasons. Some seek it out as a form of entertainment. Others escape to it as a coping mechanism. In some form or another, most addicts crave the excitement of secrecy, waiting for and even creating opportunities to be alone where they can then view it unrestrained and without anxiety. For me, I often turned to it when I felt unfulfilled; not sexually, but in the sense that I felt of little value, like I wasn't being recognized for what I had done, or because I felt I was without sufficient opportunities through which to reach my potential. Among recovery groups, it is common to see the following acronym used when speaking about other seeds of indulgence: I. B. L. A. S. T. O. F. F. It stands for: Insecurity, Bored, Lonely, Angry, Stressed, Tired, Overwhelmed, Frustrated, and Fearful. Additionally, in my own life, my addiction got to such a point that there were times I would turn to it on the heels of something good happening. Inexplicably, more than a means of celebration, looking at pornography at such times was something I did as a sort of show of invincibility. "Life is good. I am feeling strong. So I'll show you (meaning myself) that I can look at pornography and it won't even bother me." My heart breaks when I think back on these moments and the much darker ones that inevitably followed when I realized my deceit and could no longer regain the happiness I had enjoyed just moments before. In despair, I would often return to pornography within hours in a crude attempt to escape the acute sense of failure. In this sense, addictive habits are perpetually producing, then ferociously feeding off, failure. It is a nasty cycle.

No matter who we are, it is natural to experience these types of feelings as we go through life. But that does not mean they are the source of temptation or sin. Rather, they act as the servants of a greater master through whom the door to addiction is opened. And what is this greater master? Of what do these feelings all have in common? Self. Addiction, at its core, is selfish by nature. It is also very impatient, an attribute closely linked to selfishness. It wants relief now. It wants pleasure now. It wants to do such-and-such because *I'm* bored, *I'm* right, *I'm* tired, *I* deserve a break, they don't understand *me*, *I* need to do something for *myself*, and on and on and on.

We live in a Band-Aid world. When children are little and sustain an "owie" of some kind, it is not uncommon for them to want it kissed better or to have a bandage put on it right away. They usually don't want it cleaned (after all cleaning hurts); they just want the bandage. Somewhere along the way, they become conditioned to associate the bandage with a reprieve from pain. By definition, however, a reprieve from anything has never been about permanence. Likewise, as adults, when we feel bad or bored or angry, we immediately begin looking for ways or things by which to temporarily soothe the pain or escape from it, mistakenly believing that with that momentary fix time alone will smooth things over. Quite often we are so focused on temporary relief that we don't even stop to consider the consequences of our actions. We simply want the pain to abate now. Is this selfish? The desire for relief is not, but demanding relief at the expense of appropriate care is.

On this subject, Anna Williams, the eighteenth-century poet and one-time companion under Dr. Samuel Johnson's roof and care, once wondered aloud why men turn to strong drink and, in a drunken stupor, make beasts of themselves. In reply, Johnson said that "he who makes a beast of himself gets rid of the pain of being a man."[2] I want to amend the statement as follows: "he who makes a beast of himself *tries* to get rid of the pain of being a man"; for fleeting relief is the only relief that can be achieved through selfish, thoughtless bestiality.

To better apply this to our situation, let's first define *pain*. There's physical pain, of course, but most dangerous to the addict are the internal pains we can easily hide: emotional anguish and mental frustration. And when have we experienced these internal pains before? It has been my experience that they most often consume us when some goal has not been realized, or when some situation or person—perhaps even ourselves—has not lived up to our high expectations. To whom or what do we turn for comfort? We should turn to those closest to us. But often we do not communicate properly, we are embarrassed to admit weakness or hurt, or we do not want to talk to them because, perhaps, they caused the pain. Thus, when we have a bad day or feel a keen sense of inadequacy about ourselves in any manner, we begin to seek ways through which we can immediately escape the pain or discomfort and feel better by ourselves. Often, we do this by turning to things that can immediately distract us, temporarily relieve suffering, or erroneously fill the void we feel inside. In concept this is not a bad thing because our thinking is correct. We do need relief from the pain. The void does need to be filled. The trouble is we often fill the void impatiently and with things of no worth; we escape to places that promote selfishness and end up making us feel worse after the initial albeit temporary rush of relaxation or excitement.

Spiritually speaking, when we feel depressed by these mental and emotional pains, we are at our must vulnerable. Satan moves in to tempt us further and lead us by degrees into darker and more depressing alleys. Of this, the Head Devil in the C. S. Lewis novel *The Screwtape Letters* teaches that "the trough periods of the human undulation provide excellent opportunity for all sensual temptations, particularly those of sex." He later adds that the "attack has a much better chance of success when the man's whole inner world is drab and cold and empty" and that during these times he can also be "much more easily drawn into perversions."[3]

I will be the first to admit that I often looked at pornography during these "trough" periods in an attempt to feel good, and by that I do not mean physically. Yes, addicts often turn to pornography to experience sexual elation, especially when coupled with masturbation. But viewing pornography, I believe, has little to do with feeling *good*; rather, men often look at it because they believe or are conditioned to believe at that moment that it will make them feel *better*—better about themselves usually or about their current situation—by removing them for a time from the harsh reality of their existence.

With this in mind, we need to realize that these struggles and the process by which we seek to find comfort in the midst of them are common to all people. Thus, while the outward appearance of pornography addiction is different than, say, that of alcohol or drugs, the selfish foundation of the addiction is the same. This goes for subtle addictions too, such as shopping, watching soap operas, social networking, reading romance books, watching sports, eating, gossiping, and more. Taking into consideration the definition of addiction proposed earlier (something you cannot completely control), it is my belief that at some time in our lives, we are all addicted to something; something we struggle to control; something we turn to out of habit in order to escape.

This information can be hard to hear, especially because many people—particular those who are trying to help someone with a pornography addiction—do not want to consider that anything they are involved in is, in any manner, similar to something they see as perverted and base. I find it necessary to offer up this viewpoint, though, as the means of leveling the field in order to help us separate the problem, pornography, from the cause, selfishness. Let me repeat that: the problem is not, not, not pornography. The core problem is selfishness and impatience; pornography is just the fruit. Meaning if we focus all our efforts on plucking the fruit off the tree, it will just grow back in a season. To keep the fruit from growing back then, we must tackle the problem at its roots. The tree, so to speak, must be dug out; not chopped down because that still leaves the roots in the ground.

In order to successfully recover from our addictions and heal from the betrayal we feel because of another's addictions, I believe we need to get to a point where we see that this concept is true: the foundation of pornography addiction is no different than any other selfish habit any of us struggle to control. With this mind-set, the way to recovery becomes clearer, and those of us helping an addict find our ability strengthened to help in spite of our initial response of disgust or anger.

I feel it is also important that a vast difference exists between doing something for yourself and doing something out of selfishness. Doing things for yourself can be important and will even be necessary along the road to recovery. Truth be told, sometimes we are guilty of not doing enough for ourselves. On the road to recovery, there must be a delicate balanced. We will discuss this later. Suffice it to say, if we feel a need to do something to help us de-stress in order to regroup or refocus, keeping intact our goals, then this is good; it increases love for self and others and will generate the strength we need to keep fighting against temptation. However, if we are determined to do something for ourselves out of spite with a proud, even rebellious "You know what? I don't care. I deserve to do something for me, me, me" attitude, then this is bad and will surely lead to trouble.

In addition to this, when we define our self-worth solely by outside circumstances such as work, accolades, and others' opinions of us, we become reliant on their continuation. The danger here is that if someone is not constantly recognizing us, or if we are not always meeting what we deem to be the highest standard, we feel less about ourselves. This was true for me. Recognizing inside an emptiness, loneliness, and a general lack of self-acceptance, I began a search to satisfy these needs.

On this idea of satisfying needs, I am reminded of an experience my wife and I shared when we were first married. She was and is a water drinker. I, on the other hand, have always struggled to drink and enjoy the mass quantity of water recommended by people who know better than me. Each night as bedtime neared, I'd begin to sense a growing emptiness inside, a deficit of energy caused by a lack of something vital. In an effort to interpret what I thought were pangs of hunger, I'd quickly begin looking through the cupboards. In the end, however, out of habit my mind always turned to ice cream, a favorite from childhood that always seemed to be in supply. Clearly, my body needed something and by all accounts and past experiences ice cream was that something that would satisfy the cravings.

One time in particular, however, my wife turned me to and said, "You should drink a glass of water instead." Skepticism raised my eyebrows at this ridiculous suggestion. I didn't *want* water. I *wanted* ice cream. After jest-filled deliberation she finally "convinced" me that this was not about what I wanted, but about what my body needed—water.

In order to appease my wife, I promised to first drink a full glass of water. Then I would eat my bowl of ice cream. So I filled up the glass and guzzled it down as fast as I could in order to get on to "better" things. But something strange and, frankly, quite frustrating happened. My desire for ice cream evaporated. In that one instant, the real need of my body had been satisfied. My wife was right. I was so ticked off. I had wanted to enjoy that bowl of ice cream, but now my body didn't need it anymore, nor did it even want it.

Our bodies and spirits are smart. They know what they need in order to operate at full capacity. They recognize when there is sickness brewing or when there is a void of some kind. In the only way they can, they relay messages of need in the hopes we will take appropriate action in order to avoid sickness or maintain health. We, on the other hand, are not so smart—not yet, anyway. In answer to the call, our own personal backgrounds, experiences, and life-exposures have preconditioned us to turn to different things or habits through which we wrongfully attempt to satisfy needs.

So it is not that we do not recognize the need, rather it is simply that we misinterpret what the real need is, and, thus, what the real solution is, and how unfulfilling our go-to-habits are.

Think of your own addiction. At some point in your life, you turned to pornography. The effects were negative, whether you consciously recognized it or not. As a result of these negative feelings, you sought a way to assuage them or to escape. Embarrassed or afraid to tell anyone, you tried out different solutions. One of those solutions was to return to pornography, at which time you felt an immediate dismissal of the bad feelings, stress, and so on, and a surge of elation, control, and power. Just like that, your body conditioned itself to think it needed "ice cream" over "water," so that in the future any time you felt down or bad or frustrated, after subconsciously discerning a need, you relied on habit to try and fill the void. You may have felt satisfied for a moment, sure, but in the end—hours, days, weeks later—those same driving pangs of "hunger" always returned. Why? Because you were not fulfilled mentally, emotionally, or spiritually. You still had real needs that had never really been addressed. Your body was still trying to tell you that it was in desperate need of not "ice cream" but "water," without which the body eventually dies.

So what are your needs? When and where are you settling for ice cream when your body is screaming for water? To stop the unhealthy, immoral cycle of gorging, you must reverse the trend of selfish, impatient, habitual fulfillment. You must force yourself into an honest, open period of introspection where you analyze (ideally with a partner) your goals, your failures, your feelings, your pains, what you think your needs are, and how you have thus far sought to satisfy them on your own. As you do this, you will begin to discern the real needs of your body, mind, and spirit. And when you do, you will be well on your way to filling the void in the right way, selflessly, and at the right time, patiently.

9

ON LOVE AND
REVERSING THE TREND

*"The most important thing in life is to learn how to give out love,
and to let it come in. . . . We think we don't deserve love, we think
if we let it in we'll become too soft."*[1]

MOST OF US FIND COMFORT IN CONTINUITY, IN THE
patterns and physical laws that can be relied on, and out of which
at least some sense can be made. The sun rises in the morning, the moon
at night. Gravity, of course, pulls us down, while levity—in the older
sense of the term—allows for an object to rise above what has always kept
it grounded. For every force exerted upon a certain object, there is a force
equal in power coming from the opposite direction. And then there's
Newton's first law of motion, which states that an object in motion will
remain in motion and on its present course unless compelled to change
by some external force; and when that external force is equal to or greater
than the force of initial motion, the object in motion stops altogether.

These laws are universal, and as such they can be likened to many
things. Perhaps as you were reading through them now, you discerned
mental, emotional, or spiritual parallels to your current situation. No
doubt, the truths therein have been and will continue to be the basis for
change in your life.

For me, the moment I first looked at pornography, I was forced into motion, thrust forward at imperceptible speeds toward some unknown destination. In reality, though, as those first initial moments turned into weeks, then months, then years, and as the speed at which I accelerated from one episode to another increased, it became clear that there was no designated stopping point. Like an object hurling through infinite space toward unexplored universes, it seemed I was doomed to continue to accelerate into the darkness until the day I died or, worse, lost everything dear to me.

Almost every time after a binge on pornography, I would step away in horror at what I had done and wonder how I had arrived at that point and what I could do to keep it from happening again. Looking back, a number of other experiences—good and bad—similarly placed before my mind the need for change. Eventually, the culmination of these experiences and my own maturation brought about the force necessary to stop forward motion long enough to reason logically and commit to change, no matter the cost. For many of you, the doorway to change was ultimately opened by your spouse walking in on you or discovering your virtual footprints on the computer. But like me, these events only served to stop your path of descent momentarily, and they lacked the power to reverse your direction.

The greater question and principle we need to understand then is not how do we stop forward motion, but once stopped, how do we build momentum in the opposite direction. We will discuss theory first and then later in the second section, we will discuss actual steps you can take. However, they will be meaningless if we do not first attempt to understand the principles behind them.

We noted above that opposites exist in all things. With this in mind, if addiction is fueled by selfishness, then it holds true that recovery must be fueled by selflessness. If, at the root of addiction, there is a lack of love or a low self-esteem, then at the heart of recovery, you must learn to love yourself and admit your value. Just as surely as addiction sprouts from a selfish foundation, recovery and healing can only flourish when fed by love. So we need to do all we can to invite, recognize, and accept it. The natural fruits of love will, in turn, give you the strength and inspiration to increase forward motion in the opposite direction. I know this sounds overly simple, romantic, and even cliché. Perhaps it is even embarrassing to consider. But it is the truth.

Love comes in many different ways. For our purposes, though, the love I am speaking of is synonymous with respect and acceptance—as others extend it to us, and as we extend it to others and ourselves. All of us have an inherent need to love and be loved. When this transactional relationship is present in our lives, we experience a sense of fulfillment, even the purest form of happiness for which humankind was made.

In Tolstoy's *War and Peace*, Pierre, a rash young man whose passions and apathy have gotten him into a great deal of trouble, learns this same truth. Of this, the book reads: "While imprisoned in the shed Pierre had learned, not with his intellect but with his whole being, by life itself, that man is created for happiness, that happiness is within him, in the satisfaction of simple human needs."[2] For Pierre, these "simple human needs" have everything to do with love—how it is shown to him by strangers, how he finds it in God, and how he learns to give it to others. In the end, by learning to love and accept love, Pierre experiences for the first time a peace of mind and a happiness that always eluded him. This too will be the case for you as far as you apply this principle. You are in prison, of sorts, and you must learn to love and be loved.

In her simple yet powerful book *Confronting the Myth of Self-Esteem: Twelve Keys to Finding Peace*, Ester Rasband reiterates this point by stating that a "peaceful feeling of acknowledging that we are loved is what makes it possible to grow and contribute. Peace born of love is what gives mankind the strength to make effort."[3]

That is what we ultimately need: the strength to make the effort. As with Pierre's experience, three main sources of love—for ourselves, from our friends and family, and from God—can give us this strength and see us along the path of recovery. Ideally, all three sources combine to help you and love you no matter your mistakes. Love is a powerful combatant against any struggle or addiction. Nothing has the power to inspire humankind to give up sins as does love. It comes in many forms: in an embrace, in a kind word, in praise, in concern, even by way of careful chastisement. On the other hand, when love is withheld or when its opposite, hatred, is instead exhibited in speech or action, the mind and heart of humankind will rarely find the strength or desire to change. I have made the mistake of disciplining my children out of frustration and not love. Had I controlled my temporary temper and harnessed my love for them in a more constructive and creative way, they no doubt would have learned the lesson I intended to teach. More important, our relationship would have become stronger. They would have learned to trust me and not fear me. Instead, when I needed them close, I only managed to push them away. This is true of all of us, but during this process, it will be especially true for the addict.

Men, as you progress toward recovery and healing, you will most likely feel both loved and hated, and perhaps, at first anyway, the latter more than the former. This can be true for a couple reasons. First, anytime we are keenly aware of our failures, it is hard not to despise what we have become. Second, those with whom you have shared your struggles have been suddenly thrown into a pool of confusion and pain. The laws or patterns they'd always relied on and found comfort in were violently ripped from under them. In these instances, it is only natural (not right, but natural) for them to react out of anger and come across as full of malice toward you. It is equally natural (not right, but natural) for you to take these outward expressions personally.

During the first couple years after my wife and I began the long process of recovery and healing, I found her using often the word *hate*. In a public setting, for instance, a friend might mention a particular movie that I had always loved but which she associated with my addiction. "I hate that movie," she would say abruptly, and in her voice I could hear an intense surge of anger that wanted no rebuttal or compromise. For my part, I became sensitive to the word *hate*. Her pronouncements of hatred seemed indirectly directed at me. It was hard to convince myself otherwise and it hurt. But did she really hate me? No. Quite honestly, I think very few people are capable of the intense hatred we assign them. Rather, our words and feelings are often projections of what we feel inside. And as it concerns hatred, hate is often only hurt in masquerade.

I am reminded of the initial hurt I felt after learning of my uncle's premature death at the hand of drugs. I was on my bike pedaling to an appointment where I was going to teach a family about my belief that families can be together forever, and the whole time I was literally cursing his name. Out of context, to anyone who might have overheard me, it must have seemed that I hated him passionately. But did I hate my uncle? No. I loved him and love him still. Because of that abiding love I felt so much pain, and because of that pain, I verbalized my sorrow in a hate-filled way.

Eventually, my anger toward my uncle subsided, but I instead projected it upon drugs of all kinds, those who dealt them, and those who used them. Similarly, it is common for wives to feel hatred toward the objects of addiction, such as the people who make pornography, the women who pose for it, the stores that carry it, the people who buy it, poster ads in mall windows, actresses on television or in movies, women at the office, or even random women walking down the street in revealing attire. I know my wife felt anger toward these types of things too.

So what is my point in sharing this in the middle of a chapter about love?

First, in regards to all things drug-related, I justified I had reason enough to hate. I was wrong. I see that now. Likewise, as hard as it may be to hear, you wives must also learn to let go of any hatred you feel. It is debilitating and will only serve to prolong your suffering. In the end, for ultimate recovery and healing to take place, all anger and hatred must be swallowed up by love. This is most often a process. It will take time to get to that point, but if you work at it, the hatred you feel will dissipate.

Second, feeling that we are hated is rarely based on knowledge. Rather, it is something we perceive to be true. But perception, like the greatest magic trick, is often just an illusion. For whatever reason, sometimes we are so focused on what we perceive as real that we see only the trick and not the reality or the reason behind it. I realize there may be times, especially at the beginning, when those you love, and whose love you need, may do things that seem void of love altogether. But they love you—they do. Look hard and I believe you'll see that the reason they act the way they do is because they do love you and they want you to be safe and happy.

A couple years ago, the wife of a recovered addict struggled to know how to help her husband after several relapses. At what point, she wondered, does helping and forgiving in the face of relapse turn into enablement? At the forefront of her struggle was the question: should I ask him to leave our home? In the end, she decided that by allowing him to stay in the situation he was in—continuing to rise and fall and rise and fall without any greater consequence—she was not helping him. In fact, she was prolonging the suffering of everyone under that roof. And so, with tears of love in her eyes, she asked him to leave. He will tell you, if you were to ask him, that this demand made by his wife, whom he loved but had betrayed, was a metaphoric slap in the face. It was, however, the push he needed. I admit to you that I too can speak to the necessity of this push in my own life. The night I was asked to leave my own home was one of the loneliest moments of my life. I have been in dark places. I have felt very, very alone and afraid, but never as much as I did that night, sitting in my car in the dark, wondering what I needed to do to regain control of my life. As far as I knew, I had lost my wife and my children, who had never done me any wrong.

At that moment, I hated myself more than anything. These feelings of intense personal frustration projected themselves upon my wife. "How," I wondered angrily, "could she do this to me? I need her help. I need her love." With the benefit of hindsight, of course, I see clearly now it was her love that forced me out into the cold, and it was in the cold that I awoke to the need for internal revolution. I have not looked back since.

Sometimes the greatest form of love is exhibited by the hands that chasten. Certainly, this is the way the Lord works. Wrote King David, "My son, despise not the chastening of the Lord; neither be weary of his correction: For whom the Lord loveth he correcteth; even as a father the son in whom he delighteth" (Proverbs 3:11–12).

Above all, I know this: where the love of self or the love from others may falter or even seem to fail, the love of God and the Savior will not. They love you because you are theirs, and they will not love you less. This is law universal and unchanging. In that I hope and pray you will find the strength to make the effort and to see recovery and healing to its end.

10

ON OUR INITIAL REACTION

"The more efficient a force is, the more silent and the more subtle it is. Love is the subtlest force in the world."[1]

F OR EVERY ACTION, THERE IS A REACTION. THIS TOO IS an immutable law. While stressful situations often lead to stress-filled reactions, nowhere does it say that you have to react badly in bad situations. With regret, I can think of a recent instance where frustrations at work spilled over at home, so that when my son did something that perhaps deserved gentle correction, he was met instead by a harsh voice. The punishment did not fit the crime and, in fact, my overreaction only made things worse. As soon as the words escaped my mouth, I knew I had been in the wrong. In my pride and frustration, I did not want to admit I had reacted poorly, but it was the only way to make things right and restore in my son some level of respect and trust in me.

Whether you are the one struggling with addiction or the one struggling because of your husband's addiction, it is natural to feel, think, and even verbalize your pain. It is also natural to feel that no one can understand what you went through or what you are going through; that your situation is different than the other person's; or that you alone are the victim. Let me say this, there are no winners here. Everyone is hurting inside. Everyone is a victim in his or her own way. Trying to prove you are the greater victim will only make things worse. What's done is done. We must accept that we can do nothing to change the past. We can then focus our efforts on fixing the present to pave the way for a happier and more stable future. How we react from this moment forward will go a long way toward successful reparation.

To you addicts, the people helping you—the people *willing* to help you in your battle against pornography—will play a fundamental role in your recovery, if you do not drive them away. So don't yell at them. Don't throw your hands up in frustration or roll your eyes in exaggerated disbelief. Odds are if they say something that makes you feel to react this way, there is probably some degree of truth in it. They may not have said it in the best or most polite way, but that doesn't mean you have to retaliate and showcase your hurt feelings by ranting and raving. Getting mad and giving voice or body language to that anger is a choice. You, however, must choose to be in control of your actions at all times and in all places. So they said something that you felt was rude or mean. Rise above it, glean from it whatever truth you can, and apply it like a man!

That said, if you are basing your recovery on other people—to what extent they help you or how lovingly they react or don't react—you will never succeed. As hopeless as it sounds, you cannot rely on others in the end. The positive, loving reactions of friends and family can go a long ways in a short amount of time to help you maintain the strength to recover, but the ultimate responsibility to change rests firmly on your shoulders, no matter how the people around you act.

Now, a word to those of you helping your loved one overcome addiction. It is nearly impossible for someone who has not struggled with a major addiction to comprehend just how hard it is to control. This was true for my wife, I know, among others who desired my recovery. "Just don't look at it," I might hear on occasion, or "Choose to look away. You are in control." This advice, offered out of concern, was good and true. How we react is, as stated above, a matter of choice. But—and this is a big *but*—addictive substances are often so powerful that they cloud judgment and imperceptibly control choice, or at least heavily influence it. I can recall choosing to go to the computer to look for pornography after seeing something on television that aroused my interest. But I can also remember how I did so with little thought about the error of this decision or the consequences that would follow, which is why I always found myself at the bottom looking up, wondering how exactly I had managed to fall so far. In this sense, an addict might appropriately be compared to a dinghy amidst rough ocean waters, pushed this way and that by forces greater than choice, even though it was choice that got us out in the ocean in the first place. With this in mind, I will try to explain what it feels like to be addicted to something. At the same time, I want to use this description to introduce how many women commonly react when a man first discloses to her his past or the events of a recent relapse. I hope that by seeing how an addict is easily pushed along by habit without conscious choice, you will find the compassion and understanding to control any initial reactions of anger and frustration, both of which are a choice.

As strange as it may seem, there were times when I could actually feel myself falling back into relapse long before I even relapsed. A giant ocean wave approached slowly but surely, ever increasing in size and velocity until it suddenly overcame me. Of course, I did not see that this was the case until long after my limp body had been washed ashore. Depression works much the same way: those who struggle with it will tell you that they can feel it coming, that they can sense they are sinking into grave emotional and mental depths, yet they can do little to stop it.

I am reminded of a time when I was a little boy. Consumed by an intense fever, I woke up in the middle of the night with hallucinations. Among other things, bees were everywhere. In front of me and all around me, they kept zipping about at uncontrollable speeds. Everything in the room was spinning in circles too. I focused all of my mental energy on trying to stop what I knew was mine to control, but no matter how hard I tried or how bad I wanted it to stop everything kept moving at dizzying speeds. To this day, I can recall with clarity that moment and the fear that accompanied it. Of the many instances in which I succumbed to intense temptations of pornography, I felt like that little boy again. How often I realized in the middle of surfing the Internet that I needed to stop looking at pornography, how often I told myself "No more! No more! No more!" only to keep looking because at the time it was not within my power to stop.

To paint an even more vivid picture of a man drowning in addiction, listen to Daniel Dafoe's famous character, Robinson Crusoe, describe shipwreck at sea.

> A raging wave, mountain-like, came rolling astern of us, and plainly bade us. . . . It took us with such a fury, that it overset the boat at once; and separating us as well from the boat as from one another, gave us no time

to say, "O God!" for we were all swallowed up in a moment.

    Nothing can describe the confusion of thought which I felt when I sank into the water; for though I swam very well, yet I could not deliver myself from the waves. . . . I saw the sea come after me as high as a great hill, and as furious as an enemy, which I had no means or strength to contend with.[2]

Let's build upon this horrific image. Imagine you are on a dock. It stretches out into the ocean like a giant hand. Beyond the edge of the dock, the ocean roars, turned about by violent storm. In the midst of that ocean, you see a dinghy. Made of aluminum, it can barely hold its own let alone the added weight of its captain—a tired, drenched, and ragged man. You recognize him as your loved one. Maybe a son or husband, maybe a boyfriend or even your dad. You sense he is in trouble and needs help. The wind is so loud you can barely hear him, but his muffled screams confirm your suspicions.

He then hefts into the air a rope you can use to haul him in. "Yes, let me help!" You encourage him to throw you the rope. He does and it plops onto the dock at your feet. But when you go to pick it up, you see it is not just a regular piece of rope as you had assumed it would be. Rather, it is worn and tattered from the many storms he has weathered. Drenched by the heavy rains and covered in slimy seaweed, it is slippery to the touch. Perhaps it is also covered in barnacles that tear at your hands. To make matters worse, its moldy, rotting exterior emits a foul odor.

Focused on the filth of the rope, you drop it and take a step back. It slips into the ocean and is swallowed whole, and the man in the boat is left, for a time, to wait out the storm on his own.

The sudden, out-of-nowhere unveiling of your partner's past probably took you by surprise. Or perhaps you had hints along the way that prepared you for the revelation of his struggle, but even this, I wager, was not enough to minimize the actual surprise and accompanying pain. Regardless, upon learning such a horrific secret, you no doubt experienced—and perhaps even continue to experience—a violent surge of emotions including but not limited to sadness, hurt, anger, and even hatred as was discussed briefly in the last chapter. These feelings are normal and often take quite some time to run their course. But run their course they must. In light of this, it is equally important to realize that you will require just as much help as the addict and that your recovery process will be similar in scope. We will discuss the grieving process in detail in the healing section, but for now and for the sake of this topic, it is important to simplify and even undermine that particular and necessary process by saying that even these feelings of acrimony must be controlled.

On our fridge growing up, my mom used to have a yellow cardboard placard with a quote on it that has been attributed to many people over the years. In green letters it read: "Life is 10% how you make it and 90% how you take it"—good advice for all of us. How we react is of the utmost importance and, in many instances, it can make all the difference as to the outcome. Imagine if the prodigal son had returned in all humility only to find a father that shunned him because of his mistakes. What might the prodigal son have felt? What might he have done? What opportunities to grow and love might the family have been denied?

As previously mentioned, I have on several occasions shared information about my past with various friends and family. Sadly, but not without understanding, on some of these occasions my declaration—made in an attempt to seek support and fully repent—has been met with disgust and disdain. My parents and siblings were understanding and supportive. I do not know if I could have made it through this without their unconditional support and love. But when my wife and I decided to tell her folks, it did not go so well. In fact, just the opposite occurred. My mother-in-law adamantly encouraged my wife to seek a divorce; she took it upon herself to track down my parents and suggest they get me help; and she broke off all contact with our family. Over a year passed before she spoke to my wife again, and five years came and went before she ever spoke to me. To this day, my relationship with her is surface-level at best, only kept alive it seems by duty and the commonality we share in my wife and children.

We can spend a whole chapter analyzing why my parents reacted one way and hers another. But the reality is none of us are perfect. We are all just dealing with this situation the best we can and with the understanding we have. To make it harder still, we live in a society where pornography addiction is not only misunderstood but looked down upon. Anyone involved with such filth, we believe, must themselves be filthy and perverted.

It may be hard to see now, but this is just not so. As you strive to be comforted and to forgive he who has hurt you, it is imperative you try to understand that behind every sinner there is a person really no different than you, a child of God with struggles unique to and perhaps a reflection of his upbringing. All of us have weaknesses, some that we're ashamed of even, but when, where, and why these weaknesses developed is anyone's guess. From the moment we are born, countless variables, encounters, and experiences play a role in shaping who we become, but they cannot be easily traced. Some studies suggest that individuals are born with certain weaknesses or with higher propensities toward sexual behavior. Again, the evidence is far from decisive. But even if the influential experiences in our lives could be determined or the evidence of such studies clearly pointed to a behavioral disorder of some kind, I believe we are greater than our circumstances and stronger than any study might suggest.

Because of this, what the addict needs more than anything at first is for judgment to be suspended. As it pertains to society's judgmental reaction to pornography or sex addicts, I believe we can learn a lesson from observing those who have recovered from drug or alcohol addictions and how they are commonly treated. Recovered drug addicts are often forthright about their past problems, often sharing this information within minutes of meeting you. They do this for a couple reasons. One, constantly acknowledging their victories helps them stay honest and strong. Two, like any of us, they need respect and continual encouragement. And three, disclosing their past increases the number of people in their corner who will watch out for them and even go to great lengths to protect them from situations that might prove harmful. I have seen many people forego alcohol temporarily or permanently for the good of a friend they care about.

For example, take Josh Hamilton, a baseball player who openly shared his past battles with drug and alcohol addiction. When his team won its first ever playoff series in 2010, his teammates canceled the traditional champagne celebration, opting instead for two-liters of soda. Away from the celebrity spotlight and television cameras, I have likewise seen this same level of respect and support freely given to others. Whether friend or complete stranger, their reactions are virtually always the same: "good job"; "way to go"; "wow, that's tough to do;" "I'm proud of you"; "keep going strong!"

Imagine how much stronger the pornography addict would become if, after admitting the struggles of his past, he was the immediate recipient of sincere encouragement and respect. "Good job, man." "Honestly, I've struggled with that too. I'm in your corner." "I can't comprehend it, but I know it's a real addiction and it had to have been excruciating to overcome." "I appreciate you telling me." "I'm proud of you." "I'm happy for you." "You have my respect." "How can I help?" From such reactions, the degree to which the addict's strength and courage would increase cannot be measured. You've heard the phrase safety or strength in numbers. This is no exception. What are our reactions like? Are we part of the crowd that empowers the individual by our respect and encouragement or are we part of the larger crowd that does not care to associate with them, as if they were diseased? As individuals, as a couple, a family, or an entire society, we must get to the point where we naturally and happily join the first group. We must somehow progress past the initial feelings of disgust. We must look past the sick and twisted facade we are wont to paint over the sinner and see him for who he really was, is, and may yet become.

Above all, remember, if a loved one has come to you of his own accord, he is seeking your help. And if he has not come to you and you have discovered his problem on your own, then he really needs your help. So when you see that mildewed rope cast before your feet, be strong and take up the slack. At both ends is a person who needs saving.

> They that go down to the sea in ships, that do business in great waters;
>> These see the works of the Lord, and his wonders in the deep.
>> For he commandeth, and raiseth the stormy wind, which lifteth up the waves thereof.
>> They mount up to the heaven, they go down again to the depths: their soul is melted because of trouble.
>> They reel to and fro, and stagger like a drunken man, and are at their wits' end.
>> Then they cry unto the Lord in their trouble, and he bringeth them out of their distresses.
>> He maketh the storm a calm, so that the waves thereof are still.
>> Then are they glad because they be quiet; so he bringeth them unto their desired haven. (Psalm 103:27–30)

11

ON COMMUNICATION

"I was angry with my friend:
I told my wrath, my wrath did end.
I was angry with my foe:
I told it not, my wrath did grow."[1]

SOMEONE ONCE ASKED ME, "OUT OF EVERYTHING you've learned during your recovery process, if you could choose just one piece of advice to share, what would it be?" My answer: communicate. Communicate, communicate, communicate! I am positive that the majority of problems couples face could be solved in an instant or would have been prevented in the first place, if they had known how to properly and appropriately communicate with each other. I certainly did not know how to do this. My wife too had to learn. Together, we learned to share our feelings, to articulate our thoughts, to withhold judgment and anger, to be patient, to be charitable, and to listen, listen, listen.

With this in mind, I want to present three different scenarios to showcase the errors we often make when trying to communicate with one another. All of them exhibit forms of retaliation and pride.

Number one: Inevitably, during playtime, one of my kids accidentally does something that hurts the other. Often it is the result of a foolish mistake made because he got caught up in the emotion of the moment, or because he was so wound up he did not see the pending danger just moments away. Either way, the child who was hurt often retaliates by screaming at the other or even reaching out to hurt the other in a manner equal to or greater than the way they were initially hurt. This causes both to be upset and feel hurt.

Upon asking what happened to cause such a violent outburst and why the one felt justified in hurting the other, I am met with the following reply: "So-and-so made me mad."

To this I have often retorted, "No one makes us mad, son. We choose to be mad. Had you taken a step back and talked to him calmly, or had you walked away and come and talked to me first, we might have worked this out without anyone getting more hurt then they already were."

Number two: In similar situations, I have also heard the following response:

"What happened?" I ask.

Answer: "So-and-so hurt me."

"I didn't mean to," rebuts the other.

"Yes, you did."

"No, I didn't."

"Yes, you did."

And so the argument will continue until either a third party (me, in the case of my children) steps in or one of them takes responsibility to stop and voice his views in a less vindictive manner, perhaps even at a different time.

Number three: Have you ever played the game *Taboo*? It is a simple game wherein one player tries to give clues to his teammate to help her guess a key word. Looming over his shoulder, however, is an opponent who all-too-eagerly waits, watching for any slight slip of the tongue, which might reveal one of many words he is not supposed to say during his turn of play. Upon hearing the utterance of such a word or even a part of the word, the opponent immediately pushes a button, making a loud buzzing sound in his ear. It is all fun and games. But have you seen this in your own communication habits?

I have certainly seen it in mine. I cringe to think how often I have sat listening to my wife explain her feelings, answer my questions, or offer constructive criticism, only to eagerly jump in and cut her off with a rebuttal of some sort. Equally egregious, how often I have perched like a hawk, listening for a slip of the tongue that might reveal a flaw in her story, thus proving my point; or a weakness in her argument that might allow me to turn the tables so that she becomes the one at fault, and not me.

Having been on both ends of these types of conversation, let me make you a promise. If you truly want to understand your partner, then listen to her, and don't say a word. Let her work out her inner most feelings and thoughts. If you do this, rather than always jumping in to try and solve the problem or cutting in to make a point or protect your reputation, you will come to see your spouse in a new light. You will hear and comprehend the real problem, and know, if requested to do so, how to help find a resolution.

No matter the size of the issue, how we respond can seriously alter, reset, or propel forward the progress made. To bring about complete healing and recovery as a couple, you will need to continue to keep open the lines of consistent and honest communication. It is important to realize that as both of you work to undo these addictive tendencies and repair the breach in your marriage, there will continue to be temptations, temporary setbacks, relapses, hurt feelings, and even hard feelings of which you will both need to share with one another—immediately and kindly.

As you intimately share these feelings and thoughts with each other, you will begin anew to safeguard your relationship. Though it may now hang by a thread, in time it can again become a complex tapestry of beauty and strength. Above all, remember that charity given is charity received. Kindness begets kindness. "A soft answer turneth away wrath: but grievous words stir up anger" (Proverbs 15:1).

Men, if your wife yells at you, take the higher road and return her anger with words and deeds of kindness. She is hurting, and her words are simply a reflection of that pain.

Women, the same goes for you. You do not have to tolerate anger. In fact, if your husband's temper is habitual and makes you fear for your safety, then you have every right to demand respect and to flee the situation. But if you can see that his sudden burst of anger is not meant to be abusive but is, instead, a reflection of the pain he feels inside, then return his indignation with kindness of your own.

The "force of love," Gandhi said, "truly comes into play only when it meets with causes of hatred. True [love] does not ignore or blind itself to causes of hatred, but in spite of the knowledge of their existence, operates upon the person setting those causes in motion."[2]

May this love ever garnish your words, keep open your ears, and soften your hearts.

12

WHEN DESIRE IS LACKING

"And you too . . . will realize the Vision (not the idle wish) of your heart, be it base or beautiful, or a mixture of both, for you will always gravitate toward that which you, secretly, most love. Into your hands will be placed the exact results of your own thoughts."[1]

IT IS MY HOPE THAT THIS BOOK IS BEING READ BY BOTH husband and wife. Having said that, I am enough of a realist to know that in many cases, it is you, the wife, reading alone, hoping to better understand your husband's addiction, thereby discovering a way to help him change. Before I say anything else, thank you. Thank you for making the effort. I know you love him; that is why it hurts and, most likely, that is why you are here, reading this book. If your husband never does anything to change at all, I promise you will be blessed because of your selfless desires. But, for all intents and purposes, you will not change him. He alone must decide to change. If he refuses, then, of course, it is a problem that requires resolution. For this chapter, I do not want to focus on that scenario, though. We will touch on that in the next chapter. Instead, men, I want to focus on you, in particular those of you who lack the desire to change.

First, as a foundation for our discussion, let's deconstruct the addiction process with an analogy. Most of us look at pornography addicts as being in their right mind and, thus, being able to make heads or tails of what to us are black-and-white situations. They are not in their right minds, though. Studies prove pornography affects the brain on many levels. By its very nature, it subtly but surely smothers the real desires and needs of a man. Picture a thousand blankets on top of a campfire, or what once was a campfire. Each blanket represents a moment in which pornography was indulged. In the beginning, a man may be drawn to pornography only to despise it seconds after coming off the emotional, sexual high. In these cases, the resulting pain and anger are usually enough to keep him far from it for good. He rips the blanket off the fire, fans the flames back to life, and moves on. But sometimes the man does not take the blanket off. Instead, after watching it burn, he just walks away. Maybe days, months, or years go by, but eventually he returns. Another blanket is tossed on the fire. Perhaps he thinks nothing of it because he can still see the fire and feel of its warmth. But then he returns, again and again, and under the two, three, four blankets, the fire dwindles. The more often he returns, the less time goes by between episodes of indulgence and the faster these blankets pile up. Eventually, relapse after relapse, blanket after blanket, the addict no longer sees or feels the existence of the fire that once burned bright. After more episodes, he may even forget that a fire existed in the first place. The same can be said for all aspects of the addict's life: his desire to go to church, spend time with his kids, be intimate with his wife—all these things can be squelched by the thick blankets of addiction.

At some point, he steps back, looks at the pile of blankets, shivers in the cold, and assumes the fire is out for good. But is it? Or do live embers exist somewhere underneath all of those blankets?

With this in mind, men, I want to pose a question: do you really have no desire to change at all? Or is your desire simply very small?

To help in your analysis, I'd like to share an excerpt from a letter written to me by a friend who, at the time, was struggling with an addiction to pornography:

> "Why am I doing this?" I kept asking. "Why do I keep returning to this horrible thing that brings darkness into my life?" I really struggled with this question. I studied the scriptures, I prayed, I talked about my weaknesses with others, but it was never enough to help me stay clean for good. Then I came to a realization that was extremely difficult to swallow—I was doing it because I wanted to.

I remember when he later shared this realization with me again over the phone. "I know I should stop," he cried. "And I know I need to stop. But how do you stop when you don't want to?"

I want to pose again the two questions I just asked of you, but this time about him. From what you can gather, did my friend really have no desire to change? Or was his desire simply very small?

Out of everything he said, one word in particular jumps out at me: *want*. "I was doing it because I *wanted* to." "How do you stop when you don't *want* to?" This seems clear enough, *want* being synonymous with desire: okay, he had no desire. Then why was he still working to overcome this problem? Why was he talking to me? Why were these questions even on his mind? Because, in spite of a waning desire to stop looking at something that instigated sexual arousal, he knew that stopping was the right thing to do. There is, I believe, little distinction between wanting to stop and knowing you need to stop. In fact, for this discussion, I'm going to say they are one and the same. We must not confuse a lack of desire with a flat-out refusal to change. The latter has made up his mind. With stubborn pride, he has snuffed out the flame and walked away. The former, however, is trying to make up his mind, and in him exists, as small as it may seem, a flickering light of hope.

Men, you may not feel a desire to change. I understand this; the seductive pull of pornography is overpowering, to say the least. But if you are being honest, like my friend, you know there needs to be a change. You have thus far maintained two lives: addiction and family. But you also know that if you persist down your current path you run the risk of losing everything. So why not change now? Desire to desire to change.

"What? But how?" you might ask still. "I don't feel like changing. In fact, I don't feel anything, except when I'm looking at pornography or masturbating. So how do I change and start desiring something I don't— just like that?" In answer, let me share a lengthy but pertinent quote from Stephen R. Covey's *7 Habits of Highly Effective People*:

> "My wife and I just don't have the same feelings for each other we used to have. I guess I just don't love her anymore and she doesn't love me. What can I do?"
>
> "The feeling isn't there anymore?" I asked.
>
> "That's right," he reaffirmed. "And we have three children we're really concerned about. What do you suggest?"
>
> "Love her," I replied.

"I told you, the feeling just isn't there anymore."

"Love her."

"You don't understand. The feeling of love just isn't there."

"Then love her. If the feeling isn't there, that's a good reason to love her."

"But how do you love when you don't love?"

"My friend, love is a verb. Love—the feeling—is a fruit of love, the verb. So love her. Serve her. Sacrifice. Listen to her. Empathize. Appreciate. Affirm her. Are you willing to do that?"[2]

I likewise propose that desire is a verb. It is a choice more than a feeling. How do you desire to change? Make a conscious effort to start desiring change. In the spirit of self-affirmation, wake up every morning and look in the mirror, if you have to, and tell yourself that you want to change. Then go about your day and change what needs to be changed, as if it was the desire of your heart. More specifically, if you are to regain the desire buried deep within you, you must find a way to remove yourself from the problem long enough to extract the desire from under the many layers of habit and yearning. Alcoholics and drug addicts undergo an intense period of detoxification. So must you. If you are to succeed, you must choose to step away from anything and everything that has led or might lead you to pornography. This will no doubt require a barrage of strict rules, great personal sacrifice, and the help, prayers, patience, love, and constant follow-up of family and friends. Desire, the feeling, the natural fruits of these actions, will then begin again to blossom.

Studies show this to be true. Prolonged viewing of pornography changes the brain, causing men to become indifferent and numb to the real pleasures of life (family, a healthy sexual relationship, hobbies, and so on), to experience a hyper-reactivity to new types of pornography (made worse by the sheer amount of it all over the web), and eventually to discover their willpower has eroded completely. This pattern works in the reverse direction as well. As you force yourself to step away from pornography (because you know you need to or should), your brain, like an elastic band, will spring back into shape. Your willpower will increase. As it does, you will become more sensitive and opposed to all types of pornography (even in its smallest, most subtle forms). And all the while, you will again feel, not only the long-lost desire to change, but the immense joy of living with those for whom you have changed.

How long it will take for you to uncover this long-lost desire is uncertain. In the scientific world, the period of detoxification is often in proportion to the depth of addiction, meaning the longer you were addicted, the longer it will take to regain what you have lost. With this in mind, do not become discouraged if you do not "magically" feel the desire to change overnight. In many instances, desire is regained by degrees.

Having said that, allow me to close with yet another reference to my Christian faith. I know this may not apply to everyone reading this book, but I feel the need to say it. I believe there is a higher power in charge of healing. I believe that if you do everything in your power to avoid pornography, God will do everything in his power to help you rebuild the fire within. But you must seek his help. More specifically, you must seek the desire to change. Of all the powerful stories in the Bible, none are perhaps more applicable to you now than that of the father whose son had since childhood been enslaved by an "unclean spirit." In humility, the father sought out Jesus, not because he believed but because he wanted to believe. Said the father to Jesus Christ:

> If thou canst do any thing, have compassion on us, and help us.
>
> Jesus said unto him, If thou canst believe, all things are possible to him that believeth.
>
> And straightway the father of the child cried out, and said with tears, Lord, I believe; *help thou mine unbelief.* (Mark 9:22–24)

If you lack the desire but know in your heart that you want it or need it, then ask for it—"Lord, help thou mine undesire"—and I promise he will help you, just as surely as he helped my friend. Like a flame flickering to life, and with the help of family, friends, and God, my friend changed. He found his lost desire. So can you. If Jesus Christ raised the dead once, why not now? If he healed the sick once, why not now? And if he once turned water into wine, then who says he cannot now, starting this hour, begin to turn a lack of desire within you into a burning desire to change.

As Jesus said to the father, so I say to *all* of you: all things are possible *if* you believe. This caveat refers specifically to believing in Christ, but I want to step away from that religious principle for a second and apply the "if" in a general sense. Believe that you need to change. Believe that you can uncover the desire to change. And believe that you will change. Your desire may be small—it may start with just knowing you need to change—but that will be enough. If you do everything in your power to avoid pornography, even when you do not want to avoid it, I promise you will feel the desire to change, and with that ever-increasing desire change you will.

13

ON MARRIAGE AND DIVORCE

"Though nothing can bring back the hour
Of splendour in the grass, of glory in the flower;
We will grieve not, rather find
Strength in what remains behind."[1]

WE HAVE THUS FAR SPOKEN WITH OPTIMISM ABOUT the potential for healing and recovery. We will continue to take this angle, focusing more specifically in the following chapters on repentance, forgiveness, and hope for a better tomorrow. Yet we realize, that in many cases, the wounds of the past run so deep and the idea of a future under present circumstances seems all but impossible. This, of course, may be true if present circumstances do not change.

We wrote this book with the intention that it be read by both husband and wife, and with the belief that when so read, it would help initiate the introspection and dialogue necessary to bring about recovery and healing for both the individual and the couple. Yet with a measure of sadness and frustration, I admit I have seen countless copies shunned by the husbands who need the healing principles within its pages. "Why," you rightly might wonder, "is my husband not willing to read this, or not willing to go with me to a counselor or a support group, or not willing to see our ecclesiastical leader, or tell his parents, or so on?" The reasons, no doubt, vary. At the center of them, however, is a selfish pride that is not willing to forego ego long enough to get control of the problem. I know that sounds harsh, but I can speak to that. I did not go with my wife to a support group. I dragged my feet to and from the $95/hour counselor. And had someone offered me a book to read, I probably would have pushed it aside too. For me, it was not that I lacked the desire to change, but I wanted to do it on my own, or at least feel like I was doing it on my own. I also felt an unhealthy level of embarrassment and apprehension. For many of you wives, the struggle to get your husband to seek or accept help has continued and may yet continue because he has convinced himself that he is doing no wrong.

In such a scenario, you may wonder, "When is enough, enough?" Among all the burdensome questions and concerns you have thus far shouldered, whether to divorce or not will most likely be the heaviest of all, especially if kids are involved. So, do you leave your husband? While I know you crave a yes or no, I cannot in good conscience answer that for you. In fact, even if I had all the facts before me, it is not my decision to make, nor do I believe it is anyone else's to make but yours. I will, however, attempt to share a few insights that will help you make this decision, if indeed you are contemplating it now.

The effects of divorce—for better or worse, 'til death do we part—cannot be measured. My mom's parents divorced when she was young. I am not qualified to speak about the struggles she and her siblings had because of this, but I do know they were real and, in some cases, lasting. In addition to a set of grandparents on both sides of the family, instances of divorce seem to be everywhere my wife and I turn: uncles, aunts, cousins, siblings. I have often wondered how many, if any, of these divorces were influenced by the preceding divorce of parents or grandparents. Noting the significant struggles many of their children had growing up, I have further wondered how much, if at all, divorce was to blame? Take my uncle, for instance. Might he have avoided drugs had his father been in the home? I don't know, nor can I know. But I do know that it is not fair to look back and suggest that all negative things thereafter resulted because of that one act. Like a fire that makes room for new life by purging the forest floor, I believe in many cases, divorce can make room for and lead to better lives. My sister-in-law, for example, made the difficult decision to leave her first husband after sustained dishonesty proved he was not willing to change. Years later, she would meet my brother and in their union, we have all found great joy. He adores her children, and they adore him. The agony of divorce has been compensated for. My aunt also finds herself in a better situation, having left her husband after he chose to live a lifestyle that excluded both her and the children. The examples on both sides, for or against, are many. In some cases, religion and culture are deciding factors. In most cases, family, friends, and coworkers may seek to persuade you to leave or stay. While sincere in their love for you and their desire to see you safe and happy, their efforts are often premature or tainted by their own experiences. In the end, divorce is a personal decision that must be made carefully and consciously, all emotions aside. Furthermore, from a religious point of view, I believe it is a decision that can and should only be made by the guidance of the spirit made available from God to all his children.

Before broaching this subject any further, I'd like to share a story from my youth to set up my general feelings on marriage and divorce.

When I was in high school, I took a pottery class. I loved sitting down to a fresh block of clay. The limitless possibilities evoked the image of some unique, stunningly beautiful masterpiece hidden deep within the clay. For my part, I was to do as Michelangelo did: envision the masterpiece, and then, by constant re-working, set it free. The work was intense but creatively satisfying. By the end of the term, I ended up with a large teapot, a set of mugs, a butter dish, a tissue box, a bowl, and a coil vase or two. But as well crafted as they were, they all had a common problem: they were not done. I had shaped them as desired, I had let them dry for an extended period of time, and I had even put them in the kiln for an initial bisque-firing, but that was it; that was as far as I wanted to take them. I did not sand down the bumps or pores on the bisque because I was not willing to look closely at their imperfections. I was more concerned with making as many pieces as possible rather than seeing one or two pieces to the very end. I did not apply any glaze either. The paints looked flat and I could not exactly determine how they would turn out once fired, a process discovered only by trial and error; and since it would be too late to make any changes, I decided it was too big of a risk to take. Thus, the pieces on which I had spent a considerable amount of time and energy never entered the final firing process in which both clay and glaze are matured, strengthened, and made vibrant in a 2100-degree kiln. To this day, the teapot and mugs sit on the back of a shelf, covered in dust. I do not dare use them less the toxic unfired bisque poisons the guests. I wonder, then, having never become what it was meant to become, can I really call it a teapot? Or is the real teapot in there somewhere, still screaming to be set free?

What does this have to do with marriage? Too often we enter marriage thinking the block before us is in its completed state. This blinding bliss is not necessarily bad because by it we are often able to glimpse what can be if both husband and wife are willing to work together and see the job through to its very end. Like it or not, this process is all about risk; it's about trial and error and choosing the wrong glaze from time to time, or not letting a piece dry long enough, or lifting the kiln lid to discover a cracked handle or, worse, a piece that exploded altogether. Yes, these moments and mistakes can be frustrating and heartbreaking, but it's what we learn from them and how we move forward in spite of them that ensure a beautiful final piece.

Let me offer yet another art analogy. Before my aspiring pottery days, when I was young and first learning to draw, I would often crumple up and throw away a whole sheet of good paper because in the first stroke or two I made what I deemed to be a picture-ending mistake. It took lots of time and patient practice, but eventually I learned to use the eraser and keep on drawing. In some cases, I even turned those mistakes into details that made the picture better. Similarly, we live in a day when people try on marriage like it is some purchasable good, made to be used or worn or played with, then tossed away after we have outgrown it, matured beyond it, or become bored with it. I am even familiar with marriages that have been annulled within the first few months, returned like some gadget within a ninety-day grace period. The tabloids showcase such examples. Sometimes, a long history of one-sided infidelity is cited and the decision to divorce is understandable, but in most cases, I believe the decision to divorce is more about two people giving up than being unable to reconcile differences. Post-bisque firing, many couples decide the risk or fear of the unknown is too great, so they shelf the unfinished piece. Mid-sculpting, they find their strength taxed and their tools dull, so they lay them down and move on, never realizing the beautiful work of art that might have been.

I'd like to suggest that most marriages can and should be saved, no matter how bad they have gotten, if—and this is a huge "if"—both husband and wife are willing to continually work hard at it. In most cases the cure for a "dying" marriage is not divorce, but humility, charity, a desire to change, and effort.

As intimated, Michelangelo's idea about seeing the beautiful statue inside every crude block of marble has merit and application. Every one of us can benefit from trying to see what someone or thing can become. No doubt, many of you wives have stuck with your husband this long for no other reason than you have experienced such glimpses. But Michelangelo's description is also overly romantic, acknowledging little the herculean effort required to remove surplus stone. In comparison, I'd like to share a quote on the same subject offered by one of his contemporaries, Leonardo da Vinci:

> The sculptor in creating his work does so by the strength of his arm and the strokes of his hammer by which he cuts away the marble or other stone in which his subject is enclosed—a most mechanical exercise often accompanied by much perspiration which mingling with grit turns into mud. His face is smeared all over with marble powder so that he looks like a baker, and he is covered with a snowstorm of chips, and his house is dirty and filled with flakes and dust of stone.[2]

"Strength of his arm," "strokes of his hammer," "cuts away," "mechanical," "perspiration," "grit," "mud," "his face smeared all over," "covered with a snowstorm," "his house is dirty"—these are terms that more accurately describe what it means and takes to sculpt from raw material a beautiful masterpiece to be admired by generations to come. The same can be said of marriage.

But if only one person is trying to make this marriage work, then something needs to change.

Returning to the analogy of raw clay, if your husband is willing to change or, at the very least, if he has the mere desire to change, then there is still hope. So why stop now? Together, keep shaping this raw block called marriage, then reshape it, and then again and again and again; then let it dry so the water is eliminated and the clay will not crack under the heat, which *must* come if the piece is to remain intact; then sand away the bumps and the pores, apply liberally the glaze, and let the final fire seal everything together. If you stick with it together, I promise the seemingly insurmountable trials you now face will only mature, strengthen, and make vibrant your marriage and love for each other.

On the other hand, if you are alone, dealing with a husband who has made it clear he has no desire to change and is not exerting any effort of his own to change, then the situation must change. This process of recovery and healing is just that: a process. There may be slip-ups along the way, but your husband and your marriage should always be moving forward. If he is not progressing because of a lack of effort, or if by his words and deeds he is pushing you backward or in some way threatening or damaging the long-term emotional stability of you or your children, then it is your right and job to protect yourself and your kids. And if, after making it a matter of prayer, you feel the protection and the change needed are to be found in divorce, then so be it. You will have my support, for what it's worth. I further promise in such a case that when you let go, you will not be alone. If not by family and friends, then certainly there will be celestial arms outstretched to catch you, to hold you, and to carry you until peace, love, and joy can be restored.

14

SIGNS OF THE TIMES IN THEORY

*"Be watchful, and strengthen the things which remain, that are
ready to die: for I have not found thy works perfect before God."
(Revelation 3:2)*

PROPHETS, BOTH ANCIENT AND MODERN, BOTH
Christian and non-Christian, have long since foretold of the "last
days," days in which the hearts of men and women will sway and the "love
of many will wax cold" (Matthew 24:12). In terms of the toll pornography
takes on hearts, minds, and marriages, I think we can safely say this has
come to pass. In addition to these prophecies, specific signs were given,
things for which the people could watch so that when the day of reckon-
ing did come they would be ready and prepared to protect themselves and
their families against potential destruction. In our lives, we too can watch
for certain signs that will let us know when trouble is near or if a loved one
has already buckled beneath the weight of temptation. I want to quickly
address these signs as a wife might see them in a husband's behavior, and
as a recovering addict might sense them in his own feelings and behavior.

"How," a wife might ask, "do I know if my husband is involved in
pornography?" This common question is full of concern and apprehension. If you are reading this book, chances are you already know your
spouse is or has been involved with pornography. But that does not mean

you will not wonder at a later date whether he has again fallen prey to its enticement. In fact, because of the nature of addiction, both of you will need to remain vigilant, watching well into the future for signs of its influence. I say "well into the future" not because of the adage "once an addict always an addict" (though there is wisdom in this), but because there is greater wisdom in continually watching out for each other. Over the last couple decades alone, pornography has become increasingly perverse and pervasive, cajoling by subtle, seductive slight-of-hand. It will only get worse. For this reason, I have always said it takes a family to close up the inroads of pornography addiction. As you stand on the watchtower, scanning the homeland for approaching enemies that promise to come in the night when you least expect them, so your husband should watch out for you. And as you both stand ready to address and combat approaching enemies on behalf of your children, so should they be ready to fight for your integrity, and feel confident enough to come to you with concerns as they relate to your moral welfare. The safest kingdoms have always been those whose watchtowers, even in times of peace, are constantly in use—not out of paranoia for what might be but out of love for who is.

Like most addictions, viewing pornography is done in secret. But because of the physical, emotional, mental, and spiritual toll it takes on the addict, it can be hard to hide. Sudden but prolonged changes in attitude, behavior, and habit can easily betray the burdensome secret, if we are honest in our analysis. I use the word *honest* only because from experience I know how easy it is to dismiss rising concerns of this nature and, in essence, lie to and convince ourselves that something wrong does not exist when, inside, we know it does. "Not my husband," we persuade. "He is different. He would never do anything like *that*," only to have our worst fears confirmed later. Often we try to assure ourselves that all is well as the means of hanging on to hope. It can also be a mechanism by which we attempt to fend off oncoming pain. To some degree, we have all been guilty of this type of deceitful reasoning, but if you have, do not allow yourself to feel guilty. This is not your fault. Do you hear me? *Not your fault*! I need you to feel the truth in those words. Let them sink deep into your heart and mind. I know it is easy to start thinking that if you had listened to or acted on those initial impressions, you would have spared your husband this whole mess. But this is just not true. The onus will always be on his shoulders. It was he who ignored warning signs, he who turned a blind eye to the approaching enemy, and, therefore, it is he who must repair the breach. If he is sincere, I feel strongly he will succeed in doing so. His burden, like yours, is immense, but you can help him. The past is behind you. Look back only to analyze any patterns or warning signs that might have revealed or foreshadowed his involvement in pornography. Learn from them, help him learn from them, and then use them to prepare against future attacks.

I have gathered the following list of behaviors that might hint at a husband's battle with pornography. First, we tend to give lists more credibility than they deserve. By no means is this one comprehensive. It is simply based off of personal experience and the experiences of others. Second, I want to emphasize the word *might*. Realize that just because some of these signs may be present in a husband's behavior, it does not necessarily mean he has a pornography problem. In fact, I hesitated to draft this list at all because the one thing we don't want to do is turn genuine concern into paralyzing paranoia and start negatively reading into every little thing our spouse does or does not do. Most of these signs may simply affirm that he is dealing with a high level of stress to which we are all prone. But even if these signs are just stress-related, they are important to be aware of and address, for uncontrolled stress can just as easily lead a man to pornography as indicate an existing problem with it.

In no particular order, you may notice any of the following emotional and behavioral patterns in men struggling with an addiction to pornography:

1. Depression or other mental/emotional disorders

2. Increased anger or a quick temper

3. A developing habit of physical, emotional, verbal, or sexual abuse

4. Deterioration of familial relationships and values

5. Decreased problem solving skills

6. An increased desire to spend more time away from home

7. An inability to physically perform during intimacy

8. A general lack of desire to be intimate or acting distant during intimacy

9. Increased desire for control or bestiality during intimacy, or a desire to have you do certain things or fulfill certain fantasies with which you are not comfortable

10. An increase in alone time at the office or in the computer room

11. A decline in personal scripture study, prayer, or other things of a spiritual nature

12. The constant need to be on the computer or checking email or checking "something" else online

13. Late night or early morning Internet usage

14. The history on the computer or on their cell phone is consistently emptied or altered

15. He quickly clicks to a different computer screen when you enter the room

16. The computer room or house door is "conveniently" locked or barricaded

17. Cell phone Internet usage increases behind locked doors, even while in the bathroom

18. He refuses to let you install Internet tracking software, saying you don't trust him

19. Upon walking in on him, his heart pounds incessantly or you notice other physiological changes such as a flushed or red face, anxious movements, or an inability to look you in the eyes

20. He comes up with excuses as to why he cannot or does not want to attend an event or meeting with you or the family

21. He is not getting projects done at work or school anymore and performance is suffering

22. You catch him lying or being dishonest or not disclosing the whole truth

23. He has his own email account to which you do not or maybe even cannot have access

24. You discover he has created a separate email account

25. When you approach him about your concerns or ask him if he is involved in pornography, he denies it vehemently and becomes enraged.

Again, this list is from off the top of my head. The signs of a loved one's struggle will inevitably vary with the situation, personalities, and so forth. Your own experiences may yet add many other signs for which you will need to watch. Above all, though, if you are worried about your husband, address those worries now. Do not let them sit and fester. If you want to know if he is involved with pornography, or if he has ever indulged in it (and it is your right to know), then ask him. I know that sounds simple and perhaps even incredibly difficult, but open communication is and will continue to be essential to the healing of your relationship. Your heart will be pounding, your mind racing. But you can do it and then you will know. Approach him at the right time and in a spirit of love and concern—for him and for your family. Then listen to him and to your heart; and whether he admits to it or not, you will discover the answer you seek. From there, the road to healing begins.

To you men struggling toward recovery: you can watch for signs too, but they are much more subtle and, therefore, much more complicated to prepare for and protect yourself against. Think of a meteorologist. It is one thing to notice the ninety mph wind speeds and twenty-foot oceanic swells and say, "I think we're in the midst of a big storm here." It's entirely different, though, to look days, even weeks into the future, and try to anticipate the path and intensity of a hurricane forming hundreds of miles off the coast when it now appears only to be but a faint scattering of clouds. I don't think weathermen worry too much when the seven-day plan looks mild. But when it *might* prove disastrous or when they foresee that lives *may* suddenly be at risk, then you better believe they pour every ounce of time and energy and training into that forecast. You must do the same. You must become the meteorologist of your own soul.

Unfortunately, I cannot even begin to tell you how to do this, other than to say that you will need to become more methodical, more analytical, and more calculated in thought and action. The rest you will have to figure out for yourself because it is different for each person. Up until now, part of your problem has been that your response to certain stimuli is habitual. You react instead of act and by small degrees these seemingly insignificant reactions build and build until you are blindsided by their cumulative effects. The trick is to get to the point where you can recognize the first of these signs (stress, self-deprecation, or disparagement, for instance), and consciously choose how you respond or, better said, how you do not respond. For me, there were times when I'd wake up in the morning and for whatever reason I'd feel emotionally "blah." I felt of little value. I was overwhelmed by a long list of things to do. And I felt that the course of my day and, thus, my life were being determined by everyone and everything else, and not by me. Ironically, it was these feelings of a lack of control in life, when unaddressed, that almost always led me to escape to pornography, which I justified as being something I could choose and could be in control of. But it soon spiraled out of control. It took a long time before I learned that the days on which I woke up feeling this way always ended with selfish gratification by way of pornography. I had to recondition myself so that when I began to feel so in any degree, I would recognize it as a warning sign of what was to come and take immediate action to get out of the emotional rut.

To help illustrate the universality of this point, I want to share an experience my wife had just the other day. Because of a number of health issues that seemed to pop up out of nowhere a few months ago, she has to work hard to establish and maintain a healthier lifestyle. In addition to exercise and avoiding sweets, she also gave up products containing gluten for a time. She was busy homeschooling our kids, but in order to help a friend in need, she took on the extra responsibility of caring for a bed-ridden mother and her eighteen-month-old child, who, by nature, was a destroyer of bookshelves, cupboards, and the like. By the middle of the second day, my wife was exhausted and extremely stressed. Our kids reacted to this change in pattern and accompanying stress by fighting and complaining. This only increased her stress level, to which she responded by trying to eat it away. This is common for a lot of us. Looking back, however, it became clear that her decision was not actually driven by need (she was not really hungry) but was instead a habitual reaction to the stress. As is often the case in situations like this, she did not just go straight into the kitchen and eat something off-limits because she knew that sugar and gluten would make her sick. But in spite of that, a part of her brain tried to convince her that she not only wanted sugar but that she needed it to feel less stress. This part of the brain is smart. It realizes it is acting against the grain. It knows that if it is to move us to rush into something, we would most likely detect the error in our thinking and be able to resist the temptation. So, instead, its goal is to work on our mind in such a subtle way that we do not fully comprehend the path we are on until we have concluded it.

In my wife's case, she could have chosen other options to address her stress. She could have gone outside to get a breath of fresh air, for instance. Or she could have called me at work. Instead, her mind and body, having convinced her of the stressful, hard work required to relieve stress, were looking for a quick fix requiring little to no effort at all. Agitated, she first went into the kitchen, looking for something within her diet restrictions. Nothing, though, looked fulfilling to her, so she walked out. With no proper plan in place, it was only inevitable that she would return, hoping to fill the stress-induced void she felt inside. Sure enough, within thirty minutes she was back in the kitchen, looking for anything that promised fulfillment even, this time, if it fell outside her diet. She saw on the counter muffins she had made for the kids. They contained both sugar and gluten. She left the kitchen without partaking, but with still no plan in place to get the real fulfillment she needed, she was already on a path to eat one of those muffins. She just didn't know it yet. She entered that kitchen, then left, then entered again many more times until finally she took a small nibble from one. Now that she had taken that first bite, it was much easier to justify coming back to take a second nibble, then a third and fourth and so on. Over the course of the day, she took small bite after bite until the muffin had been consumed. And was her stress relieved? No. If anything, it was heightened. On top of that, she felt physically sick from having eaten something her body was not supposed to have.

Now fast forward a couple days. Under considerable stress from taking care of our own kids, who were now sick, she again looked to food to satisfy internal needs that had nothing to do with hunger. In the fridge were chocolate balls we had made as part of a Christmas celebration. Fully aware that she was reacting poorly, fully aware that she would not feel good after eating them, and even with the direct parallels to this book in her thoughts, she went back to the fridge, opened the bag, and on three separate occasions stole away to the garage (where the kids would not see her) and ate a chocolate ball. A day later, she said something that made me question why she was not feeling good. It was then, out of relief it seems, that she shared with me her momentary indiscretion.

My wife is healthy. And heaven knows she is not an overeater. I'm not really comfortable even relating this small occurrence to pornography addiction, but the principles behind it are so powerful, she and I decided it needed to be addressed herein.

We can have all sorts of discussions on how the outcome could have been avoided. At one point in what seemed like jest, she told me she was going to throw the chocolate balls away so she wouldn't be tempted to eat them. I trusted her to stick to her goals and was not worried (especially because of how healthy she had been feeling), but in spite of that trust should we have gotten rid of them? What if she had verbalized to the kids her struggle and the temptation to eat them? Might they have helped her stick to her goal? I can hear them saying, "Mommm, what are you doing looking in that fridge?" That or making the ultimate sacrifice and eating them all by themselves! Is my wife the only person responsible or do the kids and I share the blame? If we really wanted to support her, should we have even made the chocolate balls in the first place? Should we have even shopped for the ingredients? So the neighbors end up with a vegetable platter on their doorstep for Christmas instead of cookies. They'll get over it, and maybe they'll even appreciate the fresh change from sweets. I jest, but I think you get my point.

The answers to these questions and the parallels they have to pornography addiction are intriguing. As you have time to consider them, they will no doubt reveal truths that will help you along the way to recovery. For the addict, a fine line exists between the signs that can foreshadow pending relapse and the triggers that can cause it. In my wife's case, was stress the trigger or were the muffins? Or maybe it was both, with stress also acting as a recognizable warning sign? It may well be a question of semantics. But it doesn't really matter as long as you learn to recognize moments of personal weakness, control your response to them, and plan to more appropriately address your real needs. We will touch on triggers more thoroughly in the next section, but for now I want to point out a few things I hope you take away from this extended real-life metaphor. First, it is so easy to misinterpret our real needs. Second, we all respond out of habit to certain situations or feelings. Third, we need to look for unhealthy patterns in our lives and learn to recognize certain feelings or situations as signs foreshadowing relapse unless something is changed. Fourth, it is requisite to verbalize our weakness and enact a plan of action by which we offset our incendiary weaknesses. And finally, I hope it shows that because we are *all* prone to addictive tendencies, we must watch out for each other, and not let fear get in the way of speaking out when we feel inside that something is wrong.

Philosophies aside for a moment, it is my belief that these "gut feelings" often come to us in heart and mind as warnings from the spirit of God. From the beginning of times, he has warned his people in the hopes of helping them avoid bondage or certain destruction. As he warned Noah, so can he warn and help you to discern when destructive storms are brewing in the distance. On this note, I cannot say enough about prayer as both a source of comfort and a guide through which we can know if a loved one is struggling. My parents will tell you that every night they pray to know when their children are in trouble, and how they can help. Because of their prayers, they sensed in advance that problems with pornography were among their children long before I admitted it to anyone. No doubt I received strength from these prayers. I encourage you wives to pray. Pray for the spirit of discernment. Pray for insight into the problems of your spouse. Pray to know if or when he is struggling. Watch. Be vigilant. Be honest with yourself and accepting of the thoughts and feelings the Lord will give you. I know many of you may feel as if this advice is too little too late. The storm, long since raging, has already overtaken heart and home. Perhaps you feel as if your home has been permanently torn apart, or that there can be no escape from a storm that, at first glance, covers the sky in blackness as far as your eyes can see. But I want you to know that there is hope—hope for the man enslaved by his addiction, and hope for the woman suddenly racked with chains of guilt, anger, and intense suffering. Just as the Lord has often warned his people so they could avoid bondage, so he has always prepared a way for the escape of those already in bondage. As he guided Moses and the people of Israel out of the hands of the Egyptians, so he can guide you away from the storm into a land of peace and love that is "overflowing with milk and honey" (Exodus 3:8), where freedom is and conflict cannot be.

15

ON EVIL AND HATE

"Love thine enemy because they are the
instruments to your destiny."[1]

IT IS WITH A SIGH OF ANXIETY THAT I PRESENT THIS chapter, and I want to warn you now, it may prove difficult to read and accept. I beg you, though, to please hear me out. I struggled to know where in this book to place the content herein. In the end, I felt it was important to insert it here—at the *end* of our theoretical discussions on pornography and addiction, and at the *beginning* of the sections on your journey toward recovery from addiction and healing from pain.

John Newton wrote, "Many have puzzled themselves about the origin of evil. I observe there is evil, and that there is a way to escape it, and with this I begin and end."[2] I too have puzzled over the origins and the devices of evil. What, for instance, does the word even mean? In today's entertainment world, it is often associated with the supernatural, but at its core the word is humanistic, denoting the purposeful act of doing something morally wrong and injurious to one self or others. This, I feel, is a basic but important distinction to remember, and I share it to tame any errant associations we may have with this word. Is pornography evil, then? I think so. It has always been morally wrong. It has always affected mental, emotional, and spiritual injury upon individuals, families, and society; just because our culture is becoming more accepting of it, does not make it any less so. Moreover, from the beginning its intent has been unmistakable and purposeful: to promote selfishness, invite debauchery, and draw away the hearts and money of good men—all of which leads to the ruination of family. But because of my personal experience with pornography, I am more concerned with how we judge those who view it. So what of them, the good men who cannot stop looking at it, are they evil? And what about the men and women who make pornography, pose for it, and distribute it? It is here that I feel the need to make what may, to some of you, be a controversial and infuriating statement: no, even they are not evil.

"What?" some of you may want to question. "How can you say that?" "Look at what *they* made" "Look at the problems *it* causes." "Look at what *they've* done." "I lost a wife, my kids because of *it*." "*They* violated my home." "*It* destroyed my family." "*They* tore my husband from my arms. *They* reached in with their filthy hands and *they* stole my husband's heart—and *they* have broken mine." "How? Please, tell me how can you defend *them*?"

Because they deserve a defense.

Let me explain. To me, to say someone is evil seems like an absolute. But I cannot believe that any one person is completely bad or completely good; they, like us, are just people trying to make their way through life. We have all made foolish mistakes. For some, such choices led to long-term consequences. Because of this I believe every man, woman, or child deserves and even needs in his or her corner someone who is willing to look beyond the exterior and into their hearts—hearts which may or may not contain love. Sadly, for many of these performers, it is the latter case. I will not go into the common backgrounds of physical, sexual, and drug-related abuses that many of these people share. But in my heart I have to believe that they are simply doing the best they know how with what they have been given, and that they are responding to how they have been raised. When I think of them, I think of Paul Dunbar's poem, "We Wear the Mask":

> We wear the mask that grins and lies,
> It hides our cheeks and shades our eyes,—
> This debt we pay to human guile;
> With torn and bleeding hearts we smile
> And mouth with myriad subtleties,

Why should the world be overwise,
In counting all our tears and sighs?
Nay, let them only see us, while
We wear the mask.

We smile, but O great Christ, our cries
To thee from tortured souls arise.
We sing, but oh the clay is vile
Beneath our feet, and long the mile,
But let the world dream otherwise,
We wear the mask!³

In my own time, I have worn such a mask, and by my sins I too have kept friends, family, my wife and children, and my God away from the pain in my eyes, the dirt on my hands, and the struggle in my heart. Because of this I cannot bring myself to hate the sinner, for I was and am one, and ever will be until, by the grace of God, I am found worthy enough to be made perfect through the love of his Son, who suffered in both body and spirit, and bled and died for me . . . and you . . . and you . . . and all of us! Might we say of *them* as Jesus Christ said of the Roman soldiers that crucified him: "Father, forgive them; for they know not what they do" (Luke 23:34)? The Savior saw no room in men's hearts for *absolute* evil, only a deep-seeded need for *absolution*.

Wives, I know—I repeat, *I know*—how hard this might be to accept right now. It is common to feel hatred toward your husband or toward the objects of his addiction, such as the people who make pornography, the stores that carry it, the people who buy it, even the poster ads in mall windows, actresses on television or in the movies, women at the office, or random strangers walking down the street in revealing attire. I am not saying you should not feel this way. In fact, anger and hate are integral parts of the grieving process and you are not wrong to feel them. Let them run their course. Share your feelings as you feel them. Write down your thoughts as you think them. Work hard and pray hard to come to terms with these emotions. And then let them go. Healing cannot take place where hate resides.

Letting go of my anger was hard for me to do after learning about my uncle's drug overdose. I talked about the anger I had felt toward him. But I did not mention how after that anger subsided I began to project it toward others things, in particular toward drugs of any kind and those who used them or made them available to others. This subtle transition made me feel somewhat better because I no longer felt anger toward my uncle, but it was not better for me. The hate was still inside me, festering, robbing me of ultimate healing; it was just in different form.

Quite honestly, I don't think I was really able to let go of my anger until I began to see that these drug dealers and users and I were not really that different from each other. I'm not just talking about the commonality of sin or addiction here. I was an addict, yes, and I knew that if people found out they would be disgusted and they might even hate me for it and categorize me as evil or bad. But I also knew I was not bad. I knew I had goodness inside. I knew that I loved, and I knew that I needed love and help. But I didn't know where to get it, and I didn't know how to stop the double life I was living. Suddenly I began to think that if this was true for me, maybe it was true for them too. If I was wearing a mask to hide my sins, who says that they too were not hiding behind a mask of their sins?

Before we close this chapter and section, let us return to our initial question about the origin of evil. Who then is responsible for this mess— for your addiction to pornography as well as the pain and anger you feel because of his addiction? First, I want to reiterate that I am not absolving anyone from personal responsibility. For every broken law, some consequences must be suffered, and so we are each suffering in our own way. But I feel it is important to express my belief that it is Satan, Lucifer, that old diabolical adversary at war with our souls, who is the author of evil in all its forms. Everything he does is with purpose: to tempt and entice good people to make morally wrong choices without truly realizing how seriously they are hurting themselves and the people around them. He wants to destroy you and your family. I believe this is true. But equal in certainty to me is that there is an author greater than he who has a purpose and plan by which all men and women and children can be set free. It is with him in mind that I believe in the inherent goodness of humankind. *Inherent* is the key word here. It signifies something with which we have all been born. In accordance with my faith, we are the spirit children of a God in whom there is no evil, only good. Because of this, goodness, light, and love are in our genes and no matter how hard we try or how often we mess things up we cannot completely eradicate them from our spiritual makeup.

So, to me, it does not matter what the beginning of evil is. For my part now, I am only concerned with the end, the destination of happiness and peace and love that is mine and yours to choose. You have felt these things before. You can feel them again. You have people around you—friends and family—who love you, who stand ready to listen and advise, to help and comfort as needed. I believe God and Jesus Christ are eager to help you too. It is they who are "the beginning and the end, the first and the last" (Revelation 22:13). Evil is real, yes, and it must not be ignored. But we can escape its grasp. It will take effort and sacrifice, humility, patience, and love. But escape your addictions you can. Escape the hurt in your heart you can. Escape them you must. And with that I begin and end.

PART 2:
ENDING THE CONFLICT

by William A. Donne

16

THRESHOLD OF VICTORY

"And now, beware of rashness, but with energy and sleepless vigilance go forward and give us victories."[1]

JUST AS THERE ARE DIVERSE WAYS BY WHICH WE CAN commit sin, there are equally as many—if not more—ways by which we can overcome it. Even though it may not seem like it, the upper hand is always ours. However, the process by which we overcome an addiction to pornography may be simplified to three steps—namely, admitting you have a problem, repenting completely, and enduring to the end.

Naturally, the first step to overcoming your addiction is admitting you have a problem. Often this is the hard part because what we are involved in does not always seem like a problem. Regardless, the fact that you are here now and have read this far tells me you have accomplished this first step, or are at least trying to because of the love you have for those who have perhaps put this book in front of you. When you opened this book and began reading, you stepped across the threshold of understanding. No doubt, a new world of sorts has been opened up before your eyes. If read, considered, discussed, and applied as intended, the principles you have thus far uncovered have propelled and will continue to propel you toward recovery and healing. Do not underestimate the power of these preceding principles. In my experience, they are foundational.

Many before have failed to achieve recovery because they did not understand the principles or were in such a hurry to recover that they did not give the principles the time required. But as powerful as the principles can be, they are not enough. You must do more. Having said that, this very page constitutes yet another threshold upon which you stand: the threshold of victory. With theoretical principles in place, you are now ready to apply them. Beyond the doorway, over the subsequent chapters, we will walk the final paths of recovery, repentance, and ultimate forgiveness together. You will continue to experience pain and suffering and heartache. You will feel anger and deep sorrow. At times, you may want to turn back. Don't. You must keep moving forward. It is this process that assures your victory.

It has been said that "across the plains of time bleach the bones of countless thousands who, upon the threshold of victory, sat down to rest, and resting they died."[2] Often in my past I toed the threshold of victory; often I stood at the cusp of receiving great blessings, answers to prayers, even additional strength for the task ahead, only to falter at the finish line. No doubt this has been true for you too.

But no seasoned runner would run his best race only to stop to take a breather just feet from the finish line. So why do we falter? The answer is simple: we stop because we cannot see the finish line. We do not know what it looks like, we are looking beyond the mark, or we believe it is too far off and we are not up to the task. But you are up to the task. The finish line is closer than you realize. In fact, in life, there are multiple finish lines along the way. We just need to recognize them. The final finish line will come in time. For your part now, you simply need to worry about getting through the little races. Every hour, every day, every week, and every month—these are races you can win. Plan for success and do not settle for less than your best.

When I was a sophomore in high school, a good friend of mine and I decided to try out for the cross-country team. We both made the team. The coaches were impressed with the muscle mass in my legs. They said I could become a great runner if I wanted to. In the back of my mind, I assumed that promise was a guarantee regardless of the conditions they placed upon it—namely, desire, work ethic, and sacrifice. It did not take me long to realize that running was not going to be easy. I had dealt with exercise-induced asthma as a kid, so inconsistent breathing and the side aches that followed inhibited my natural abilities during each practice and race. While I could employ breathing techniques and general running strategies to alleviate this problem, I chose not to discipline myself enough to do so, thinking I could last long enough on my own to finish the race. In this, I failed.

One race in particular stands out in my mind. I was confident and felt good physically. However, every other runner thought just as I did. At the starting line, with the three-mile course ahead of us unseen and the uneven lay of the land un-run, we each believed we were the best runner on the starting line; so much so that, in our imaginations, we had already claimed the coveted blue ribbon. Signaling the start of the race, the gun went off. Our bodies and minds seemed up to the task. We raced ahead, each at our best, propelled onward by the cheers from family and friends who were lining the first hundred yards of the course.

By the end of the first mile, I grew a bit weary. But that exhaustion came at the exact moment I circled back around and faced the crowd. My parents and friends again cheered me on. They believed I was the best. I knew they believed in me, and I did not want to let them down. So I raced ahead, feeling and looking like a top-notch runner.

But as I ran up and over the hill, away from the encouragement of the crowd, a fierce battle began. My legs tired and my breathing began to labor. I was sure I could feel a side ache forming below my ribs. I continued to run, but slower, waiting vigilantly for that side ache to appear. It did. The battle waged on in my mind as I contemplated whether I should stop or keep on running. At this point, I was deep on the other side of the course, and everything around me was silent. By all accounts, I appeared to be running alone; because I could no longer hear the crowd, I forgot about them cheering me on. The side ache worsened. My breathing too. In an instant, I made up my mind. I stopped, to rest, I told myself, just for one second.

It did not even take one second, however, before—*Whoosh! Whoosh! Whoosh!*—runner after runner began passing me by, leaving me now entirely and truly alone on that section of the course. Frustrated at how quickly I had fallen behind, I convinced myself that it was too late for me to make up the lost ground. So I continued to walk a little longer. When I decided to run again, I did so only for a little bit at a time, choosing to stop again and again. Because I had stopped the first time, it had become far too easy to stop the second time, the third, the fourth, and so on. The minutes ticked away, and I can only imagine that my once-excited family began to wonder where I was. Eventually I rounded the final grove of trees and picked up the pace—for the crowd. My family cheered just the same, but inside I knew I did not deserve it.

That one race set the tone for the many races that followed—both on and off the cross-country course. To this day, I regret stopping during that race. I became nothing more than a middle-rate runner with a collection of purple participation ribbons. I have often wondered why didn't I just push through it? Why couldn't I run the race I knew I was capable of? If I went back now, could I bring myself to run through the pain, all the way to the finish line where rest was guaranteed?

In the Academy Award-winning movie *Chariots of Fire*, Eric Liddel teaches a sermon to a crowd, in which he says, "I want to compare faith to running in a race. It's hard. It requires concentration of will; energy of soul. . . . I have no formula for winning the race. Everyone runs in her own way or his own way. Then where does the power come from to see the race to its end? From within. Jesus said, 'Behold, the kingdom of God is within you. If with all your hearts you truly seek me you shall ever surely find me.' If you commit yourself to the love of Christ, then that is how you run a straight race."[3]

We must ask ourselves: What are we in this race for? Are we in it to win? Or are we just running for the first hundred yards because that's where the crowd is? If we truly want to win, and it is the desire of our hearts, then we must do everything in our power to run the race straight. We must be willing to discipline ourselves and take correction, and cease to persist in our old ways simply because that is what we have always done. As has been said in a hundred different ways, if you want something you've never had before, you must do something you've never done.

This will never be as applicable in your life as it is now. You will have to sacrifice much. You will have to declare a revolution on all you know and are. You will have to transform. It will be hard. It will require faith and concentration of will. You will have many emotions as you humble yourself and, in your weakness, lean upon the shoulders of those who are willing to help. Above all, there is one upon whose shoulder you can always lean, even that of Christ—the Redeemer—who suffered in mind and body the pains you now feel. But he was up to the task then, and he is up to the task now. When you turn to him, he can and will help you. The victory has been purchased by him already; the victorious end has been decided. It is up to you to take it; when you do, it will be yours, Christ's, and your family's; and you—all of you—will experience the joy and peace and love you now so desperately seek. It is just a matter of time.

17

HOW LONG WILL IT TAKE?

"We are for today; when tomorrow will come we shall see what we can do" "The future is so much in the hands of God, I find it much more easy to accept today because yesterday is gone and tomorrow has not come and I have only today" "And that is the wonderful gift of God that He has not given us—that is His great love for us that He has not given us to know the future. We fear the future because we are wasting the today."[1]

AFTER SUFFERING AN INJURY OF ANY KIND, IT IS ONLY natural to try and determine how long we will be incapacitated. "When do I get the cast off?" "How long before the medicine works?" "Will I be up and about in time to do this or that?" Physically speaking, it is easy for a doctor to look at patterns, cite statistics, consult charts, and say with some level of assurance that "your cast will be off in three months" or "your pain will dissipate in three days" or "why don't you go ahead and plan on doing this then." In the interim, we often rely on prescribed over-the-counter medicines to temporarily alleviate the throbbing pain until actual healing takes place. However, in regards to deep emotional and spiritual wounds, there is no pattern, statistic, or chart that says you will only suffer for three days, months, or years before you can with confidence proclaim yourself completely recovered or healed.

The time frame in which recovery and healing are realized will vary by wound, person, and circumstance. It will also depend on the effort and sacrifices you are willing to make along the way.

In terms of recovery—addicts, I believe the healing process is entirely in your hands. I have often been asked, "How long can I expect it to take to overcome my addiction to pornography?" My answer is one second, if that. It takes but a moment to make the decision to turn away from a pornographic image. From then on, you are free from pornography as long as you work together with your family and friends to honor and protect that decision. But this latter part (in the same way you only officially earn an A at the end of class) will take the rest of your life to prove. Just because healing may come quickly to you does not mean other areas of your life will heal as easily. As part of enduring to the end, you must consistently turn your focus to any relationships shattered by your actions. With this in mind, get to work. The problems that belabored you spiritually are behind you. So leave them there. Do not look back with wantonness. You will be surprised at how fast healing can come when you begin to communicate properly and repent completely; by *repent*, I mean that you talk to those you need to talk to, forsake what you need to forsake, and prove yourself from here on out however you need to do it.

Be cautious, though, of feeling and then declaring your miraculous recovery too early. For me, during the first couple months after telling my wife about my addiction I felt like I was done with pornography for good. I felt little temptation, which I mistook as a sign that I was completely and permanently healed. I recall sharing these feelings with my wife, counselors, and ecclesiastical leaders. They believed me because I believed myself. This is a common occurrence among all men, but rarely are such personal beliefs actually the fruit of true recovery. More realistically, an addict will rarely feel the tempting pull of pornography during the first few days and weeks because, in the back of his mind, the consequences that have already been suffered are clear, as well as those potentially worse consequences he knows will come about if he messes up again. In this case, it is the subconscious fear of punishment that keeps his mind, heart, and hands clean. This is not a bad thing at all—if the addict can recognize and admit there are other forces at play keeping pornography at bay. What the addict must do, then, is use this time to further protect the wound from reopening. As pessimistic as this sounds, it is important for both husband and wife to realize that few simply recover without some sort of relapse. Temptation will come, especially as you distance yourself from the initial date of disclosure. If driving desire draws your eyes toward pornography again, do not despair. Communicate your error, analyze your failure, and re-dress the wound.

Wives, your process of healing is just beginning. When I think of you, I think again of *War and Peace*, in particular of the pain Natasha felt at the death of her fiancé, Andrew: "When it is a beloved and intimate human being that is dying, besides this horror at the extinction of life there is a severance, a spiritual wound, which like a physical wound is sometimes fatal and sometimes heals, but always aches and shrinks at any external irritating touch."[2] Right now, I know it feels as if your husband is dying, your marriage is dying, and even that you are dying. And I know that every day, perhaps on the hour, you are seeing, hearing, thinking, and feeling things that aggravate the pain you feel inside and cause you to shrink at the slightest touch. But I promise the ache you feel can dissipate. You too can experience a healing more immediate than prolonged. Like your husband's process, your process of healing starts now. Unlike his process, however, it will take more than just a split-second decision to overcome the pain you feel.

Whether consciously or not, your husbands have been healing or, in other words, working toward recovery since they first looked at pornography. Because of this it is plausible that they will feel recovered long before you feel healed. They may even question why it is taking you so long. Don't let them. Husbands, don't do that. I admit I often felt frustrated with my wife and with what seemed like a never-ending healing process. I even questioned whether she was going about it correctly. There is not necessarily a right or wrong way. It is a personal process. You must remember that she is suddenly dealing with a whole load of stuff you took years to come to terms with. To voice frustration will only further hurt her feelings and delay healing.

You have probably both heard the phrase "time heals all wounds." Is there any truth to this image of time as the ultimate healer? My knees and elbows are covered with childhood scars that certainly testify of time's rejuvenating powers. Yet there is not a scar on my body that, when a fresh cut, was not first cleaned and cared for by someone—either by myself, a family member, a doctor, or sometimes all three. Under such care, the cleansing process—the rush of water or the gentle repetitive daubs from a hydrogen peroxide–soaked cotton ball—was often more painful than the actual moment in which the wound was first received. As we all can agree, though, this pain is necessary, as it is an indicator of the inner battle that is taking place where the cleaning agents fight and kill invading germs. But when the sting of alcohol finally fades, is the healing process complete? No. Open wounds are then immediately wrapped in a bandage designed to stop the bleeding and protect the sore from getting infected. Even then, additional, daily care must be taken to keep the bandage and the cut clean. Only after some time has passed (how long depends on the severity of the cut) is the bandage finally removed. It is then, perhaps in awe, that we observe that where the gash was, a new layer of skin has miraculously regenerated.

In light of this analogy, I ask again: *Is it really time that heals wounds?* Yes and no. They heal in time but not by time. Give your wounds time to heal and do not get frustrated if it takes a while; they run deep for both of you. But don't just sit there on the couch, either, waiting for things to get better on their own. Rehabilitation takes work. If you do not exercise the injured muscles of your body, atrophy can set in lightning-fast, further debilitating the wounded area. Apply this emotionally and spiritually. We spoke before about *desire* being a verb, not a feeling. To some extent, this can be said of healing too. It is common to wait for a feeling of healing to suddenly wash over us. But more often than not, with hindsight we see that healing and recovery often come one drop at a time. Healing, recovery—these things are subtle processes that may take significant amounts of time. But you can start now. Perhaps, for today, your first step toward recovery is simply keeping the computer off, no matter how bad you want to use it or how vital you think it is to check your email. And, wives, perhaps the first step toward healing will be as simple as deciding to get up and move forward with your plans for the day, even if it's the last thing you want to do. From there, increase your efforts daily. Obey the guidelines you have put in place. Communicate openly, honestly, and cordially. Write out your thoughts. Analyze your habits. Make continual changes as necessary. Take the time to do things that bring you joy. Accept help from others, then, in turn, find people who are struggling and help them. These are just a few things that can help ease the pains you feel. Over time, I promise these small decisions will yield the fruits of healing and recovery that you crave.

Having said that, from my faith-based perspective there is another component to healing that is more vital than time. Of his purpose on earth Christ said, "They that be whole need not a physician, but they that are sick" (Matthew 9:12). He, then, is a doctor who knows you personally. He has a perfect understanding of your body, your mind, and your heart. He has felt every type of injury and, therefore, knows how to help you; he stands by 24/7, especially in times of despair when you do not think you can bear the pain any longer. Thus far I have tried my best to explore principles and theories, but in the end I believe in the power of Christ to change lives. I believe he is the ever-living water, the cleansing agent by which all traces of germ and disease can be washed away and cleansed— permanently. His atonement can temper the necessary sting of an open wound. And when we keep his commandments, a protective pavilion can be placed over us—one through which no infection can enter, and under which healing can take place. Because of faith and obedience, by miraculous means he once restored to the blind their sight, cast out devils from men, and breathed back life into the dead. If he did so then, why not now?

Turn to God and let him heal you. He can begin to do so now. This does not necessarily mean you will wake up tomorrow without addiction or pain, but it does mean that he can help you overcome your struggles as fast as possible. To open this chapter, I mentioned how doctors often prescribe temporary medicinal relief. It has been my experience that the relief you seek can only come through personal prayer. Sometimes this relief will be just enough to get you through the day or a particular trial, but it will come. Seek comfort in this manner. Ask for strength, guidance, wisdom, patience, and, above all, charity. There were so many times when the only thing I could do was fall on my knees or onto my bed and cry for help. In one way or another, that comfort always came. As Peter began to sink into the sea, the scripture reads that, in response to his cry for help, "immediately Jesus stretched forth his hand, and caught him" (Matthew 14:31). I promise if you seek his help, you too will find the comfort you need when you need it. As hard as the days to come will still be, that collective comfort will be enough to carry you along toward happier days when the pain you feel has been lifted and replaced by love.

Now, I wish I could end here, but I feel the need to say three last things by way of admonition.

First, do not resist help, especially God's. As strange as it may seem, it is in our nature to do so. Think again of the child who pushes away the helping hand prepared to anoint a cut with peroxide. It is not that the child does not want to feel better; it is just that he or she is afraid of the pain required for proper healing to take place. It is this mind-set, in part, that allows addiction to settle in and continue. It will likewise prevent proper emotional healing. Fear too can be swallowed up by the atonement of Christ.

Second, because of the indefinite time frame for healing and recovery, it is common for both husband and wife to look for people with similar struggles and use their healing process as a gauge by which to judge their own. On many occasions, I have heard couples say something similar to "Well, I read in this article that it took this lady five years before she felt spiritually healed. So I think I'm doing pretty good considering . . ." Or "You know so-and-so. Well, it took him two years to give up looking at pornography. So I think I'm doing pretty good considering . . ."

Two problems are evident in this line of thinking: one, while it never hurts to learn about the recovery process of someone in a situation similar to your own, it can hinder your progress if you use their experience to justify bad behavior. Two, they are not you, nor is their process yours. Suppose an addict you know was able to stop looking at pornography immediately, or a wife you know felt she was able to forgive her husband after one month. In these cases, an unhealthy comparison may lead to greater depths of despair. "What," you might wrongly wonder, "am I doing wrong?" In reality, you may not be doing anything wrong. The wounds you feel inside are different than hers or his or theirs. Therefore, they will not heal in the same way. Remember, your job is to simply do the best you can to protect and keep clean the wounds long enough for healing to take place. To me, the biggest problem with these types of comparisons, though, is that by looking to another person, we are putting our trust in man and not God as the ultimate source of healing. We are saying that it is time that heals and God and Christ have nothing to do with it. We are limiting ourselves, damning our progress, and robbing our family of peace and joy now.

Third, be careful not to confuse healing and memory, or a lack thereof. "Forgive and forget" is a common adage that, I believe, is often misused. I have heard it said in religious circles and among bantering couples in an effort to instruct someone about forgiveness. "If you really have forgiven me, then you wouldn't bring that up or even remember it." I know I have felt and said similarly. But I have not always been right to feel or say so. Yes, as I have forgiven myself, there are many things I do not recall. That is a blessing. But I can and do recall many situations with searing regret.

I do not do so on purpose; sometimes, they just pop into my mind or haunt my dreams. I believe there is a purpose in this. Returning to our on-going wound analogy, it is true that in some cases the body's skin heals so perfectly that scars are either nonexistent or imperceptible, usually when the wound is small. Because of this we may forget the accident altogether. In most cases, however, especially for severe cuts, both scar and memory remain. These scars can serve as reminders that help steer us away from dangerous situations. Below my elbow, for example, is a fading scar that reminds me of the time I rode my bike over an open manhole cover and crashed. I will never do that again. On my thumb is a trench-like scar from a nail. I now always wear gloves when working with tools. In terms of pornography, as much as I loathe reliving painful mistakes, I have to believe they help me stay safe. Such memories for my wife often prompt her to ask me how I have been doing lately in regards to temptation. This is never a bad thing. It too helps her feel safe and at ease. With this in mind, I have come to believe that forgetting is less about having an event stricken from memory than about choosing to leave in the past what belongs in the past. If something which you have already forgiven or been forgiven for comes back into your mind, don't let it linger. Learn from it, grow stronger from it, and be grateful it is just a memory. At first, when you are not far removed from the actual receiving of the wound, the memory will be just as painful as when you received it. But in time that pain will also fade, and the memory of it will takes its rightful place behind a long row of happier recollections.

18

BUILDING
A FOUNDATION:

The Four Corners of
Accountability and Recovery

"He is like a man which built an house, and digged deep, and laid the foundation on a rock: and when the flood arose, the stream beat vehemently upon that house, and could not shake it: for it was founded upon a rock" (Luke 6:48).

FROM OUR EARLIEST DAYS BUILDING THINGS WITH blocks, we have learned about balance and the need for a strong foundation. Where foundations lack, stability can never be. This is true of addiction recovery too. Before we get into the practical side of the foundation that you will need to fully overcome your addiction, I want to further set up the principle by sharing another story.

When my wife and I were in the market for our first home, we fell in love with the second or third one we looked at. It was older, but we were so eager to find a stationary roof for our growing family that we did not pay sufficient attention to its deficiencies. In our defense, we also did not really know what deficiencies to look for. After making an offer and having it accepted, we paid an inspector to look the house over for us. It was in his report that we first discovered a problem with the home's foundation. We arranged to meet the inspector there for a follow-up, at which point he escorted us to the far corner of the house and proceeded to go under the house through a hatch located in the master bedroom's closet. With the aid of his expert eye and the ever-handy flashlight, we were able to see for ourselves the problem. Built on a once-stable dirt floor, over time the land had begun to settle, widening the distance between the stick-built home and the ground. Consequently, this corner of the house had begun to shift downward. The effects became clear when the inspector pointed to the wall and ceiling of the closet, and we noticed, for the first time, a pretty significant crack forming as a result of the stress-induced settling. With most new homes, some degree of settling is expected, especially if the ground has not been properly leveled and compacted. But the settling of our potential home was more violent because the home had been built in an area that was once wetlands. To make matters worse, we discovered two more issues connected with the first: the crawl space would fill with water during the winter months and, instead of getting professional help for the settling, the owner had jammed a car jack under a corner beam of the house. As needed, he would drop down into the crawl space and raise the jack a little higher to try and keep the house level. This, of course, was a problem for many reasons. Even if the house was stable on the jack, the jack's foundation was the ever-subtly settling land. We wanted a house so bad that we considered it for a time, but eventually we came to our senses, deciding it was better to start our search over. It did not take long for us to find a better house and feel grateful we did not buy the first.

For all of us, recovery is about fixing or, in some cases, completely rebuilding a home. In doing so, we are faced with the decision of applying a quick, cheap fix or expending the necessary funds to exert the required energy to build it right so that come winter storm, our foundation, and thus our home, stays strong. It is expensive—mentally, emotionally, spiritually, physically, even financially—but it must be done.

Every home's foundation has four corners. Likewise, there are four corners to recovery that must be set in stone—four pillars you must erect if you are to rebuild a stable home with a leak-proof roof that will keep your family safe and happy. More plainly, there are four groups to whom you must disclose your struggle, to whom you must be held accountable, and from whom you can and should receive constant, perhaps even daily, support.

These corners are your *family, ecclesiastical* or *professional leaders, friends,* and your *employers* or *coworkers.*

I can hear some of you balking at these already. I understand your concerns and fears, and the potential embarrassment you feel. But, like yours, my addiction continued because I did not allow others to help me combat it. I wanted to spare them pain. I wanted to beat it on my own. So I tried to do just that, day after day, year after year, until it became painfully clear that I could not do it alone. By erroneously thinking I could, I had wasted sixteen years of my life and built all of my relationships on a shaky foundation.

It is no coincidence that the four corners account for every facet of life. The reason for this is so that you cannot go anywhere without being accountable to or receiving support from someone. You've heard the boxing phrase, "I'm in your corner." There are all sorts of parallels we can draw between boxing and addiction recovery, but there is one glaring difference. If we are to win, encouragement cannot be limited to the corner with the trainer wearing your colors. It must come from every corner, from the referee, and ideally from the crowd. Granted, sometimes the crowd beyond the ring will be cheering for you, and other times they will be acting as if they despise you. But if your corners are true, what the crowd thinks will not matter. Nor will it make a difference in the outcome you earn in the ring and, more important, in your heart and mind.

A closer look at these groups will show us how they, like inspectors, contractors and builders, can provide us with the expertise and extra sets of eyes needed to build a straight home on a firm foundation.

Friends

Because I want to use the subsections on talking to family and ecclesiastical/professional leaders to lead into the chapters that will follow, we will start with the need to tell friends. While, in the order of things, friends should not be the first ones to whom you disclose your struggles, they are no less important. A corner is a corner and serves the same function no matter when formed.

Telling select friends is a necessary part of recovery. You may want and need to tell a friend for several reasons. I told friends because I felt I had betrayed their friendship and trust—at least indirectly—by engaging in things they would have found hurtful and offensive. I also told friends because I felt like I needed their support, and I knew I could trust them to help me. Sometimes it was clearly the right thing to do, and I did so without apprehension. At other times, I was afraid they would react with disgust or anger. Among my friends, never once has my confession been met with such a response. In all cases, they expressed gratitude for my telling them, pride in my decisions to change, a deeper love for my wife and me, and a determination to help. In many cases, I have seen them make changes in their own lives (Internet and media viewing habits) in order to strengthen their own families and so as not to be a source of temptation for me.

Clearly, these were the right people to tell. They are true friends. At the end of such conversations, I always give them a chance to express any questions or concerns. I also tell them they have my permission to discuss it with their spouse, and that they should feel free to follow up with me at any given moment. "I need your help," I've said. "I don't care if it's two in the morning. If I come into your mind and you are concerned—right or wrong—give me a call or give my wife a call."

In contrast, I recall a time when I was ten and a friend invited me to spend the night and watch a PG-13 movie that was popular at the time. The movie was against my family rules, though, and I knew it. I had been dying to see it, so I called my dad and asked to watch it. He reminded me of the family rules but told me it was my decision to make. I told my friend I couldn't watch the movie. What did he do? He put it in anyway because he wanted to watch it. To this day, I remember lying on the couch, my back to the screen, listening to the movie until I fell asleep. Among true friends, this type of scenario would never occur. My friend, respecting my rules, should have found another movie.

With regret, I recall another time in my life when I was the friend who failed. While using a relative's computer, I stumbled upon a series of pornographic images saved to a special folder. I was in shock. For his sake and safety, and for the sake of his family relationships, I should have brought it to his attention and encouraged him to talk to his wife. But he was much older than me, I did not want to offend him, and I was not even sure how to bring it up. At the same time, how could I bring a man under condemnation for the issue I was struggling with myself? A similar thing happened just months later when using a roommate's computer at college. I went to save a document, and the "Save As" box revealed several pornographic images. Sadly, in both cases, I did nothing. I do not know what became of their addictions. What I do know, though, is that whatever the struggle, I am partly to blame.

In these instances was "I my brother's keeper?" (Genesis 5:9). No. I was no better than the priest and Levite who passed by the traveler who had been beaten, robbed, and left to die on the side of the road to Jericho. I can only hope that somewhere along their way a Good Samaritan had enough courage and charity to stop and answer their silent calls for help.

Encourage your friends to do the same for you. Wives, I know this section is not about you, per se, but if you think you should ask your husband about this problem for whatever reason, even if it could end up being a senseless worry, do so. Don't hold back, but approach him in love and out of concern for his well-being.

How many friends you tell is a decision only you, the addict, can make. It will, I wager, depend on how bad your problem is, who you feel you have sinned against, and how often you need support. I can only hope you will have with your friends such luck as I. The reality is, though, you may come across friends who do not support you. If you do, move on.

Wives, you too will likely have the need to confide in friends. This will go a long way in building a support system and helping you feel less alone. We will discuss this later in the wives' section. But for now, if you and your husband are working together toward recovery and healing, I encourage you to only tell a friend if you have permission from your husband. I know this may not make sense now. He has hurt you, and you need help and he can tell whomever he wants. Well, on that matter, you should probably be in on whom he tells too, but you are right; he has less to worry about since he is the one in need of help. Again, it has been my experience that you should tread carefully when telling your friends in order to seek their support. I have seen many instances where such a disclosure, made without the husband's foreknowledge, has led to hurt feelings, damaged relationships, awkward situations, and gossip, by which his mistakes have been quickly spread across a network of women who are in a fiery mood to protect their friend at the expense of her husband.

Another benefit to having friends in your corner will be that you can turn to them in moments of weakness or temptation. While you should always make your wife aware of such moments, sometimes she is not available or, for whatever reason, the time is not right. In these times, a quick text, email, or call to a friend can keep you from a disastrous relapse. Many therapists refer to this type of go-to person as a sponsor. Personally, I'm not a fan of the word "sponsor." It is too clinical for my liking. In the end, it is camaraderie, respect, and love that lead someone to make himself or herself available to help you as and when required. These attributes must not be overlooked or forgotten. In all cases, a friend must be worthy of receiving this sensitive news. He or she must be strong enough to be leaned on, dependable enough to follow-up, and loving enough to help you rebuild.

In all cases, a friend must be worthy of receiving this sensitive news. Friends must be strong enough to be leaned on, dependable enough to follow-up, and loving enough to help you rebuild.

Employers, Coworkers, and Employees

You might ask, "Of all the people to involve in my past, why involve my employer, coworkers, or employees?"

Telling a coworker is, in principle, much like telling a friend. They may even be the same person. If you have a coworker you trust, with whom you share everything—perhaps over lunch or during the commute—then you may consider telling them and seeking their support.

The same goes for employees. On occasion, I have told my employees. Sometimes I have told them simply to explain why the office computers have filtering software installed. Other times I have told them so that they can be a support to me and I to them.

As for telling the boss, in my case, several times I used work computers and time to access pornography. In some cases, I accessed it at hotels while on business trips. Yes, it was in my off time, but I was still there on company business. In all these instances, my accessing pornography was against company rules and was certainly not an honest use of company time or equipment. As mentioned in the section on friends, if this is or has been the case for you, this step will be an important part of seeking their forgiveness for your dishonesty and immoral behavior. If you work with computers and have used them or been tempted to use them to access pornography, or if you simply sense the opportunity to use them in this way might present itself, this step will be an important means of preventing further relapse and finding a support system in the very place you spend much of your time.

It can be hard to tell a boss, especially if you have nothing more than a boss-employee relationship. In my case, my boss and I had developed a good friendship. But that does not mean I did not worry about it. "What if telling him affects our relationship?"; "What if he tells someone else?"; "What if he fires me?"—these were and are valid concerns. True, the fear of dismissal is real, but I believe a pink slip for pornography will be rare. In most cases, you will find people at work to be understanding. This is especially true when you confide in people of the same sex. One hundred percent of the time, when I have told male friends, associates, coworkers, or employers, my admission has been met with empathy and a general attitude of "How can I help?"; sometimes they share stories of overcoming similar struggles.

So how can they help? In many cases, an employer might be in a position to install Internet filters or Internet accountability software, or to set time limits for Internet use so that you are not able to access it before others arrive at the office or after the doors have closed for the night. Maybe you don't even need the Internet at all. Or perhaps you can move desks or change offices. The possibilities are endless. And who knows, maybe any changes that come about because of your confession will help those around you. Maybe your boss or coworkers will refrain from sharing inappropriate stories, jokes, pictures, or video clips. Or maybe the changes will prevent someone else at work from falling into similar traps on company computers. In fact, I'd bet on it. By telling your employer and seeking his help, you can be the means of helping someone else.

Do be cautious, though, if your employer or employees are female. Such a conversation may be uncomfortable and even inappropriate. Your struggles may not be easily accepted or understood. Remember the ultimate goal here is to build a support system. If you and your wife feel this is not going to happen by telling your employer, then it is best to leave it alone for now. But if you have looked at pornography at the office, you will still need to come up with a plan with your wife and friends to help you avoid that problem in the future.

As with your friends, letting the appropriate people at work know and giving them permission to check in with you will give you that extra advantage needed. If you know they can follow up at any time, if you know they can see what you are looking at, if you know your job depends on staying clean now, you will be less likely to make an impulse decision, type in a search term, or return your gaze to something you know you should not.

Family

In the order of things, family should always be involved first. This can be emotionally difficult for many. In fact, I'd say as uncomfortable as telling a friend or employer may be, talking to your family is going to be harder. Why? Because he or she will be hurt the most by your admission.

You may have reasons why telling friends, employers, or church leaders won't work. You may not have a friend ready to hear your confession, or it may not be right to talk to your employer, or you may not have any church leaders at all. But when it comes to confiding in your family, I believe there are few exceptions. They, above all, have been betrayed by your silent addiction. And they, above all, can give you the support you need.

After telling my wife, I told my parents within a week; my siblings within a few months; and then my uncles, aunts, and many of my cousins within a couple years. Not only have they been able to help me, but I have been able to help them. On more than one occasion, a relative has come to me, thanking me for sharing my story. "It has," I've heard some say, "helped me stay strong." "What you've written here is so needed. I'm proud of you for sharing this." Or "I gave it to a friend who has been struggling with this problem and it is helping them." Or "I've struggled with this too." Can anything be more empowering than family helping family? No. Emphatically, no!

With this in mind, I'd like to share with you a part of my story as it relates to telling family: both the family of my childhood the family unit of my adulthood that had expanded to include my wife.

I was fourteen when I finally worked up the courage to see an ecclesiastical leader about my problem, which, at that point, was two years old. Soon after telling him, he asked if I had told my mom or dad. I had not. Our meeting ended fairly quickly, and I was dismissed to go home and talk to my parents. Clear in my mind is the moment when, later that day, I asked my dad if I could talk to him. There, standing in his room behind closed doors, I disclosed this embarrassing vice. I do not recall his words other than that he wanted to talk to my mom about it first, because it would be hard for her to understand. What I do recall is his reaction and lack of reaction. He simply took me in his arms and squeezed me tight. I sensed no anger or disappointment. Perhaps it was there, but he knew then that I needed help, not censure.

In retrospect, that instance of confession was relatively easy when compared to a similar moment fourteen years later when I found myself on the verge of telling my wife.

As background first, for years I had told myself that I would never tell her because of how much I loved her. "I am not going to be the one to break her heart," I said, as if the withholding of information somehow negated my previous actions. On several occasions, I even recall wrestling in thought and prayer before God, telling him, in essence, "I will go to hell first before I break her heart. You want to damn me because I will not tell her, so be it. I don't care. I don't want to hurt her." I hoped that such a protective attitude and promise would count for something at the judgment bar. "See, God, how noble I was. I didn't tell her *for her*." But this too was about me. I was angry with myself. I should have passionately protected her innocence and love by fending off the seductive temptations of pornography in the first place. That's where nobility is to be found. But in this, I had failed. I had already hurt my wife. She just didn't know it yet. Subtly and selfishly, my thoughts and desires to protect her were nothing but a cover for the fear I felt inside. Deep down, I was fighting what I knew had to happen. I had to tell her. For her, yes, but, above all, for me.

I was terrified. I loved my wife, and because of her love for me I knew telling her would all but destroy her. I remember sitting in church one Sunday, though, when a friend said something that opened my eyes long enough to see the path before me clearly. To paraphrase, he said: "Your kids are not yet yours. They have been loaned to you from your Father in Heaven, but you must earn them. In this life, they are yours to keep or lose." As if for the first time, I looked at my wife and my little boys, whom I loved more than life itself, and I was suddenly consumed by the awful reality of my addiction. It hit me—hard. I needed help and I needed it now, or I was going to lose them forever. No matter whom I had to tell, no matter the consequences, no matter the cost, I had to get my problem under control.

The terrible possibility that my wife might take the children and leave me after I told her loomed like a heavy shadow upon every thought and action from that point forward. I was sick to my stomach over the idea of life without them. But I also came to realize that whether they stayed or went didn't really make a difference. With or without them (preferably with, I prayed), I needed to turn my life around. "For what shall it profit a man, if he shall gain the whole world, and lose his own soul? Or what shall a man give in exchange for his soul?" (Mark 8:36–37). These were the questions at the forefront of my mind.

According to my beliefs, I was going to lose them forever unless I changed. So this was my chance to try and make things right and hopefully bind myself to them anew, not only here and now but eternally.

So I set out to tell my wife, all the while searching for and praying to recognize the right opportunity to do so. But there was never going to be a right time. Thankfully, as happens often, I believe, the Lord began to prepare my wife for the news. In her thoughts, she began to wonder if I was having a problem with pornography. At first, she shoved the idea away: "Not my husband!" But such thoughts continued until she began to suspect I was indeed struggling with an addiction to pornography. One night, after an indirect conversation about pornography (it is not that hard to bring up; it is everywhere: among friends, in the news, in sermons at church, and so on) she asked me if I had ever looked at it before.

With such a direct question, I was, for the first time in my life, able to give a direct answer. "Yes, I have." This immediately opened the door for other questions: "When?"; "Recently?"; "Today?"; and "How often?" I was again able to answer them as directly as they were asked, and I cannot accurately describe without shedding tears the weight that was immediately lifted from my body, mind, and soul, as if a giant boulder that had restricted my breathing since childhood had been suddenly removed. More painful, however, was the abrupt realization that admission alone had not removed my burden; rather, it had simply and quickly redistributed the weight of it. My boulder was not any lighter. I just wasn't the only one holding it up anymore. A glance to my side was all it took to see in my wife's once-bright-now-trembling eyes that I had shifted part of this tremendous weight onto her delicate shoulders. Oh, to see her knees buckle under that weight, and the agony bead up across her brow; it pains me like nothing else ever has to know that such suffering was because of me. In the suffering painted across my bride's countenance, I also came to see clearly the pain I had caused the Bridegroom, Christ, who above all first shouldered the tremendous weight we now were both feeling at that moment.

From there the long and arduous journey toward recovery and healing began, leading us countless times to church leaders' offices and marriage counseling and therapy sessions. On one occasion, we even gathered in the living room of my parents' home where, according to plan, we confided to all of my siblings and their spouses the full details of the addictions of my past and the road to recovery. We pled for their help and prayers and issued a warning that they beware of the subtle inroads to pornography within their own families. This was a defining moment in the lives of all of my family members. My siblings shed tears for their brother and sister-in-law. These were not tears of sorrow but rather empathy. In that single moment in which all truth came forth, we became a family in the purest, most sacred sense of the word. There was nothing but absolute love and support in that room, and it empowered us all. I believe if a family is willing to share one another's burdens, they will become stronger, and eventually, they too will share in the joy to come.

I often tell this story as I meet with recovering addicts. To my surprise, almost every time it is met with varying degrees of surprise and disbelief: "I can't believe you told your whole family" or "Why did you tell your siblings?" More surprising at first, though, was to hear several men state, "I could not get that kind of support in my family; my parents would kill me." I hear about so many good families that support their sons and brothers in their undertaking to deal with a personal problem. But I also hear about many good families who do not. Sadly, anger is a common reaction among parents and siblings. "In these cases," I am asked, "am I still supposed to tell my family?" Yes. First, I believe we owe it to them. They have a right to know. Second, while support may not come immediately, I have to believe it will come eventually. They just need time to get over the shock. Third, if they react out of anger or threaten to disown you, then I really think they needed to hear your confession, because they too need to learn lessons from it. They need to learn to be forgiving; they need to learn to be humble and charitable and patient. Your mistakes and your admission of them will simply be the catalyst for those life-changing lessons that can, in the long run, bring your family closer together. And who knows, but your disclosure will help them too deal with problems of their own.

I once worked to help a teenage boy overcome his addiction. He was accompanied at recovery meetings by his father, who was, at times, visibly flustered by the principles we taught. I could sense there was a struggle ensuing inside, and based on what he was saying, I was pretty sure he had past indiscretions of his own that he needed to divulge. As they joined us week in and week out, the dad slowly softened toward the recovery process. It was some months later when, in the midst of our meeting, he shared with us impromptu how he too had been struggling with pornography addiction, how he had fought against what we were teaching at first, but how he had finally told his wife, and how he felt so much better inside. He was on the road to sure recovery. He had tears in his eyes when he shared his gratitude for his son whose courage and honesty had set the example for him, the father, and prepared the way for his escape. Never have I seen a more beautiful moment in such meetings. This is the purpose and power of confession. We are here, all of us, to learn how to become sons and daughters, brothers and sisters, mothers and fathers. We are here to learn how to repent and how to forgive. We are here to learn how to support, how to save, and how to be saved. There is no more sacred place designated for this to happen than in the home where love should ever prevail—and prevail it will. In that I have faith.

Ecclesiastical & Professional Leaders

Throughout the various religious texts of the world, teachings speak to the last of the foundational corners we will touch upon—namely, the commandment to confess mistakes to an ecclesiastical leader as a part of the repentance process. Where training may lack, religious authority prevails. Acting as spiritual judges in Israel, they have the right to spiritual discernment and can help mediate the repentance process between you and Christ, so that "though your sins be as scarlet, they shall be as white as snow; though they be red like crimson, they shall be as wool" (Isaiah 1:18).

Religion often requires you to confess your sins before an appointed person within the church. But what if you are not religious or do not have a religious leader in whom to confide? The principle is not null and void. Telling a leader of some sort is still a crucial step to recovery. Perhaps you can tell a therapist or counselor. It does not really matter who you talk to, only that outside of work, friends, and family, there is someone with experience or wisdom to guide you, watch over you, advise you without judgment, mediate between you and your spouse as needed, and help you conquer this destructive habit.

In many cases, it will be necessary, or at least wise, to meet with both religious and professional leaders. This was true for my wife and me. We met with the equivalent of a pastor. At his encouragement, we also met with a local specialist in compulsive behaviors, in particular pornography addiction. His unbiased, nonjudgmental approach made him someone to talk to as well as someone to learn from. His goal was simply to help us analyze ourselves and the addiction and its catalysts, and help us learn for ourselves how to help each other avoid the crutch of compulsive behaviors.

Counseling can be extremely expensive, though, and many counselors design their program to be ongoing. You will find some who are in it for the money and others who truly want to help. Either way, care should be taken to not overtax your finances. Yes, you need to escape the chains of pornography at all costs, but doing so should not throw you into a new set of chains, albeit fiscal ones. Bondage is bondage and can take a heavy toll on a marriage no matter its origin. If you feel the need to see a counselor but cannot afford it, you might consider asking one about alternative options. In many cases, counselors have sliding fee scales based on income, or they may know of local low-income or nonprofit programs that exist to offset fees. For us, it was hard to swallow ninety-five dollars an hour, two times a week. If I'm being frank, I didn't want to go in the first place. My wife did, though, so we went. Good things came from our sessions. They were especially helpful for her. But in the end, we came to the conclusion that everything he was teaching us came down to open and honest communication. After a couple months, we decided we had gained what we could and began to only meet with our church leader, as needed. This was free of charge. He listened to us, advised us, prayed for us, and helped us "work out [our] own salvation with fear and trembling" (Philippians 2:12).

I want to make this clear: I am not saying counselors are a waste of money. I am saying, though, that as husband and wife, you are in control. Counselors are just a tool to help you. Use them as you need. Just as often as our therapist said things we agreed with, he also said or did things we did not agree with. This was not necessarily a bad thing, though, because in our disagreement with his methods, we became united. Afterward, we always discussed the principles highlighted in our session. As a result, we came to our own conclusions. His counsel simply became a tool that we used as we saw fit to work out our own recovery and healing.

In the previous subsection of this chapter, I briefly mentioned part of the experience I had when confessing my addiction before a church leader for the first time. For the sake of this chapter and the two to follow, I'd like to go into a little more detail about it and another time I sought guidance from my church leader.

As mentioned, I was fourteen. For whatever reason, several experiences and sermons at church combined that day, like waves off the coast, to have a powerful effect on me. I felt compelled to go to my pastor and get help. I had no clue what to expect. All my life I had heard about repentance and going to confess your sins, and I had heard words like *dis-fellowship* and *excommunication*. I didn't know exactly what they meant, but I was filled with all sorts of irrational fears and concerns. To make it harder, the leader over the congregation at the time was my best friend's dad. Still, I knew what I had to do. Before I could change my mind, I quickly made my way down the hall toward his office. When I turned the corner and saw him standing there, my heart began to pound. I took a breath, walked right up to him, and asked, quietly, if I could talk to him. He must have sensed the urgency in my request, because he invited me in without an appointment. In that instant, my emotions ran the gamut. No sooner did his door close than I burst into tears, sobbing like a little child. Taking a seat in front of me, he surveyed the broken boy, looked into my eyes, and with a smile said, "Why don't we start with a prayer." In the moment it took for that prayer to be offered—a prayer which sought God's spirit to guide us and which requested courage and peace to be with me—I managed to calm down. When it was over, I told him about my problem. I don't remember much of what was said between us other than he understood it was a problem for many people and, as I already related to you, he wanted to know if I had told my dad. With a hug and a few other encouraging words, he dismissed me to go tell my parents.

Over a decade later, I found myself in a similar situation. The problem that began in my youth was now a terrible monster. While on my way home from a meeting, I was reflecting on the need to get control of my life. "How?" I kept wondering. "And when?" A favorite quote then came to mind: "You cannot run away from weakness; you must some time fight it out or perish; and if that be so, why not now, and where you stand."[1] Overwhelmed by the truth of this statement and my building desire to change, I immediately took an earlier exit and drove straight to the church. My leader was not there. To make sure I did not have time to change my mind, though, I wrote a letter explaining my mistakes and asked to meet with him; then I slid it under his office door so I could not retrieve it. I experienced a whole slew of emotions: relief mixed with doubt mixed with absolute fear. Because the mistakes of my past were allowed to run rampant and had worsened since I was fourteen, I was certain I would now be subject to the laws of the church. I feared being disfellowshipped or excommunicated. I worried about what people would say about me and how they might whisper about my family. I dreaded the call from my pastor in response to my letter. But when it came he was sincere and understanding. I was not kicked out; rather, I was embraced. We met often, and he helped me down the road toward repentance and forgiveness. In the mirror of confession I saw for the first time the ugly face of my collective sins as they really were. I was forced to relive over and over again the things I had done of which I was ashamed. As a result, at times our meetings were painful for me, but I came to understand the necessity of this pain.

When I think of the principle therein, I think of the few times a fishing hook has become lodged in my finger. The initial moment when the barb breaks the skin is somewhat painful, but after that virtually all pain disappears unless something agitates the hook or its surrounding area. Of course, we all know that if the hook is not taken out, the wound will become infected, thus leading to a more serious problem. So we pull it out, a process that also causes pain. However, because barbed hooks are designed to easily penetrate skin and stubbornly hold on afterward so the prey cannot escape, the removal process often causes much greater pain. This is true of repentance. It is a process that will ultimately offer you relief and peace of mind, but before you experience those things, you must painstakingly remove from your life the sins you have so stubbornly held on to.

I am grateful for those ecclesiastical and professional leaders who did everything within their power to release me from the awful grasp of pornography. I only wish I had been strong enough to free myself when I was fourteen. How much pain would have been spared us all!

"So wait," you might suddenly wonder. "Why were you caught again by pornography addiction? When you were fourteen, if you did as you have just told us to do, if you confessed before your church leader and you sought the help of your family, then why did your addiction to pornography return?"

Answer: Because I did not tell them everything.

19

AN ANALOGY ON COMPLETE REPENTANCE

"Be ye clean, that bear the vessels of the Lord" (Isaiah 52:11).

I HAVE MENTIONED TWO TIMES WHERE I SOUGHT OUT an ecclesiastical leader to whom to confess my sins. But the reality is, I have met with and confessed before many church leaders. In fact, out of the ten or so different pastors I've had, I've met with six. Why? Because I always had something new to confess. Why? Because I never really confessed correctly in the first place. How? I was always purposefully leaving some sins out. I wanted forgiveness with the least amount of effort and embarrassment possible. The following real-life analogy represents the importance of complete repentance now, and I share it as a preface to the two chapters that will follow.

As a kid I often remember my mom making dinner and afterward my dad doing the dishes. Partly because of this example, after I married I automatically started doing the dishes after every meal. I am embarrassed to say that with our work schedules as they were, many times those dishes piled up in the sink. This would have been disgusting enough if it weren't for the discovery one day that the apartment complex was home to cockroaches that delighted in our gift of dirty dishes.

I would come home from work, tired and just wanting to eat and relax, only to see that menacing pile of dishes. I would wonder how it got so out of control, yet quite often I lacked the energy or the motivation to dive in and clean them up. Instead, I would make dinner then sit back to enjoy a much-deserved albeit self-appointed period of relaxation. As a result, those dishes only got worse. As a kid and through most of my adult life, I always preferred a clean room to a dirty one. The problem with the dishes was that I didn't want to go through the work to clean them. If they were just cleaned up, it would be so much easier to keep the kitchen clean. Finally, out of frustration, I would roll up my sleeves and begin scrubbing.

It took time and lots of hot water and soap. But finally the dishes were all clean. Well, almost all clean. Inevitably, at the bottom of every pile of dishes was one dish that seemed to be more disgusting than the others. Usually this dish was a crock-pot or a casserole dish or something like that—something that in the process of cooking had gotten caked with sticky residues or petrified crusts or impenetrable grease. Upon further inspection, at the bottom of the stagnant water filling that dish I'd often find yet other bowls, cups, and silverware that needed to be washed.

I would fish out the smaller dishes and clean them. They were easy. But as for the big, disgusting one that still needed a good scrubbing? I was tired of doing dishes and lacked the desire to clean this most disgusting of all dishes. So I'd hang up my scrub brush and kick back on the couch. "I'm going to let that big one soak a bit," I'd tell my wife. "I hate those things. I wish someone would invent a lining of some kind for those dishes—something that could just be thrown away and didn't require all the soaking."

In reality, it was an excuse to not do something I should have just pitched in and done.

Days would pass and I'd come home, tired and in need of "me time," only to open the door, shoo away the cockroaches, and find a new pile of dishes—seemingly larger and filthier than the previous pile.

"What?!" I'd exclaim to myself. "How did this get here? Didn't I just do these dishes, like a few days ago?" My thoughts would trail off as I recalled the last few days over which I set my dirty dishes on the counter and promised to get to them later that evening or in the morning, because "right now, I'd rather relax or go out or play a game."

Grumbling all the way, I'd again roll up my sleeves and sink my hands into the grease and grime. I'd run the hot water. I'd add soap. I'd scrub and I'd rinse and I'd scrub and I'd rinse some more. And at the end, or where the end should have been, do you know what I would find?

That same old, stinking crock-pot just sitting there where I had left it last. Finally, finally, I would clean it.

Again and again in my life I have had this experience, where at the end of doing dishes I find a larger dish previously ignored. "Why," I've asked myself, "is this pot always the first dish at the bottom of the sink?" The answer, of course, was that it was not always the first dish; it was simply the one dish I never wanted to deal with. When the sink is clean, it is so much easier to clean the other dishes as they come, and keep the entire kitchen clean. But I had convinced myself that a long soaking was what this particular dish needed in order to soften up the grime. Because of this, that one pot was the seed of all the other dirty dishes.

It took years before I saw this pattern in my own life. When I say I was addicted to pornography for sixteen years, I do not mean that I looked at pornography every day. In fact, days, weeks, months, even years would go by when I didn't look at it at all. I was sure I had beaten it on my own. But I had not. It always returned. Why? Because in my confessions, I had always left out certain pieces of the truth, and most of the time they were not your little forks and knives; rather, they were significant sins which I felt particularly afraid or embarrassed to admit. It never failed. "I did this," I'd say. "And I looked at this. And I struggled with these thoughts. And I did this and this and this."

"Is that everything?" I would then be asked by my parents, my church leader, or my wife.

"Yes," I'd answer, hoping they wouldn't see through me, "that is all."

But it wasn't. Sitting deep below the surface, I could still see the outline of a sin I did not want to bring up. Quickly, I'd transition into sharing my thoughts on the atonement and my gratitude for the Savior who suffered for all of our sins. In part, this personal testimony came from my heart. But it was also a sly, underhanded way of switching the subject. By sharing these feelings, I was also trying to convince myself that I did not need to share everything. "I have gone through the motions of repentance," I told myself, "and I think I've given them a pretty clear idea of my problems, and that is good enough. The Lord should cover the rest." This, of course, is false. For everything to be forgiven, everything must be confessed.

Sometime later, after a major relapse, I would find myself sitting in front of my ecclesiastical leader again, going down a long list of new mistakes, at the end of which, still lurking in the murky waters, was that one sin in particular. Like a speck of mold never cleaned from a piece of fabric, it had again been the culprit from which a thousand new sins had spawned. I am convinced that my addiction returned as often as it did because of my selfish refusal, when I had the opportunity, to properly scrub from my life every last mistake.

"Is that everything?" came the familiar question.

"No." Big breath. "There's more."

As soon as I pulled every sin from the grimy water that my life had become, and presented them to the appropriate people for help in cleaning, I overcame my addiction. By offering up every sin, we are in essence offering up our whole selves, including the pride and ego we have not wanted to part with. No longer content to hang on to certain sins to protect our worldly name and reputation, we become the humble man with the "broken and contrite heart" that God requires for repentance to work (Psalm 51:17). It is then and only then that Christ's atonement can put that heart back together again.

With this in mind, I encourage you to give up your whole self, pride, ego, heart, and soul. If you are sitting in the office with a pastor, if you are on the phone with a parent, or if you are face to face with your wife, then the hard part of getting there is over. This is your chance. Don't leave certain mistakes unconfessed. Admit them, admit them all, then move on and watch the atonement work. I promise it will be a turning point in your life. Your ability to overcome your addiction will increase in proportion to the honesty and diligence with which you confess and forsake your sins.

As a side note, about the time I learned this lesson, I decided that, as a symbol and reminder, I would never let another dish soak again. On occasion, I have filled a grimy crock-pot with hot water and soap and started to turn away to let it soak. But I always stop. "My hands are already wet," I tell myself, "and if I leave it undone, I'll have to clean it later when my hands are dry, and then it will probably be worse—all full of cold water and the same grime that disgusts me now. I have to clean it at some point. So . . . why not now? It'll take a few extra minutes of my time, but it will be worth it to have all of the dishes clean with none festering in the sink for later when I have better things to do."

And so, to this day, I do not let a single dish soak. Why soak them for later, when you can scrub them now?

20

TELL THE WHOLE TRUTH

"Now Faithful play the man, speak for thy God,
Fear not the wicked's malice, nor their rod;
Speak boldly man, the truth is on thy side,
Die for it, and to life in triumph ride."[1]

WE ARE ALL FAMILIAR WITH THE PROCESS OF SWEARing in a witness in the courts of law. "Do you swear to tell the truth, the whole truth, and nothing but the truth, so help you God?" Some tell the truth no matter how it implicates them. Others, for many reasons, try to hide it. But, in the end, the truth always gets out. The truth must, you might say, be free. Ironically, in order for you to be free, you must be 100 percent truthful.

Mark Twain once said, "If you tell the truth, you don't have to remember anything."[2] This was true for me. I cannot begin to tell you how often I racked my brain trying to remember what I had told someone to cover up my problem. One lie had led to another until my entire life was covered in a thick blanket of them; and I could not tug at one edge without pulling a corner back somewhere else, thus revealing my deception. In response, I always made fabricated yet another lie in order to cover what had been exposed. Oddly, I did not see them as blatant lies.

I justified telling them in order to keep the peace and happiness in my marriage and home.

I am positive your life is full of lies. Your wife might even suggest that your entire life has been a lie. I don't think this is necessarily fair, but it doesn't really make a difference. If you've lied to your wife once or a hundred times, you have been unfaithful. Going forward, there can be no secrets.

On occasion, I have heard of therapists or church leaders who preach otherwise. There is a time, some have said, for secrets. Respectfully, I disagree. I can't think of any situation where dishonesty is okay. Experience tells me we justify keeping secrets or withholding truths because we are not charitable or wise enough to recognize how to tell the truth in the right way. No doubt, this is something we can all work on. I find there is no better option than careful candor, respectful replies, attentive albeit apprehensive answers, and timely truth-telling. Only in the fertile soil of absolute honesty can trust and love reach their full potential.

I am often asked why my addiction continued for so many years. The answer is just as I alluded to: I kept *all* of it a secret. It was not that I kept the whole problem a secret, though that was true for many years; but rather, when I did first confess, I never once revealed all of the truth. When I met with my pastor for the first time, I actually went to see him about a problem with masturbation. As we have discussed, masturbation and pornography are almost always linked. But I did not mention to him that I had looked at pornography too, and he did not ask. But my dad did. After seeking his help, he specifically questioned if I had looked at pornography in conjunction with masturbation. I answered that I had not. This, of course, was not true. However, I wasn't purposefully trying to be deceitful. I just didn't see how telling or not telling my dad or my pastor made a difference. Furthermore, I didn't recognize full disclosure as being such a vital component of repentance. I justified my actions by telling myself that "I had not known any better, but now I know, so I will just be better from here on out." In fact, at the exact moment I said "no" to my dad, I made a mental resolution to stop looking at inappropriate pictures too.

I do recall wondering if I should go back and talk to either of them about my dishonesty, but I always convinced myself otherwise. It had been so hard to get my courage up to talk to them the first time that it just seemed easier to let it go and stop the habit rather than initiate embarrassing dialogue a second time. Also, these were not expressly pornographic pictures, I justified, as much as they were seductive images in fashion or celebrity magazines. Besides, I figured it would be easy enough to stop looking at them on my own. I was wrong.

On the heels of the little victory gained by talking to my dad and pastor, life went on without further incident—for a couple weeks at least. Then, one day, I slipped. I shook it off, reminding myself not to do it anymore, resolving to do better. But then I slipped again a week later, and then a couple days later again, and then again and again, and just like that the pattern picked up where it had left off pre-confession.

Each time, I talked myself out of going back to my dad or pastor. "I only need to tell them if it's a problem," I kept saying, "and it's not a problem anymore; it's just a one-time occurrence because I'm stopping—starting right now." But I never could. Without any accountability, I never progressed past the commitment to "stop the problem—starting right now."

As a result, sixteen years would pass before I learned this one truth: it is the truth, the whole truth, and nothing but the truth that will set you free. Not "so help you God," but so God can help you.

And help you he will. In your situation, freedom from sin and from the desire to sin will come in time as you consistently begin to tell the truth in all things—specifically to yourself, your spouse, or any of the people in the four corners we have previously discussed.

I said it before, I will say it again: there can be no secrets. Some men and women mistakenly believe they do not need to hurt their spouses or fiancés with details of past indiscretions prior to marriage. This is not true. As hurtful as it may be, everything must come out into the open.

Anytime I bring this up, it is inevitable that someone retorts, "Yeah, but if we've repented, I don't know why we should bring them up later." This is a valid concern. In reply, I pose the following question: "If it is not now a problem, and if you have truly repented and been forgiven, why then are you afraid to bring it up?" Also, to those of you yet to marry, might your future spouse not have the right to know just what kind of person she is marrying?

A look at the basis of the "Lemon Law," which offers consumer recourse after the selling of a car with known faults, might help us better understand the necessity of having no secrets. It might also help us come to terms with exactly what past secrets should be revealed.

Not long ago, my wife and I weighed the pricey decision of paying ten thousand dollars for a van, with which we intended to transport our growing family to all of our desired destinations. People rarely buy a car without running a detailed report proving an automobile's excellent record. In my excitement to buy this van, however, I simply asked the owner, who seemed like a genuine guy, if the car had ever been in any accidents. He told me he had bought it from his brother, and it had a perfect record. I took his word for it, feeling further convinced by the clean look and feel of the van. So we bought it without asking any other questions. However, as major components quickly began to fail and various mechanics weighed in, we discovered to our frustration that the vehicle had a laundry list of accidents and mechanical failures. Worse, it had been totaled twice, the odometer had been tampered with, and gold wasn't even its original color. By the time we discovered these major red flags, it was too late to take any legal action. We made do with it as best we could, but when the transmission went out for a third time, we washed our hands of it once and for all.

After that experience, I vowed to follow the common practice of asking for a history of maintenance before purchasing a vehicle. Why do people ask for these? Because we all want to know that what we are investing in is as good as advertised. With the professional-grade cleaners and waxes that are available at any part's store, any car can be made to appear presentable and without defect.

On the road to life, we all sustain damages of some kind. Is this something to be ashamed of? Only if we did not appropriately fix the problem and it continues to resurface. I have seen many people try to hide the need for maintenance in order to sell their car at the highest price possible. I have also seen people try to hide the fact that certain maintenance has just been performed, as if the knowledge of such will reflect poorly on the reliability of the vehicle. I understand both of these concerns, but if a new transmission has been installed or the breaks fixed or the clutch replaced, who cares if they know? Do these things not signify that the car is now in working order? While any buyer may hesitate for a moment and devote extra time to do a little more research, at least they have a clear and honest idea about their investment. No one wants to be sold a lemon. Yet so many of us, out of fear or greed, do not hesitate to sell someone else one. In such cases, it is only a matter of time before the need for maintenance becomes abruptly clear. Sometimes the problems under the hood are discovered in the driveway or a store parking lot. Other times, though, they are not discovered until either we are far from home, barreling down the freeway in the middle of a storm, or we experience an accident.

"But what if I don't struggle with those problems anymore?" Then again, I ask, "Why does it matter?" If they are gone from your life, you have nothing to fear. Your relationship, if it is to succeed now and forever, must be founded on absolute honesty and openness. As contradictory as it may seem, making known past mistakes now will solidify your relationship in the future. When a spouse knows there are no secrets, it is easier for him or her to trust the other completely. To have that trust will never be more important.

I have a friend who committed to not only tell his wife if he ever looked at something he should not, but to show her what exactly he looked at. This was an extremely hard thing to do the first couple times he slipped. It was extremely embarrassing to look with his wife at the single image he had not been strong enough to turn away from. But through her eyes, he suddenly saw how ridiculous and perverse his obsession was. Since then, this potential consequence, among others, has been enough to help him stay clean.

Like icebergs in the ocean, what you see when you first discover a loved one's pornography addiction is usually only 10–20 percent of the real problem. The rest discreetly and dangerously lurks below the surface. To those of you on the receiving end of these personal confessions, please realize that in most cases it will take several periods of confession before all secrets have been excavated from the recesses of the addict's mind. This is often the case for a couple reasons. One, it can be extremely painful and embarrassing to share every little mistake all at once. The confessor may not be ready to deal with certain things yet, and frankly you may not be ready to deal with them either. Second, until addicts really start to examine their lives in full and on paper, they may not realize just how bad their mistakes have been. For most of them, the addiction has been going on for years, and it can be nearly impossible to recall everything they have done wrong in one single moment of conversation.

To you addicts, just keep the lines of communication open—with your spouse and with your Father in Heaven. As you do, he will bring things back to your remembrance. Mistakes that have long laid hidden, but that need to be confessed and forsaken, will pop into your mind. Whenever they do—no matter how long it has been since you last shared past mistakes, or how painful you think it will be for your spouse to hear yet another and perhaps even worse mistake—muster up the courage to disclose everything and let the truth set you free. In recovery groups, it is a common practice to write down the history of your mistakes. This, of course, can take a significant amount of time. It is not meant to be accomplished in one day or even one week. It may be an ongoing list that you continually add to. This can be valuable to you for many reasons. One, it will help you come to terms with everything you have done wrong (this will be extremely hard but necessary to accept). Two, it can help you discover other people in your life you might need to repent to or seek forgiveness from. Three, it will ensure you are not withholding any details of which you need to confess, for, if you are like me, it can be hard to remember what you have and have not confessed already. By virtue of the list, you will be able to determine rather quickly whether you have previously brought it up. Finally, writing can be quite therapeutic. I have seen some men jot down their mistakes in list form. I have seen others write theirs out in a running narrative. And I have seen others work their mistakes into the lives of a fictional character. It doesn't matter how you write them down, but do it. Eventually you can destroy the list, but for now, it will be helpful as you work to confess all your sins before God, family, and friends.

In addition to making known your past, you must make sure that you are not continually concealing present moments of relapse or temptation. If you look or slip in any degree, you will, I promise you, catch yourself wondering: "Do I need to tell my spouse about this? It was such a small thing. I don't think I need to tell her. It will only make her worry." Or "If I tell her, she will become concerned or agitated and it will ruin our evening. There's nothing to worry about anyway. It was just once. So I don't think I'm going to bring it up now." But you need to. If you slip back into an old habit and click over to a pornographic site, you need to tell your wife. If you return your gaze, purposefully or subconsciously, to a woman's body, you need to tell your wife. If you put in a movie, scan a clothing catalogue, watch a music video or video clip to satisfy your lust in any way, then you need to tell your wife. Even if you simply feel weak and vulnerable, telling your wife can help. Often the key to overcoming temptation is stepping away long enough to get past that initial moment of desire. By simply telling your spouse of your perceived weakness, you will find the strength you need to stay clear of pornography.

I have again heard some counselors and church leaders advise men that disclosing moments of weakness should only be done to a sponsor, or friend. Again, I respectfully disagree. Yes, depending on your situation (maybe she's not available or not emotionally ready to hear it), in the heat of the moment, it may be wise to call a friend and say, "Hey, I'm feeling really vulnerable right now" or "I just looked at this, and I need help." When it comes right down to it, get help however you can. Still, the best thing husbands and wives can do is talk over these potential scenarios and determine together a course of action. Maybe your wife would rather you call your friend first. So be it. But at some point during that day you still need to tell her you called your friend. Or maybe she wants to be the go-to person every single time, no matter where she is or what she is doing. So be it. That's her right.

True, after telling her, she may get upset—probably with good reason; and perhaps she does need to work on controlling her reactions, as you may very well think, and perhaps she does need to come to a better under-standing of how this problem plagues men on a daily basis, but right now you shouldn't be worrying about that at all. You should, as we've probably all told our kids before, "only worry about yourself." As far as telling the truth is concerned, your partner's reaction cannot matter. This is not to say you should not care about her feelings and it is also not to say that her reactions are not valid—because they are; it is just to say, "men, tell the whole truth no matter what." You cannot afford to let how she might react prevent you from doing your part and telling her everything. In fact, doing so will give her the needed opportunities to work on her reactions if needed, come to terms with the problem's prevalence, and become a sup-port to you. It might even help her share with you problems of her own. I am aware of men who, on more than one occasion, after sharing mistakes from their past, were met with confessions from their wives' past. They were both able to help each other.

Having said that, let me say once again how important it is that you tell the truth and leave nothing out. Remember it is the justification of the small things that has always allowed your addiction to continue. By the subtle turn of a tiny helm, mighty ships can and have forged ocean waters and discovered new lands. But by those same small turns, they have also been steered off course, led in vain pursuit of false treasure, run aground, and been destroyed. If you don't tell her, subtly but surely, degree by degree, you will find yourself getting closer to the edge until your small allowances turn into great sins. But if you do tell her, this small, seemingly-insignificant decision will be the means of reversing your errant course and bringing about great change—in you, in her, in your relationship, and in your family!

21

IT'S THE LITTLE THINGS THAT COUNT

"'Are these the shadows of the things that Will be, or are they shadows of things that May be, only?'

Still the Ghost pointed downward to the grave by which it stood.

'Men's courses will foreshadow certain ends, to which, if persevered in, they must lead,' said Scrooge. 'But if the courses be departed from, the ends will change. Say it is thus with what you show me!'"[1]

IT TOOK A HORRIFIC ENCOUNTER WITH HIS LONG-DEAD business partner, Jacob Marley, and a timely visit from three other ghosts representing the past, present, and future, for Ebenezer Scrooge to learn one lesson: that if we are to alter the destination toward which we are headed, we must change our position on the path, and, in many cases, we must change paths altogether. Of course, this principle works in the opposite direction too. You, men, are reading this book because at some point you took a detour, ended up going in the wrong direction, and didn't realize it till it was too late. In order to get back, you will need to very carefully feel your way back. To understand how to do this, though, you first need to understand how you got so lost. With this in mind, I want to explore this concept first in theory and then with specifics from my own life.

For the sake of simplifying, let's just say there are two possible end-points toward which every person is headed: happiness or unhappiness. The trouble the addict often experiences is that usually he knows he wants and needs to stop looking at pornography, but he doesn't know where to begin. Everything he is feeling tells him he is unhappy. He can see way across the way to the path that leads to happiness, but he cannot figure out how to get there, assuming that the distance between unhappy and happy can only be traveled in one giant leap.

This error in reasoning is largely due to the fact that he thinks he reached his current location by a giant leap of sorts. And this false idea is due to the blinders that form over eyes and memory when an addict begins to wander down the forbidden path of pornography. In the heat of the moment, so to speak, he does not realize many things. First, he does not see the warning signs: "Steep Grade"; "Sharp Curves"; "Falling Rocks"; "Stop!" He dismisses or overlooks every single one. Second, he does not comprehend how fast he is going, nor does he recognize just how many steps into the path he has taken. Think, addicts, of any time you binged on pornography and tell me if this is not true. Seconds, no doubt, turned into minutes and minutes into hours. You started by stepping off the path just for a moment, just to look at one little thing. But when it was all over and you opened up your Internet history to wipe clean the foot-prints left behind, you, like I, were shocked to see just how many sites you ended up looking at. One site led to another then to another, and then pretty soon you had multiple sites you wanted to look at, so you opened another tab then another and another. Pretty soon there was not enough room or time to see everything, so you started scribbling reminders and addresses on scraps of paper so you could look at certain sites another time. Imagine, for a moment, if you drove this way. Scenic view by scenic view, back road by back road, you'd be so far into the deep woods of the Yukon you wouldn't know your north from your south. Home would be a distant memory, a dying hope. In your heart, you want to simply jump all the way back, but doing so is not possible. You must work your way back—step-by-step—with as much frenzy and passion as you worked your way into this mess.

Let me use a quick sports analogy. Let's say I was your coach and our team had set a goal to score a hundred points in a game. Using the principle I am describing above, it would be like us wasting the whole game away trying to figure out how to score a one-hundred-point basket, when, in reality, the way to score a hundred points is to make fifty baskets, one basket at a time. In life it is the simple things we do that add up collectively to help us overcome the big trials. Recovery, healing, happiness—these things can only be achieved one step at a time.

"Man's mind cannot grasp the causes of events in their completeness, but the desire to find those causes is implanted in man's soul."[2] At home, we have a garden. If we are not constantly maintaining it, the weeds will take over. When they pop up, we pull them out. But imagine if we had to go into the soil to find the weed's seeds before they sprouted. Well, that is exactly what you have to do.

Thus far, as I said earlier, you have fallen because you have failed to filter or consciously define and separate the potential dangers from your lives. Our bodies are amazing machines. They are built to constantly analyze our surroundings and communicate our perceptions, and then act accordingly in order to maintain a safe and pleasant existence. In a car barreling down the freeway, we have the capacity to smell something burning or feel the engine awkwardly shudder. We likewise can hear a car racing up from behind us or see a pothole in the road ahead. In all cases, our brains immediately and almost subconsciously go into emergency mode in an attempt to determine what might be wrong and subsequently avoid the obstacle. But sometimes the most dangerous obstacles are not those large ones that we easily recognize.

We have all watched the child ignore his dangling shoelace because he either does not want to stop playing, does not know how to tie it, or does not think it is a problem. Then, some moments later, he trips and falls and hurts himself, and playtime is interrupted. Furthermore, overcome with emotion, he is no longer in the proper frame of mind to learn how to tie his shoe. We tie it for him and life goes on.

In my life, there have been many "dangling shoelaces" that eventually led to falls and scraped knees. Perhaps you have heard of the *butterfly effect*. In chaos theory, the butterfly effect is the sensitive dependence on some initial condition. More specifically, the phrase, coined by meteorologist and theorist, Edward Lorenz, refers to a theoretical example of a hurricane created in part by the flap of a butterflies wings weeks before. In essence, it is a theory based on progressive consequence. One thing leads to another then to another, and so on. There have been just as many times when a seemingly insignificant flap from a butterflies wings has led to massive storms off the coast of peace and happiness.

In light of this, if you are to completely overcome your addiction, you must seek out and deal with the butterflies. You must train yourself, upon first noticing a dangling shoelace, to stop and get help. This can be very hard for two reasons: one, "shoelaces" can be hard to notice, and two, "butterflies" are pretty and we don't always want to give them up or don't feel it is even necessary. Generally speaking, addicts are often so focused on the obvious causes of their addiction they do not see the small ones.

Now, let's segue into specifics.

It is in our nature when we fall to look back and see what tripped us, or even to look for something to blame other than our own lapse in judgment. In my life, after every single relapse, when I found myself face down on the ground, I would do the same. "How did I get here?" I'd plead, remembering with incredulity how just that morning I had been so happy.

I immediately started looking at the "storm clouds" as the cause of rain: "Okay, my family left for the day or for the weekend," or "I used my computer at night when everyone was in bed," or "I chose to stay late after work," just to name a few common ones. Now, it is true that these occurrences and decisions very directly put me in dangerous situations where it was too easy to give in, but they were not the "dangling shoelaces" I needed to address. Instead, they represented the act of stepping on the shoelace, and looking at pornography became the fall.

So where, then, are these tiny seeds of addiction? Where you least expect them.

Let me share specific examples that took me years to see. Often, the root of my fall could be found in something as simple as glancing at a lady on TV, or in an ad in a newspaper, or even at a female jogger along the side of the road. Sometimes just my pupils would move—ever so slightly—so that others would not notice. Other times, I justified I was looking at something else ("Oh, hey boys, look at that dog she's walking"), but I knew it was so I could steal a quick glance. Other times still, when no one was in the car with me, I would consciously choose to turn my head, focus my eyes, and take it all in. "I mean, men do this, right?" That was my justification. "It's just part of my nature, right?" Wrong. But even if it is part of our natural makeup, so is sickness. But when illness settles in, we don't just sit there, do we? No. We take care of it as fast as we can. We wash our hands and sanitize our surroundings and we even avoid people and places where sickness might be spread.

For me, it was always this small choice to look in *any* degree that quickly led to bigger and worse things. So my pupils ever so quickly glanced to the side as if I was just curious to see who was there. It was enough to doom me. I just didn't realize it yet. Whether I continued to think about her or not, she never left my mind. She just kept on running in there, somewhere. Like the first domino in an endless line of them, the carnal exhilaration I experienced in mind and body when I looked at her, as imperceptible as it may have been, was ever pushing me toward the next time I saw someone or something I felt compelled to gawk at. And when I did look, the degree of exhilaration increased, then again and again and again, object by object, until the simple female jogging down the street, whom I passed at fifty-five miles per hour on my way to work at 6:00 a.m. two days before, had snowballed into a website with women purposefully placed there to tempt, seduce, and destroy.

And so my advice is? Don't look. We are people-watchers by habit, all of us. Without even thinking, we turn our head to look at people because they are there; we turn our eyes to an ad on the side of the screen because it is there. But we don't have to. *You* don't have to. You can be in control of your eyes.

Once I was able to identify the seeds of pornography for me, I began to notice just how often I was turning my head out of habit. Aware of this, I was then able to consciously analyze each situation. I'm in my car; out of the corner of my eye I sense there is a group waiting to cross the street; do I look? Normally I would have because, what's the harm? But I don't because I cannot afford to be "normal." I instead force myself to keep my eyes straight ahead, thus blocking out any and every exterior influence. It is hard to do. In fact, it still takes effort for me to accomplish this. But it can be done.

To this day, when I am in the car with my wife and boys, and we see a jogger, we shout out "jogger!" then look away. My boys are too young to know yet why we are doing this, but they enjoy it. More a joke now than anything, the jogger may be male or female, young or old, attractive or not so much, but we still shout away. It is a good reminder to be always watchful of our eyes.

What "joggers" exist in your life? Maybe they are hiding in your movie collection, in your love for fine art, in that series of books you love, or behind the lyrics of the music you listen to. It doesn't matter; find them, address them, and make the change.

22

ON SACRIFICE

*"I will freely sacrifice unto thee: I will praise thy name,
O Lord; for it is good." (Psalm 54:6)*

AS A YOUNG MAN, MY GRANDPA LIVED ON A RANCH. A self-proclaimed cowboy from Arizona, there was nothing he loved more than being outside working the land. His dad loved it too. It was their life. But then, one day, while my grandpa was out in the field with horses and plow, all that changed. In my imagination I can almost hear the screen door creak as my great-grandpa stepped outside. Maybe the sound of the screen door caught my grandpa's attention too, I don't know. But I can see him as he pauses from his work, wipes the sweat from his brow and watches the darkened silhouette of his dad slowly make its way across the field. Did he notice a slight sag in the otherwise broad and strong shoulders of my great-grandpa? Did he sense change on the orange glow of the desert horizon? With few words, my great-grandpa looked at his son, told him he'd sold the ranch, then turned back and headed inside. Tears must have fallen from both their eyes, moistening the parched land below. My grandpa was crushed. He unhooked the plow and never looked back. "Why," he must have thought, "did Dad sell the ranch? He knows how much it means to me. I know how much it means to him. It doesn't make sense."

As is often the case in life, the answer came later. My great-grandpa sacrificed the ranch for his son—because he loved him more than he loved the land; he was afraid that his son loved ranching so much that he would never go on the church mission he had promised to go on. My grandpa would later admit that his dad's fears were correct: because of the ranch, he wouldn't have gone on that mission. But because he went, he received great blessings: he met his wife with whom he would later raise a beautiful family; he developed a binding faith in God that would uplift him during the dark times of World War II. Even had he been able to see the blessings that would come from selling the farm, they would not have made that initial moment of sacrifice any less painful. Without them, though, his sacrifice was monumental—especially considering the fact that my great-grandpa did not know ahead of time whether his sacrifice would pay off or not. There was a chance it would; that was it. But he sensed it was the right thing to do, so he did it. He sacrificed for the unknown.

Many years later, married and far removed from the rancher's life, my grandpa returned to see the land he had loved so much. To his surprise, the people who originally bought the ranch never ended up working it. It remained as he had left it, even the plow still lodged in the ground, as if frozen in time. Was this, then, a pointless and wasteful sacrifice? If he had never looked past the things he had to give up but continually mourned their loss, then perhaps it would seem that way. But if he focused instead on the many things he had gained because of it, then there is no question; it was the right thing to do.

So how do we measure the cost of freedom? In war time, it is most often calculated by the casualties and destruction that occur. Whether we see those losses positively or negatively largely depends on whether we believe in the cause being fought for. If we do not believe in the cause or do not want to win the war then, yes, any sacrifice is wasteful and unnecessary. But when we do believe in our cause and see it as a necessary means to protect and set other men free, then the lives lost become heroic symbols of ultimate sacrifice and love. So what else are you willing to give up? And *willing* must be the key here. If the sacrifice you make is to have power enough to save, you must make it of your own free will and choice.

Think of Siddhārtha Gautama Buddha, the great Hindu spiritual teacher. He was born of a royal family. From his birth on, his parents spared no expense to protect him and to provide him every joy in life. But around the age of thirty, he gave it all up—every last pleasure, every last treasure. Why? Because in them, he had found suffering; in selfish pleasure, he had found pain. So he opened his mind and heart, and in so doing discovered the means by which suffering can be replaced with peace.

Are you likewise willing to make room in your heart for other more important things? Are you willing to give up all of your sins to feel this peace? While I was in Taiwan as a volunteer missionary, a young man asked a visiting church authority if he would give his life for his belief in Jesus Christ. "Son," the leader's voice boomed, "I am giving my life for it." Of you I ask similarly, are you willing to give your life for recovery and healing? Are you willing to give up all of your anger, sins, and pride? If you seek recovery, it will come. If you seek forgiveness, it will come. If you seek healing, it too will come. But before it does come, you must learn to live a life of sacrifice. When we live a life of sacrifice, or are at least willing to sacrifice everything we have been given (whether asked of us or not), then everything that has the potential to enslave or depress either falls out of our lives or becomes subject to our will.

Sacrifice, however, is not easy. If it were, it would go by some other name. As it is, by definition it is a word that signifies the giving up of something prized for something deemed of even greater value. Whenever I am faced with the prospect of sacrifice, and I feel to wallow in self-pity because of the need to give up something I love, I picture in my mind that plow, covered in rust and desert dirt, sitting half-buried in the exact place my grandpa left it. For me, it is a powerful symbol of sacrificing for that prize of greater value—namely, the people we love.

In the next chapter we will talk about specific sacrifices you can make. As we do, you will, no doubt, think of other, more personal things with which you will need to part in order to fully recover and heal. It will be a hard task to see to its end, but if you feel to falter or you lack the strength to make the sacrifice for your sake, then think of those you love and do it for them. I promise that as you sacrifice for the unknown, countless unseen blessings will await.

23

U-TURN SACRIFICES

"Let me not injure the felicity of others, if I say I am as happy as any. I have that in me that can convert poverty into riches, transform adversity into prosperity"[1]

W HEN WE SPEAK OF SACRIFICE, CLEARLY THERE ARE all sorts of things, habits, or hobbies that addicts may need to give up—either because these things directly showcase pornography, or because they may indirectly lead to its doorstep. I cannot rightly tell you what you will need to sacrifice; I can only plant ideas in your mind. I am familiar with men who have had to give up going swimming, or more specifically going to public pools or beaches. I know couples that have opted to avoid cruises because of the swim attire often flaunted by many women on the cruise. I know men who have been asked to give up playing video games, hanging out with "the guys," driving to and from work alone, going to exercise at the gym, watching television, reading books, going to the bookstore; the list goes on and on. I am likewise familiar with many families who have, in the interest of the addict, decided to cancel magazine and newspaper subscriptions and cable and Internet access. Televisions, computers, laptops, tablets, e-readers, cell phones, music devices, video game consoles, you name it. For many, sacrificing these objects is just par for the course we call recovery. I am even familiar with a man who walked away from his business because the contract required him to sell pornography in the store. Despite the family's concerns, they never once went without. He found a new job and a new life free from the influence of pornography. Ultimately, you will have to sacrifice anything that promotes selfishness, pits itself against your family and God, or parlays temptation into sin.

Friends and family, too, will need to reevaluate their habits, hobbies, and priorities. Wives, are there things in your life right now that might prove harmful to your husband? Unknowingly, many of us serve as a conduit through which temptation and pornography enter our home. Remember the boy who admitted struggling with the seductive content of a popular dance show his parents loved to watch. I have also seen women take husbands or sons to the movies, or flip on a TV show when their husbands or sons are with them, and then cover their eyes during certain inappropriate parts—as if the ears and imagination do not have the power to absorb the limited data, build it into a vivid scene of its own, play it over and over again until it loses its excitement, then seek similar experiences elsewhere. In these things, we have to be so very careful. But I am not worried. I believe you will find the strength to give up what you need to because your husband is in need. With proper communication, I further trust you will be able to search out and distance yourselves from such sources of temptation.

But in many cases, even this level of sacrifice may not be enough to curb the selfish tendencies of addiction. Sometimes, for ultimate recovery and healing to be realized, an even greater sacrifice is required. I speak of giving up the one thing you are not willing to give up. I refer to this type of sacrifice as a "U-turn sacrifice."

In driving, the U-turn refers to the act by which a vehicle is rotated 180 degrees, thus reversing the direction of travel. We have spoken several times now about my uncle. What took his life, do you remember? Not drugs. Cigarettes. Cigarettes robbed my uncle of his future. "And how," you might ask, "is this so?" Because cigarettes were the one thing he could not or would not give up, and step-by-step they led him back to drugs. In this case, cigarettes became, what I call, a secondary addiction. Secondary addictions are simply something that we turn to, often subconsciously, to replace our addictive habit. They are a variation that may not look anything like the ugly face of sin, but they are just as dangerous.

With this in mind, I first want to speak again about the entertainment we currently justify having in our homes.

"Ugh," I can hear some of you groan. "We get it already. Why do you keep talking about these things?"

Well, because it's important, that's why. In our media-driven world we often make allowances for immoral content based on story, special effects, actors, and so on. Sometimes we even pretend that these elements are why we are watching the show, when in reality it is a convenient cover through which we can view pornography and not feel guilty. It is no different than me pointing out a dog being walked so I could look at the jogger walking the dog.

But let me be even clearer: more than anything, it is the entertainment in our lives that propels addiction. It is the biggest, most beautiful butterfly in the room, and we do not want to give it up. But if we do not properly take care of it now, it will be the means by which the horrific storms in our lives continue to wreak havoc. Giving up the entertainment we love so much, though, can be an extremely hard thing to do. I remember well the day I took most of my movies and either sold them, threw them away, or taped them up in a box and put them on a shelf, where some of them still remain to this day. Those that I sold or tossed had content in them that was clearly a temptation to me and a threat to my recovery. My wife was a good barometer for this. If it offended her, it went away. As you can guess, it eliminated a majority of our movies. But we were far from done. Additionally, we removed from our collection many other movies that, by all accounts, did not contain offending material at all. Rather, they simply did not promote the spirit or a general feeling of good—movies, for instance, that were scary or particularly dark in theme or content. There was one movie in particular, a favorite of mine since childhood, which I was asked to give up because of the amount of foul language in it. Its story was very inspiring and personal to me and giving it up hurt quite a bit. But I did it, and it was only afterward that I saw clearly how it had always promoted selfish feelings of entitlement. I began to learn then what I know now: it does not have to be bad to not be good for you. This was the first turning point on my road to recovery.

Let me share one more "movie" example about a best friend of mine. Having worked in the movie industry, his love for film was greater than mine. He too tried for years to overcome an addiction to pornography. On several occasions, we discussed the idea of giving up not only movies, but his career in them. "I know," he once told me, "that I should consider it, but it's so hard. Movies are *my life*." However, after many relapses and prayers, he decided he would give up his job if the Lord required it. He then did something he had up until then resisted doing: he grabbed a handful of his movies, drove down to the local pawn shop, and sold them at a loss (when compared to what he bought them for). But the real gain, a gain that cannot be calculated in dollars and cents, was his. That simple act changed his life immediately. It was the U-turn that put him back on the right path. From that day forward, he went on the offensive, and pornography and the desire to seek it out disappeared from his life. He was not required to give up making movies. His willingness to do so had been enough.

In this example we see first-hand the transforming power of sacrifice. "But how, exactly," you might wonder, "does this work? And why?" Honestly, I don't know, but I promise it is true. I've said it before: if the root of addiction is selfish in nature, then the key to recovery has to be found in selflessness. By giving up the one thing he never wanted to give up, the one thing that defined him more than anything else, he exhibited to God just how much he wanted to overcome his addiction. In essence, he made the ultimate sacrifice by giving up, not his life, but what was his life. Let me be clear: it was not the giving up of the movies that made the difference here. That was merely a symbol of an inner-commitment to do anything required to overcome the addiction. The power is not necessarily in the giving up as much as it is in the attitude of humility it takes to willingly sacrifice.

This paradoxical truth has foundation in a number of religious teachings worldwide: when we let go of our desires, we gain freedom; when we let go of who we think we are, only then can we become who we should be. Of this, Gandhi said, "One finds a readiness to suffer imprisonment and assaults but not loss of goods"; later adding: "This struggle . . . can give us victory only if we become indifferent to everything [that] . . . can press us into subjection to its will."[2]

As noted, for me, giving up movies was a key to recovery. But it was not *the* key. I did not realize it at first, but there was something else I was not willing to give up, something that defined me more than anything else: my writing. As a matter of brief background, writing creatively was the "love of my life." From the time I was first able to write, I knew it was something I wanted to pursue. In my childhood, I wrote stories all of the time. In my adolescence, especially when I began to struggle with pornography, I turned to it as the means of expressing myself. At times, it was very therapeutic. In my adult years, it continued to give me comfort in times of frustration. More than that, though, for the sheer love of writing,

I began to work very hard to establish a creative writing career. To some extent, I was successful. I had a book published, I visited a network of schools, and I received district approval to host a regional young author's conference. But then, after more than a year from the time I was certain I had overcome my addiction, I went through a pretty intense period of relapse. Because of this and other reasons, my wife asked me to give up writing and focus on getting my life in order.

I was crushed. "That's not fair," I cried out in my heart. "My problem is not writing. I promise I won't make any more mistakes. Just don't ask me to give up writing. Not now. Please. Anything, I'll give up anything but that. Writing has been the only thing always there for me. It has been the one thing to which I could turn for comfort. Writing is *my life*!"

It was then that it hit me. More than a secondary addiction, writing had become my God, so to speak—the only thing I consistently turned to in times of sorrow as well as joy. Like my friend and his movies, writing was the one thing in which I had invested everything that I was: my time, my talents, my mind, my heart; it had always been about me. But this wasn't about me, I later realized. Yes, I needed to get in order *my life*, but more important, the life of my family. A great struggle ensued inside of me. It seemed, indeed, to be one of life or death. I was angry because I knew I had screwed up, and by doing so, I had ruined the one chance that I had for so long been dreaming and preparing for. I did not know how I was going to be able to move on. It was then that my grandpa died—the man after whom I was named, the soldier who never forgot his values or his family, the self-proclaimed cowboy from Arizona. I was there, in the room with him, with my dad by my side, when he silently slipped away. Of that moment, I wrote in my journal, "The Captain of OUR Salvation intends to lead us back HOME—to heaven. So do his Angels . . . and his Cowboys from Arizona." I thought of my grandpa unhooking the plow; I thought of the then-unseen blessings that followed because of his willing sacrifice for the unknown; I thought of his faith and his family and his victories in time of war; and I laid down my pencil.

From that moment on, the conflict for me was over. In my heart, where selfishness had been, there was now room for recovery, healing, forgiveness, love, and peace. I pray that you too will have the strength to make room in your heart for such things.

In the New Testament we read about a rich young man who wanted eternal life. "Keep the commandments, then," Christ admonished. "I have since I was a child," the young man replied. Then "go and sell that thou hast . . . and come and follow me." Heartbreaking is the nonverbal reply of the boy, who "went away sorrowful: for he had great possessions." (Matthew 19:16–22).

May we instead become like Peter and John, the beloved disciples, who, after catching more fish than they had ever before caught, dropped their nets at the beckoning of Christ and followed him (Mark 1:16–18). Yes, fishing was their livelihood! Yes, they felt like they needed the money or the food these fish would provide! Yes, they had been up all night and were tired and sore and in need of nourishment, and they probably deserved a break. But in Christ's voice they sensed the eternal importance of his call. So they left their nets, and, in hindsight, they received nourishment and treasures beyond their initial comprehension.

As for the young man who walked away from the promise of treasures in heaven, no amount of possessions could ever fill the void in his heart.

24

FILLING THE VOIDS

"Life did not stand still and it was necessary to live."[1]

IN THE LYRICS OF THE SIMON AND GARFUNKEL BALLAD "The Boxer," Paul Simon makes reference to a fighter who remembers that in his weakest moments "there were times I was so lonesome I took some comfort there."[2] Ironically, in the song, "there" refers to spending time with prostitutes. For our discussion, however, I am not so concerned with *where* he went, but rather *why* he went there. According to the words, he went there believing, however erroneously, that it would bring him comfort.

As we have discussed, this is also one of the main reasons men turn to pornography. In a twisted, complex way, they believe it will offer relief from their burdens. Perhaps, to some degree, it does, meaning it at least makes them forget their burdens, but only temporarily. It is crucial you realize that it is in your efforts to satisfy needs and find fulfillment that you have always turned to pornography, because when you finally give it up, those needs will still exist, and you must somehow deal with them still. In fact, if anything, once you give up pornography it will feel as if your needs have increased and have become more demanding. This is not true, but by it you may know just how much room pornography was taking up in your heart and mind.

It is in response to the continual need for fulfillment that men often turn to secondary addictions—those other habits that simply take the place of pornography. These may not necessarily be bad habits, but if you are not careful, they can, over time, easily lead you back to pornography. Remember, you are not trying to give up pornography, per se, as much as you are trying to give up selfish compulsive behaviors. When you give those up, pornography, along with any other addictive behaviors, will simply fall away.

To completely recover and heal, then, you must find lasting fulfillment in appropriate ways. In my experience, there are only two people to whom you must escape, only two people who can truly and completely fill the voids left in your heart in the wake of repentance and great personal sacrifice. Those two people, of course, understand sacrifice better than anyone. You must escape to God, he who "so loved the world, that he gave his only begotten Son, that whosoever believeth in him should not perish, but have everlasting life" (John 3:16). And to Christ, who made the ultimate sacrifice—for everyone; for me and you, for the ones we've hurt, and for the people who have hurt us. He has felt the pain and loneliness you now feel. You must turn to him and Heavenly Father and let them fill the voids inside you.

I remember one time in particular when, for various reasons, I felt a crushing weight of emptiness and loneliness in my chest. My wife and kids were running errands somewhere. I was home alone chipping away at a work project. My computer was before me, as was the realization that in times past I would have turned right then to pornography. But I couldn't. I wouldn't. So my mind immediately turned to my movies to which I had so often escaped, but they were not there anymore. I could write my sorrows away, I realized, but I didn't have the desire to write. There was nothing to be done, it seemed, no one to turn to—except God. This seems like a no-brainer now, but at the time it came as a lightning bolt of personal revelation. So I got on my knees and simply prayed for comfort and strength. Then I rose to my feet and went back to work. The temptation, the emptiness, the loneliness—it all disappeared. I don't know when, exactly; all I know is that at some point I realized I no longer felt alone. This too can happen to you. God can fill the voids inside of you. But your faith in his power to deliver you from pain and loneliness must come before your faith in your movies or music or books. As you turn to God, the pain in your heart will begin to dissipate, your wounds will begin to heal, and your voids will begin to be filled. But remember, "[Peace] comes not so much in 'outcome' as in 'process'."[3] The culmination of this process will be up to you, meaning that God will do his ultimate part to comfort and strengthen, but only after you do yours. For your part, you must learn to fill your life with good things.

The danger we face in the wake of massive personal sacrifice is that we can get so caught up in giving things up that we forget to do things for ourselves—not out of a selfish need for fulfillment, but out of a necessity to be uplifted and empowered. Sacrifice is a necessary component of recovery, but if all we do is sacrifice, we will find our souls do not have the nourishment necessary to flourish. We need to find the proper balance.

In my situation, I was so afraid I would slip again that I cut out of my life virtually everything I once loved. I did not want to chance doing anything for selfish reasons. So for over a year, I did nothing but bury myself in religious things. They were a great strength to me. However, as the months carried on, they began to lose their power. Why? Because I found myself unable to apply them. Why? Because I was not living a balanced life, and it is a balanced life that allows for spiritual truths to germinate and grow. Thus, I became spiritually, mentally, emotionally, and physically exhausted.

In spite of all the struggles we experience in life, and how exhausting it all can be, I believe we were made to experience joy. I promise this joy will come as you proactively seek to fill your life with things that inspire, uplift, and enable. Spend more time with your family. Spend more time cultivating your talents. Spend more time studying scriptures. Spend more time praying. Spend more time helping other people. And if you want to watch a good movie or read a good book, then by all means do it—not to escape, but because in it you find joy and strength. The Talmud specifically speaks to this principle: "the more [law], the more life; the more study, the more wisdom; the more counsel, the more understanding; the more charity, the more peace."[4]

On the latter of these, it has been my experience that nothing is so calculated to drive away temptation or depression as charity. It "never faileth" (1 Corinthians 13:8). And neither will you if you do your part and then let God do his.

25

CONTROL YOUR SURROUNDINGS

"Treat a man as he is, and he will remain as he is;
treat a man as he can and should be, and he will
become as he can and should be."[1]

HAVE YOU EVER FELT YOUR CAR TIRES LOSE TRACTION and slide over a patch of ice? We are all familiar with that sudden moment of panic. Not long ago, this happened to me while I was driving my wife and kids through the mountain passes to visit family for Christmas. Our van began to slide forward then off the road toward a guardrail with a steep and deep ravine on the other side. In that moment, I must have offered a thousand prayers as I sat powerless to do anything, hoping and waiting for our tires to catch and regain control. To my relief, just as quickly as we had lost control, our tires hit a patch of sand and regained control, and we carefully steered back onto the road. Prayers of thanks and requests for further protection were offered the rest of the way until we safely arrived at our destination.

As you work to maintain the victory you have earned thus far, and as you find yourself advancing quite confidently on the battlefield, you will most likely begin to feel that your addictions are completely behind you and you cannot be affected anymore by temptation. I am quite familiar with these feelings of invincibility, but if we are to avoid relapse, we must not allow ourselves to think we are invincible. The proud man says, "Hey, I'm fine. I don't need to be followed up on" or "I don't need these Internet filters or these sites blocked." We like to be in control but hate to admit that we are not. The reality is this: no matter how old we get, no matter how strong we become, we can never allow ourselves to underestimate the enemy. He is continuously preparing for war. But to avoid this war, we need to properly and constantly prepare for it as well. All weapons and personal shields aside, we must first erect walls and barriers and towers so high that we will be able to see the enemy coming from far off; so when he does come, he will not be able to penetrate our strongholds.

We have talked about giving up movies, video games, television shows, books, comic books—whatever it takes. We also need to sit down with the people designated as our four corners of accountability and come up with rules and boundaries for our life, home, office, and other places we may frequent. These rules will serve as a safety layer on which your tires can gain the traction needed to reverse the course of disaster brought on by slippery patches of unseen ice.

The more specific these rules are, the more protected you will be. I have heard a story about an ancient army captain who commanded his people to make the walls of their fortress taller than they had ever been before and then to add tall timbers on top of those walls, before moving to the ground, where they dug deep ditches around the entire fortress. Finally, he manned every possible post with soldiers well protected by armor and weapons. When the enemy inevitably arrived and saw how well their opponents were protected, many fled for fear of losing their lives; and those that did not flee were quickly picked off by arrows and stones.

Was this excessive? In hindsight, no. What about the people under his command, though? Did they think it was overkill when they were building it all? Possibly. But it saved their lives. And that is what you must remember: the rules you establish may at times feel excessive, but they are there to save lives, yours in particular. Because of this, never allow yourself to think that because you have a proven track record of recovery, you can steer directly into dangerous conditions without actual consequence.

In college, I decided to throw a celebration for friends and bake a king cake, a dessert often served in various cultures around Christmas time to celebrate the moment the Son of God was revealed to the "three kings." Traditionally, a small doll or trinket is placed within the bread, and the guest who gets the slice with the doll in it bakes the cake for the following celebration or, in our case, hosts the next get-together. I poured the ingredients in an electric bread machine. The doll being the only thing lacking, I then scoured my apartment until I spotted on my shelf, behind some books, a little LEGO figure, a soldier decked out in full medieval armor, which my oldest sister had given me years ago as a reminder to always "put on the whole armour of God, that ye may be able to stand against the wiles of the devil" (Ephesians 6:11). In fact, she had written this scripture across the front of the box.

In a hurry to get the bread done in time for the party, I quickly grabbed the little soldier, full armor and all, and tossed him smack into the pile of ingredients. Before the small puff of flour had fallen, I closed the lid and turned the bread machine on. From there, the ingredients bore the brunt of the mixing hooks for several minutes, before finally enduring the fiery inferno that was the cook setting. Suffice it to say, my little soldier guy did not fare so well.

Fast forward a couple hours to the actual celebration, when invited guests sat down with some level of excitement to partake of the bread and see who, by virtue of finding the figure, would throw the next party. It was not long before someone found him, or rather a part of him. If I remember correctly, a plastic hand surfaced first. A helmet was then discovered in another slice and the head in yet another. Piece by piece, the soldier in his armor of God was gathered into a single pile of what-once-was-and-what-might-have-been. His legs had been crushed into several smaller pieces. The neck part of his head, melted and warped, would not fit back onto his body. His shield was scuffed up. And his other hand, in which he once wielded his sword with selflessness and courage, was never found again.

I still keep the remnants of this knight on my shelf next to the words of that scripture as a constant reminder to me that no matter how strong you think you are or how much armor you have on, you cannot march into enemy territory and come out unscathed. The life rules you establish will keep you far from the enemy and save you as long as you keep them throughout your life.

Ultimately, it is up to you and your wife to create these rules. You might also consider talking to your other accountability partners. To help in the formation of these rules, I have included below a list of things to consider:

1. **Computer Location:** Move the computer to an open room or, at the very least, to a room with windows and where the door can remain open at all times. More than protection for you, this will serve to keep your kids and other family members safe too.

2. **Internet Filter and Accountability Software:** Install them! That's really all there is to say on the matter. No matter how restricting you feel they are, how embarrassed you are to let others use a computer on which they are installed, or how sure you are you do not need them anymore, make sure you have them on every computer, then keep them there. You can never be too safe. Yes, you can find pornography even with filters installed, but the extra wall these filters put between you and pornography can make all the difference—for your entire family. I am often asked if there is tried-and-true Internet filter I recommend. There are a number of programs to choose from, and there are pros and cons to each. In most cases, your decision will come down to personal preference. NetNanny, McAfee Safe Eyes, Cyber Patrol, the list goes on and on. These, I'm sure, are great options, but there are two in particular I would like to mention for no other reason than I have used them and found them to be excellent options:

   K9 Web Protection (www.k9webprotection.com) is a free Internet filter that also includes parental control software. It blocks sites and offers simple categorized reports based on searches made and pages visited. The parental controls and the reporting functionality are robust. Reading and interpreting the reports can be a bit overwhelming since ads, pop-ups, banners, chat boxes, etc. are also reported. You or your husband may not have even noticed, let alone looked at, a certain ad or section of a site, but, as is the case with most filters, it will still report it as if you did. This can be disconcerting to a wife reading the report on her own. To properly deal with this potential concern, my wife and I made a rule to always look at the report together. Doing so gave us a chance to communicate openly, honestly, and respectfully about every line item on the report. The one downside to filters in general, though, is that the reports can often only be accessed from that computer.

   Covenant Eyes (www.covenanteyes.com) is another great option. They too offer a robust Internet filter solution, but they also offer accountability software that can be set up on and accessed from multiple computers. While they are not free, the cost is so very minimal. Based on experience, it is worth the nominal fee. Getting set up is easy. Download the software to your computer and set up your accountability partner, someone who will receive reports on your behalf. The software simply runs in the background. As you use the web, every search made and every page visited is recorded in a live report. More than an Internet history report, everything you search for or view is actually assigned a rating. At a glance, you can tell if there is something to be concerned about. Perhaps most important, these reports can be accessed whenever and wherever you have an Internet connection. That way, if your husband is home alone, you can still be tuned in to his struggles and his victories. The accountability software also has "panic button" functionality. Say you are surfing the web and feel tempted to look at a certain site, by pressing a designated key on the keyboard, the program will immediately lock you out and prevent you from further using the Internet. Access can be reset, but only by calling the *Covenant Eyes* support center. It has been my experience that in the midst of temptation, there is always that one fleeting moment when you think "I shouldn't do this" or "I need to stop now." Too often, I failed because there wasn't anything in place to help me carry through with that internal call for help. The panic button is that safeguard.

Both *K9* and *Covenant Eyes* are available for Windows and iMacs. They also have solutions for most cell phones and mobile devices. If you'd like to give *Covenant Eyes* a try, you can get your first month free by using the promo code: *OurVictories.*

3. **Filters at Work:** If you have accessed pornography at work, you need to tell your employer. Ask them to install filters or accountability software on the computers. If for some reason this cannot work, then set rules to avoid going into the office early or staying late. You might also consider asking for a change in location so your computer faces a window or is in a more open space.

4. **Cell Phones, iPods, iPads, Gaming Consoles:** Do you need to get rid of them? Is there software you can place on them? Do you

really need texting capabilities or Internet access?

5. **Frequency of Follow-Up:** The more often, the better. Consider setting a specific day or time to go over the Internet history and reports together. This builds trust and allows for open communication. Wives, learn to ask specific questions and talk about what you see or don't see in these reports. Men, if you have nothing to hide, then you have no reason to be upset with constant follow-up. Remember, you have to regain trust. It can take a long time to rebuild, but your reactions, or the lack thereof, can go a long way to helping the process along.

6. **Computer Hours and Access:** Is your computer on all day? Do you use it at night? Most filtering software includes time locks that will allow you to set the times the Internet can be accessed. There will be little reason to have the Internet on through the night. I was once an accountability partner for a friend whose failures always came in the middle of the night when he should have been sleeping. Also, consider setting a rule that no one can use the computer or Internet unless someone else is in the room.

7. **Specific Sites:** You know as well as I do that there are sites through which you have accessed pornography that filters won't block. Maybe some of these sites were blocked but you had them unblocked because they are not specifically pornographic and you use them for other purposes. Or maybe some of the sites that pose the most danger are ordinary ones that sell swimwear or underclothing. Regardless, be very specific and discuss the dangers of having open access to them. In my experience, some of the most dangerous sites are those that have seemingly little, if anything, to do with pornography. But don't forget the "jogger." Such sites may include but are not limited to: social media sites where people post personal pictures (Myspace, Facebook, Twitter, Pinterest); chat or video chat sites or programs (Skype, Yahoo! Chat, MSN, and so on); media share sites where people can post images, videos, movie clips, and so on (YouTube, Vimeo, Flickr); media sites that offer images, video clips, and so on for business purposes (iStock, Shutterstock,); photography sites where professional and amateur photographers advertise their services and post portfolios; entertainment sites that offer movie clips,

trailers, reviews, streaming movies or television shows, or music videos (Hulu, YouTube, ScreenIt, IMDB, Netflix; music sites like MTV); celebrity news and gossip sites; classified sites that offer products and services (Craigslist, eBay); shopping sites that offer apparel and swimwear.

The list can go on and on. For my purposes, it does not need to, but for yours, it should. This should get the ball rolling. Be honest. Be blunt. Make your own rules and stick to them. Your victory is just around the corner.

Above all, to you accountability partners: if something bothers you or raises concerns, bring it up. And to you addicts: be humble. If your spouse feels it is a concern, then it *is* a concern. If your spouse wants a certain site blocked, then she has the right to block it. Remember, you are in this situation because boundaries were not first established or you purposefully went past them. The boundaries are in place to protect you and your family. Welcome this safety net. The building of it can be painful, and you will perhaps feel like you are being babysat or that you have no control. Well, you are and you don't. Not yet. But that will come. In the meantime, you must not allow yourself to rebut or get frustrated or angry. Communicate your feelings as calmly and as honestly as possible, and together you will find the answer that will help you stay free from temptation and relapse.

26

EVER WATCHFUL

"Victories attained by right thought can only be maintained by watchfulness. Many give way when success is assured, and rapidly fall back into failure."[1]

IT DOES NOT MATTER HOW FAR REMOVED YOU ARE now from the last time you looked at pornography. You will still need to be ever watchful, and you will certainly need others to watch out for your safety too. Even if you feel strongly that you have completely conquered your addiction, this is just good old common sense.

In this day and age, when it is virtually impossible to *not* come in contact with pornography, avoiding it can be a full-time job. So pervasive is pornography, in fact, that people would have to stay inside their houses, in their rooms, and under their blankets with the lights off from the moment of their birth to the moment of their death in order to never encounter it. Such a scenario reminds me of a comic I saw once of a boy hiding under his covers from the "monsters" that come out when his lights are off. In order to survive long term, he had under the covers with him a snorkel through which to breathe. Just like staying under your covers and breathing through a snorkel to avoid monsters, hiding from life to avoid pornography is neither wise nor practical; and doing so will actually rob you of the opportunities necessary to gain eternal experience, faith, and knowledge; not to mention that man cannot live on air alone.

The key to avoiding spiritual monsters, then, is not to hide from them, but to turn on the lights. "It sounds deep, but what does it mean?" To say nothing of controlling what we look at or don't look at, I'd like to propose instead that we can actually control to some extent what comes in contact with us. We accomplish this by employing the same type of thought process we used to seek out pornography. You see, as addicts we became experts at knowing where and when to find pornography. For example, in the past, perhaps you went shopping in the mall only to purposefully meander down one aisle or one side of the store as opposed to the other because you knew there was something on that side you could get a glimpse of in order to satisfy your lustful desires. Or perhaps you have navigated to a specific website to "innocently" look something up, knowing full well that the ads or featured content on the home page tend to showcase lewd images or seductive clothing lines. No doubt you have flipped through ads or magazines or books for these same reasons. I've rarely met an addict who did not feign an interest in photography or art at a bookstore so they could justify looking for inappropriate pictures. And if you are like me, by interpreting the shot selection, tone, tension, or dialogue of a show or movie, you can often sense if and when an inappropriate scene is coming up. Surely you have noticed that being home alone has nearly always led to setbacks. Now, we simply use this near-perfected intuition to avoid pornography. Much like the FBI uses reformed criminals to understand how the mind of criminals work and thus fight the inroads of crime, you, a reformed addict, can now use your past experiences to know well in advance where danger is and how to avoid it.

Let me take this concept of anticipating danger one step further. An elderly lady I know grew up in Europe during World War II. As the German army turned increasingly hostile and began to invade various countries, the people in the surrounding cities and countries became increasingly alert. This was true for her town. Even if Hitler had no intention of rolling onto their streets, they did not want to take any chances. Even as life continued as it always had for them, consciously and subconsciously they began to focus their minds on the sights, sounds, and smells around them. They were on a 24/7 watch for the enemy.

Every day before she would set out to ride her bike to school, her father would ask her the same question: "You know what the German planes sound like, don't you? If you hear one that you know is not a British plane, get off your bicycle, hide it, and hide yourself." On one occasion, as she pedaled her bike along the dirt road to school, she heard the ever-so-faint rumble of a plane in the distance. Though it was far away on the horizon, and she could not determine whether it would fly by or even see her, she took the predetermined steps to protect herself from potential harm. Hiding under a tree, she watched the plane come and go. When all was clear, she stepped out from her hiding spot and raced to school.

Pay attention, men, to your surroundings. Listen to your hearts, be honest in your thoughts, and be methodical in your actions. As you do, I promise many times you will be able to sense pornography when it is just around the corner and take the appropriate actions to avoid it. Sometimes you may hear the plane coming a mile away. Other times you may look up and see it hovering right over top of you. Either way, get off your bike and hide! Change the channel. Turn off the TV. Suggest another movie. Shut off the computer. Choose another store. Pick another book. Sit somewhere else. Close your eyes. Look away. Walk away. Fall to your knees and pray. You are in control of your surroundings.

About praying, let me add this: I believe prayer is the ultimate source of strength and comfort. But sometimes we can be so caught up in temptation that it can be hard to turn to God sincerely. Other times, if we are kneeling by our computer, that may just not be far enough away to usurp the temptations that will again be accessible moments after rising. In these cases, I have found it necessary to establish points of inspiration, or rather places to go, people to serve, things to do, or movie clips or songs to play that have personal significance and that can, in an instant, inspire me, instill selfless feelings of love within me, and lift me up beyond the temporary moment of weakness. I encourage you to also find and utilize these inspirational points through which you can distance yourself from the temptation that will come.

The more you distance yourself from pornography, the more in tune with the spirit of God you will become. It can guide you and help you further discern areas of potential danger. Listen to it and heed its warnings. Additionally, with its help you will be able to sense more vague areas of danger, such as those inevitable moments of personal weakness and vulnerability. When you feel these things settling in, address them right away by talking to your wife or other accountability partners. Then regroup. Maybe you do this by stepping away from work or the computer for a moment. Maybe you take a walk. Maybe you cancel a meeting and spend time with your wife and children. Whatever you decide to do, wait until you are sure it is safe before you get back on the "road," so to speak, and continue with what you were doing.

Now, wives, two facets of this principle apply to you. First, you too will be able to sense when weakness, depression, or vulnerability is on the horizon. Take the proper precautions to address them, control them, or even talk them out as needed. Turn to God and let him comfort you.

Second, it is your right to occupy the watchtower, ever on the lookout for enemy planes. To help your husband, you will need to be a constant voice of concern and love. If you think you see or hear something, don't hesitate to sound a warning at that moment. Remember the dangling shoelace? If you know it's just a matter of time before the child trips on it and hurts himself, why let him continue playing?

Let me reduce this to a simple saying: as a friend, if the thought ever, in any degree, crosses your mind that your husband is in trouble, ask him. Take him aside, pick up the phone, write an email, send him a text message, and talk to him about it. "Honey, did you see anything inappropriate today?" Or "Have you seen any pornography lately?" Or "Have you heard or seen anything at school or work?" Or "When we were at the beach, did you look at any of those girls today? Was that hard being there?" Or "Listen, this may be nothing, and I don't want you to be mad, but there has been something on my mind lately, a possible concern I have for you, and I need to ask you . . . are you looking at pornography again?"

As a spouse, as a friend, you must be willing to take a stand. Whether your thoughts find root in paranoia or are guidance whispered by the spirit of the Lord, the end result is that your husband knows you care. If he is involved in pornography again, it may be hard for him to admit, and his reaction may, at first, be one of anger. If he has not suffered a relapse, though, then he should be grateful for your concern. Either way, your courage to talk to him can prove to be instrumental in his life and give him the strength he needs to come clean and stay clean.

On several occasions, I have been the recipient of such calls—even in the middle of the night—because someone loved me. I have also made those same calls to others because I loved them. We are indeed on the lookout towers for one another, and who knows but that our warning voice, raised in the dead of night, will be the means of keeping our friends safe.

To end this chapter, I feel the need to reiterate that if your homes and marriages are to remain protected, both of you must ever occupy the watchtower. Wives, I know from experience that somewhere in your mind exists the nagging question: "What if his addiction returns?" Most likely this fear is founded on a combination of past experiences and scientific reports that tell you the addict's brain is never cured. Trust me when I say these fears also badger the thoughts of your husband. They are valid concerns. But I feel confident in saying that if you both will consistently look out for each other, and constantly and honestly communicate about what you see or don't see, things will be all right in the end. If you both do everything you are supposed to do, recovery and healing are guaranteed. Put your faith in God, in the tools he has given you to work out your salvation, and in his protective promises, and *not* in scientific research or reported patterns of addiction.

"With men this is impossible; but with God all things are possible" (Matthew 19:26).

27

BUILDING FOR CHAMPIONSHIPS

"As the forces around us increase in intensity, whatever spiritual strength was once sufficient will not be enough."[1]

AIMLESSNESS IS A VICE, AND SUCH DRIFTING MUST not continue for him who would steer clear of catastrophe and destruction."[2] If we look back over the failures in our lives, we will find, I believe, that we were most vulnerable when we were idle. The opposite of this is true as well. Proactivity is a virtue. Proactive behavior earns victories. Along these lines, let us look at how winning organizations establish winning traditions.

A longtime sports fan, I have seen many teams over the years achieve greatness when, by all accounts, they were not expected to do much. On the flip side, I have seen so-called dream teams fail. Why does this happen? What is the difference between these two types of teams? The difference is to be found in the off-season.

On the heels of a championship, the best teams immediately start building for the future. They take advantage of a fleeting window of success, power, and money to recruit, negotiate, wheel and deal, hire, and even fire. Regarding the latter, it is common to see the best teams upgrade their overall talent by getting rid of key players or sentimental favorites. Rarely are these moves popular with the fans, until, of course, such changes help the team achieve greater heights.

In contrast, I have seen great teams win championships, only to fail to better themselves in the off-season, believing somehow that the team they have in place now will also be good enough next season. Meanwhile, their opponents are in a constant state of building.

This can be applied to addiction recovery on so many levels. I admit that during my own season of recovery, I made similar mistakes many times. After a significant period of abstinence, I was often quick to congratulate myself. Doing this is not wrong, as long as your head remains in the game. Mine did not. Assuming I had already earned the victory, I allowed myself to relax, taking no thought for the morrow because I believed this was an instance where "the morrow would take thought for the things of itself" (Matthew 6:34). Thus, I made no plans for how to maintain the level of cleanliness I then enjoyed. All too often this quickly led to relapse, bitter disappointment, guilt, stress, and suffering—for me, for my team, and for my beloved fans who had invested their hopes and dreams in my success.

If this has been true for you, change your tactics. What was good enough yesterday and what is good enough today will never be good enough tomorrow. You have to constantly be in a state of improvement. It is at the pinnacle of success, even the moment in which you find yourself lifting the trophy, feeling stronger and more prepared than ever before, that you must start planning for the next season. Don't just settle for one championship; plan for more. Establish higher goals, and then, with the help of your family, friends, and God, pour into your goals all of the resources and efforts you have. By doing so, you will not only secure another championship, but you will earn the respect of your team and the trust from your fans. With such support in place, victories will become commonplace.

28

PROTECTING YOUR VICTORY, AN ANALOGY

"By bloodless victory, the fetters which despotism had been long preparing for us were broken; the rights of the people were asserted, a tyrant expelled, and a Sovereign of our own choice appointed in his room. . . . and that era of light and liberty was introduced among us, by which we have been made an example to other kingdoms, and became the instructors of the world."[1]

ON A SHELF IN OUR HOME STANDS AN ELEVEN-INCH marble statue of the *Winged Victory of Samothrace*, also known as the *Nike of Samothrace*. In Greek mythology, Nike was a goddess who personified victory. The replica on my shelf is of personal significance to me as it is a constant reminder of the victories in our lives and the price paid for them.

An unknown sculptor was commissioned during the second century BC to carve *The Winged Victory* out of marble to celebrate a significant naval victory. She was made to look as if she was descending from the heavens to meet the triumphant fleet after it returned from its hard-fought battles. Over time, she fell into decay, and then into the ocean. The bulk of her was eventually recovered in the late 1800s.

Since 1884, *Victory* has been prominently displayed at the Louvre and is one of the most beloved sculptures of all time. She is seen as an iconic depiction of the triumphant spirit in the face of the enemy. The sculpture's arms, once raised to her mouth in a celebratory shout, were never recovered. Nor was the head of the sculpture. Still, to many, the personal meaning of *Victory* is enhanced by the very fact that these components are missing.[2] In life, is it any different? The price of battle is steep. We all make mistakes. Yet the scars we bear can be a reflection of the battles we have won; and in this there is honor. But we must protect our victories once they are ours.

In 1939, at the outbreak of World War II, Hitler and the Nazi elite made a point to steal art they coveted and destroy those pieces made by artists not of German descent. As the threat of German invasion increased, the people of Paris decided, at all costs, to protect their art, including the *Winged Victory*. That same year, on the night of September 3, *Victory* was carefully packaged and painstakingly removed from her perch, after which a team of people guided her down the staircase onto a makeshift wooden ramp. With great effort, the team then carried her down the stairs. It was again as if she were descending from the heavens in victory. Her preservation was miraculous. When it was safe to do so, she was carried again, up the stairs, and back onto the pedestal upon which she still stands.

What price are you willing to pay to protect your victory?

29

IS THE CONFLICT OVER?

"Accordingly he signed the manumission that day; so that, before night, I who had been a slave in the morning, trembling at the will of another, now became my own master, and completely free."[1]

I HAVE HELPED MANY MEN WORK THROUGH A TWELVE-step program for pornography addiction. For many, it takes months, even years to get through all of the steps. I have, however, seen others breeze through the steps in a matter of weeks. Regardless, after closing the final meeting during which they reported on their successful completion of the twelfth step, I have often heard them respond: "So that's it? Am I done? Is pornography really behind me?" Perhaps you too are asking this question.

I reply to you, then, as I have before to them: Yes, you are done. Pornography is behind you. But it has always been behind you, remember. The trick is keeping it there, and in that you are never done. It will take the rest of your life to make sure you never turn back to it, but I have all the confidence in the world in you. You now know how to keep it there, and I trust you will.

So what's the difference between our past—when we gave it up only to return to it later—and now—when we feel strongly we will never return? The difference is time.

Previously, you returned to pornography because it was only behind you in terms of time—as in yesterday or last week or last month or last year—but all the while, it remained in your heart and mind. In that sense, it never was behind you, really, because it was always inside you.

But this time is different. By humbling yourself, by repenting completely, by establishing four corners of accountability and allowing for follow-up, and by making great personal sacrifices, you have proven to God, the Savior, yourself, and your family that not only is pornography behind you in terms of time, but it is far from the desires of your heart.

This, of course, does not mean the conflict is over because the enemy never stops preparing for war. As long as he is strengthening his strongholds and crafting his weapons, you too must constantly guard yourself, lest he become more powerful than you and overtake you in the night. The war will always be won by those who continually prepare for battles both seen and unseen.

So go forward with confidence in God, in the tools you have to secure recovery long into the future, and in the family, friends, strangers, and angels willing to fight in this fight alongside you not until death but until the victory is ours!

"Fear not: for they that be with us are more than they that be with them. And Elisha prayed, and said, Lord, I pray thee, open his eyes that he may see. And the Lord opened the eyes of the young man; and he saw: and, behold, the mountain was full of horses and chariots of fire round about Elisha" (2 Kings 6:16–17).

So it is with you. If you feel to falter, know that we are on your side. I am on your side. You can do this! You already have. Continue to turn to your wife. Continue to turn to God. As you do, you will find the voids in your life will be filled, the power of the tempter will be weakened, the eternal purposes of suffering will be made clear, and the conflicts will end no sooner than they attempt to arise.

30

PURPOSE IN SUFFERING

"I know this for a certainty: it is often in the trial of adversity that we learn those most critical lessons that form our character and shape our destiny."[1]

I WANT TO PREFACE MY COMMENTS WITH THE FOLLOW-ing personal experience.

I have good boys. "They are good at being boys," as my grandpa used to say of his own boys. I've rarely had to spank them, However, I remember a time quite a few years back when my oldest did something that warranted a spanking. I don't even remember what it was, and it doesn't even matter, really. I calmly took him into his room, talked to him about his wrong choice, and explained the consequence. Then, out of love, I laid him across my knee and gave him three firm swats. My heart broke for him, but I knew he had to suffer the consequences of his actions and learn from them. When I had stopped, he crumpled to the floor, sobbing. I immediately picked him up and took him into my arms, giving him a hug and expressing my love for him.

He looked at me with tears in his eyes and then asked one of the most honest questions I have ever heard: "Dad, why are you hugging me right after you hurt me?"

How often I have asked this question of my Heavenly Father. And in my naivety how often I have not been able to comprehend the answer he has offered; the same one I tried at that moment, however inadequately, to explain to my son: "Child, I'm hugging you for the same reason I allowed you to suffer—because I love you."

Husbands, wives, I cannot accurately say why you have had to go through everything you have thus far gone through. Nor can I honestly say why you will yet go through many hard times. It is beyond my comprehension. The answer, if there is one, is also something you must seek to discover for yourselves. But I can say that I do know that God loves you, and that, if you turn to him, you will find purpose in your suffering. In this may you find hope and be comforted.

Suffering is everywhere. We need only watch the news to see examples of it far and wide. Explicitly, we suffer because of choices we make, choices others make, and sometimes as a result of things out of everyone's control, such as natural disasters. Regardless the origin of suffering, it is natural for all of us amid the rubble of our lives to look up and question God, wondering what we did wrong or why, after doing so much right, we are being punished or hurt. This type of questioning, however, to me, has everything to do with cause and effect, and very little to do with purpose, or, in other words, aim or intent; and by intent, I mean your own.

We can spend all day discussing the law of consequence as it relates to an addict or why bad things happen to good people, in the case of an addict's wife, but to what end? Instead, I want to suggest we spend time talking about what we are going to do with our experiences. That is where purpose is to be found.

For a long time, I struggled to come to an understanding of my past. "Nine years old?'" I often bemoaned. "Did I really choose a life of addiction at nine, or was it beyond my control?" "Why did I have to go through all of this?" "Why didn't someone talk to me about it when I was younger?" "Why didn't my pastor ever follow up with me?" "Why didn't I say something to my wife early on?" "Why did it take me so long to figure out how to overcome it once and for all?" "Why? Why? Why?" In the end, I realized it doesn't really matter why the past happened. What matters is what I do with it now.

I'd like to share one final quote from *War and Peace*. This one is about Prince Andrew and Natasha. Prior to this moment, they had both made mistakes, such harsh mistakes, in fact, that not only ruined their engagement but promised to keep them separated evermore. Natasha was distraught. Andrew went off to war. During a battle, however, he was mortally wounded. To get him the help he needed, he was transported to a nearby home: Natasha's. The moment in which they met again was beautiful, filled with utterances of repentance and forgiveness. Of this moment, Tolstoy says, "they had spoken of the past, and he had told her that if he lived he would always thank God for his wound, which had brought them together."[2]

In essence, this too could be said of my wife and me. Our marriage is stronger and happier because of the wounds overcome. Now, don't get me wrong. I am not grateful for the spiritual wounds of my past. Frankly, I wish I had never gone through any of this. Above all, I wish I had never put my wife through it. Rarely a week goes by when I do not catch myself wishing we could have had at the beginning the marriage we have now.

But let me ask you this: if this book has been an answer to your prayers, or if it has helped you gain the help you would not have found elsewhere, might you say that you are grateful for the sins of my past and the struggles of my marriage?

In this, I found purpose. I came to the conclusion that if I didn't do anything with what I had learned, if I didn't try to help anyone overcome similar problems, then this whole process would have been just a really painful sixteen-year waste of time.

So I started carefully talking to people about my past. I let the spirit of the Lord guide me. It did not take long for me to find someone who needed help. In fact, not long after I began letting people know, it came to my attention that a close friend of mine was also struggling with pornography addiction. To my surprise, he, like me, had been struggling with it for years. Imagine! Two best friends silently struggling, side-by-side, year after year, unbeknownst to one another. The scenario is more common than you think. Further along the road to recovery than he, I was immediately put in a position to help him, pray for him, and follow up with him. While I was still working hard to establish distance from the problem myself, the more I worked with him, the stronger I became, until finally I was in a position to teach and testify that God does indeed deliver his people from bondage.

At that moment, I didn't care how painful my past had been. I was simply grateful for the opportunity to help a friend in need.

Not so coincidentally, the more you are open and honest about your pasts, the more often you will encounter individuals and couples who are in need of your help and the wisdom you have gained through experience. In such cases, strength given is strength received. The more you reach out to someone in trouble, the stronger you will become.

With this in mind, I submit to you that the final component of recovery and healing is to be found in helping other people. Perhaps this was God's intent all along. Experience, of course, makes us wise. More than that, though, experiences, good and bad, make us empathetic. For this reason, among others, Christ suffered for our pains and sins: so that he could help us in times of need and lead us back to God. If God allowed suffering, then, for the benefit of others, might he also allow it now, albeit on a smaller scale, for the benefit of yet other children? I think so. Set on bringing all his children back to him, and omniscient enough to use the adversary's plan against him, God, I believe, will use reformed sinners to rescue other sinners; he will use those who have been healed to testify that he heals. In this sense, for many, "the cell door is the door to freedom."[3]

"Have mercy upon me, O God, according to thy loving kindness: according unto the multitude of thy tender mercies blot out my transgressions. Wash me thoroughly from mine iniquity, and cleanse me from my sin. For I acknowledge my transgressions: and my sin is ever before me . . . Restore unto me the joy of thy salvation; and uphold me with thy free spirit. *Then* will I teach transgressors thy ways; and sinners shall become converted unto me" (Psalm 51:1–3, 12–13).

The scriptures are replete with many examples of men and women who, once freed and healed, became powerful testators of deliverance and equally powerful soldiers, fighting for the spiritual freedom of God's people. When I think of them, I think again of my grandfathers and of all the men and women who served with them in World War II, and of all the men, women, and children across the world who supported them, and sacrificed for them, and prayed for them. On the lapel of my jacket, in their honor and in the honor of people everywhere fighting to overcome personal struggles, I wear the "V for Victory" pin. Of these pins, the Belgian Minister of Justice, Victor de Laveleye, said in 1941: "the occupier, by seeing this sign, always the same, infinitely repeated, would understand that he is surrounded, encircled by an immense crowd of citizens eagerly awaiting his first moment of weakness."[4]

To the enemy, then, I shout: you are surrounded! And you are outnumbered. And you will not succeed. Together, we will defeat you, because we can. With God as our captain, it is in our power to end the conflict now.

31

PREFACE TO MY WIFE'S SECTION: ON HEALING

"In the deserts of the heart
Let the healing fountain start,
In the prison of his days
Teach the free man how to praise"[1]

HOW LONG WILL IT TAKE? AS WE HAVE MENTIONED, healing has no timeline. Healing depends on many things: your specific situation, the degree of hurt you feel, the efforts you make to overcome your struggles, the people available and willing to help you, even your personal religious beliefs. Still, much of the debate might be better resolved if we spent time defining what we mean by healing. For if we do not have a clear idea of what this nebulous goal is, how will we ever recognize it when it comes?

Without healing properly defined in our minds, it is too easy to continually wonder whether we have healed from the deep wounds caused by our partner's addiction and betrayal. Furthermore, it is just as easy to sell ourselves short and convince ourselves we are healed before we really are. Any mother knows that a deep wound, if not cared for properly, can continue to fester underneath skin, which, on the surface, appears back to normal. Just like hidden addictions, buried pains never cared for can and often will, in time, serve to hurt us, our partners, our families, and the progress we have been so vigorously working toward. Of equal danger from not defining our goal is the real possibility that we set our expectations so high that we never recognize or admit healing in any degree, thus robbing our spouses and ourselves of the blessings that gradually come through progressive healing.

By healing, perhaps you mean that day when you will be able to trust again, when you will not hurt anymore, when you can say and honestly believe you've forgiven him, when you will feel like you can finally be intimate again or when you are intimate and don't think of his addiction, or maybe you mean that day when you finally know you want to have another baby with him. These are just a few of the many sub-goals that often subconsciously get lumped into this end-all term called healing.

The problem with using the term *healing* is that most of us subconsciously associate it with a panacea or, in other words, a mythical cure-all. We think that healing means we will at some point no longer hurt, no longer remember the hurt, and miraculously be restored back to our previous state "when life was good and all was happy." Yes, restoration is a component of healing, but it has nothing to do with going back to what you once were; rather, it has everything to do with becoming something new, someone who is better and stronger in spite of and because of the pains and illnesses experienced.

On that note, I want to draw your attention to the muscles in the human body. We can all agree that without muscles, we would not be able to function as intended. From the moment we are born, we begin to develop stronger muscle mass, which, in turn, allows us to progress from sucking to eating, from babbling to talking, from lying on our back to sitting up, crawling, walking, running, and so forth. But exactly how do our muscles form? Simply put, they grow because they were damaged; they grow when they heal. As we force our muscles to work harder than they are used to, microscopic tears form amid the muscle fibers. Over the next day or two, our bodies make a biological effort to repair these torn muscles. This reparation, however, does not restore them to their previous form; rather, it creates new muscle fibers with which to fill in the gaps caused by injury, thus making the body stronger and more capable. Now, imagine if the process by which the body repaired muscles simply restored them to their previous state: why, we'd all be lying on the floor still, cooing or crying, and slowly wrapping our fingers around a rubber pacifier in a basic attempt to temporarily satisfy our need for sustenance. Clearly, this cannot be; there is a reason healing must not just restore but instead build upon. The same can be said of the spiritual, mental, and emotional healing process you have undertaken.

Without question, every ounce of your soul aches, consumed by a barrage of feelings, including but certainly not limited to sorrow, loneliness, depression, guilt, anger, even hatred. "Why me?" you have probably asked yourself. "I have worked so hard to be faithful, to honor our marital vows, or to obey God's commandments. I have given him and this family everything, everything that I was and am. I gave him my heart and my mind and my body. I sacrificed my body and my time to bring kids into the world with and for him. I tried so hard to do everything right and for the right reasons. But it wasn't enough." No doubt, there are and will yet be days in which such thoughts weigh heavy on your mind and heart. There will be days when you do not want to get up and maybe days when you don't get up. There will be times when you cry yourself to sleep or cry in the shower or cry to a trusted family member or friend or even just start crying at random strangers. "How are you doing?" someone might casually ask only to be met with a barrage of tears and confessions. If this has been or is the case, do not despair. These feelings are natural and they must be allowed a release.

But even these emotions, while natural, will need diligent attention so as not to make the wounds worse or leave them exposed to outside germs that can lead to malignant infection. Sadness, when unaddressed, can quickly turn to depression. In such darkness, anger can turn to hatred, hatred to revenge, and thoughts of revenge can ever so quickly open the door to temptation and destructive behaviors, even those you now passionately shun. In a sense, it is a wonderful time for you and your husband. As you work together to piece your relationship back together, you will get to know each other in a way you never have before. You may feel sometimes as if you are courting each other like you did after you first met. Your marriage can become even stronger. But it is also a dangerous time for you. I believe Satan will subtly and not so subtly try to use your emotions to confuse you, hurt you, tempt you, keep you wallowing in self-pity and anger, and further destroy your family. Whether you want to assign these potentially destructive attempts to a spiritual adversary like Lucifer is up to you, but the reality is, you will, if you have not already, deal with such emotional struggles.

I remember, with acute pain, moments when I could only sit there, alone in the living room or the bedroom, and listen to the heaving sobs coming from my wife behind a closed door or huddled up next to me on the bed. I remember with equal pain the moments in which her heartbroken voice boomed with anger and doubt, questioning everything she once knew, even my love for her. "If you really loved me, how could you do this?" While it may be hard to believe now, the addiction of your loved one doesn't necessarily have anything to do with his love for you or the lack thereof. The key to proper recovery and healing, on the other hand, has everything to do with love; the love we accept and the love we give.

"Love never claims, it ever gives. Love ever suffers, never resents, never revenges itself."[2]

It is because of love—the love of my wife, the love of my family, the love of my friends, and the love of my God—that my wounds and the wounds I caused others were healed. And for that, I am eternally grateful. "Come unto me," said Jesus Christ, "all ye that labour and are heavy laden, and I will give you rest" (Matthew 11:28). His promise, I believe, is true. In my darkest hour, I was not alone; in her darkest hour, my wife was not alone; and neither are you.

PART 3:
FROM WIFE TO WIFE

by Mae Donne

32

YOU ARE NOT ALONE

"I will not leave you comfortless: I will come to you" (John 14:18).

I AM NOT A WRITER, BUT MY HUSBAND AND I BOTH FELT it important that this section reflect not my thoughts converted into his writing, but my thoughts, my voice, *and* my writing. My goal has always been to approach you as I would a friend in need. I recognize that you are dealing with so much right now that this section could and should be a book all unto itself. It is for this reason my husband and I have thus far tried to introduce and discuss principles. By them and in them, truth can be discovered as it relates to you and your personal situation. It is my hope and prayer that you will find comfort, understanding, and direction for yourself as I share my thoughts with you.

I remember keenly the pain my husband's addiction brought me. During those intense days, months, and years, I would have snatched up any opportunity to read about the experience of someone who had been in my position. I am grateful for this opportunity to share with you some of the insights I have gained during my journey toward healing: healing from pain, healing from sorrow, healing from anger, and healing from suspicion. As you read these chapters, I hope you will find value in them. It is also my hope that you will find strength and understanding in the section written for men. Do not overlook the benefits this main text has to offer. It has been written for you as well as for your husband, and within it are truths that also address what you are going through. They will likewise help you find the understanding and strength you desire.

Initially I began this section by telling you my story: how I discovered my husband's addiction to pornography, and the negative effects that addiction had on not only our family but especially on me, his wife. I wanted to capture the pain of those moments so that you would know you are not alone in this struggle or in the struggles to come. As I continued to flesh out the details of my story, I realized that if you have sought out this book and if you have read thus far, you are already intimately aware of the pain pornography brings into a marriage. I find little reason, then, to tell you of the agony I have suffered. Why? Because there is a fine line between helping you feel validated and understood, and sharing so much of my story that it only increases your pain. And because, above all, this book, our lives—they are not about suffering. True, suffering plays a part, but in the end, this book and our lives are about hope and, in time, they can also be about healing.

Over the last few years I have had several opportunities to speak with women about the pain caused by a loved one's pornography addiction. Although details vary, our stories are very similar. The hurt, the feelings of betrayal, the lies, the anger—the list goes on—are very much the same from experience to experience. My husband, who has worked with many addicts, will likewise tell you that the stories of the men ensnared by this disease are also similar.

What does this mean? It means you are not alone. Others before you have traveled this path. I am one of them. I have tasted the bitterness of betrayal, and I have struggled through intense suffering—mentally, physically, emotionally, and spiritually. Experiences both good and bad can be the mother of wisdom, and I hope that within my stories you will at least find a small measure of that, as well as comfort. In response to hard times, my grandpa has often said, "Granddaughter, this too shall pass." And it will. The intensity of your pain will pass. Feel the hope and truth of those words. They are real. At some point, you will look back and see just how far you have come, and you will realize that where pain once resided, joy now consumes. This is my hope: that as I share with you some of my own experiences and the insights gained through them, you will find the strength to take the first steps toward peace, which can and will come if you seek it.

As you read through this section, you will notice at the end of each chapter a small "refocus" segment. These are designed to help you quickly recall what has been discussed. Some days will be harder to get through than others. During those particularly trying days, I hope you will turn to these and find at a glance the guidance and strength you need to sustain you along your path to ultimate healing.

33

THE TOLL OF
ADDICTION

*"When He talks of their losing their selves, He only means
abandoning the clamour of self-will; once they have done that,
He really gives them back all their personality, and boasts
(I am afraid, sincerely) that when they are wholly His they
will be more themselves than ever."[1]*

Closing the Gap: A Note about Communication

During one of the harder times my husband and I went through, a
good friend asked me how we were doing. I replied that there had never
been a "greater distance" between us. He was working long days made
even longer by a long commute, and when he arrived home, we seldom
spoke. I was so depressed by our failing relationship that I would often
go to bed as soon as the kids were asleep. I was lonely. He was lonely. We
both were hurting. To all of this, my friend then said, "Well, distances
can be quickly traveled!" I remember thinking she must have had little
experience with marital conflict. Since that time, however, I have come to
learn the truth in her statement, and that communication is the vehicle by
which these distances can be traveled across and the gap closed.

Because our relationship had been unhealthy for so long, breaking
negative cycles of communication was hard for me. Anytime I blamed my

husband for our situation, he would understandably protect and defend himself. In turn, I struggled to communicate clearly and without excessive emotion. I became hesitant to share my feelings and concerns, in part because of the way I felt they were being met with nonchalance or straight-up disregard—sometimes purposefully but other times unintentionally or out of habit. So I stopped sharing my feelings altogether. He too exhibited this same pattern. We were wrong. On an individual level, our ultimate unwillingness to communicate naturally widened the distance between us as a couple.

So how do we revive communication when it has been dead for so long? Practice. Learning to communicate positively will take a lot of it. We must force ourselves to start sharing anew our thoughts and feelings. We must also force ourselves to listen to our spouse without rebuttal. Do not give up! Communication is vital. Without it, you will not be able to move forward together.

As you begin practicing positive communication, there will probably be times where you both say things or use tones that are hurtful. Intended or not, neither one of you has to tolerate personal attacks. It is your right to expect and require respect. But you too must be respectful in your communication. Your response in these situations will either escalate or eliminate tension. By choosing to speak calmly, both temperament and circumstance will remain under control, and your chances of being understood will increase. If the situation becomes tense, angry, or even dangerous, take a time out to reset. Having said that, many times I just needed to cry it all out. This may be true for you too. But if you want to be heard and understood, and if you want to hear and understand, you will need to avoid anger.

For a while, one of our children was quite the little firecracker! Any small thing would set him off on a tantrum. I was usually quick to respond in a similar manner, which only served to amplify the conflict. Eventually my son and I realized we were not satisfied with our relationship. We had a meeting and discussed possible solutions. After much discussion, we came up with the idea of employing a secret sign. The sign was to be used when either he or I recognized the other person was about to respond harshly. This worked wonders. If you still need help communicating kindly, consider developing a silent signal that either one of you can use if you feel belittled by the other person. When the sign is given, both of you must stop talking and take several deep breaths. You should only continue when you are ready to be respectful. I know it may seem rather juvenile a thing to do, but so is arguing.

Remember, to be successful, communication must be initiated with a humble desire to understand the other person's needs, both those spoken and unspoken. Being understood, after all, is what both parties seek. For my husband and me, once we started communicating our feelings with the other person in mind, the distance separating us quickly diminished.

Pornography creates many problems in a marriage. It will take time to work through them all. If either of you thinks of things during the day that need to be addressed, you might consider scheduling an appointment to discuss them with your spouse at a more appropriate time. This will give each person the time needed to compose him- or herself and prepare his or her thoughts. My husband and I made much headway using this approach. Our appointments would sometimes last late into the night. At times, this was a great sacrifice. We both had things to do the next day. But it was worth it. The time you invest in positive communication will likewise give you a far greater return than any other investment in your life. It will be essential for your relationship to progress, recover, and heal.

Refocus:

- Be willing to practice communication.

- Do not allow destructive comments about yourself.

- Be willing to invest time in communication.

- For sensitive concerns, make an appointment with your spouse for a time that works for both of you.

Mend Your Fences: Defining Personal Boundaries

I grew up on a dairy farm. Whenever we moved our cattle to a new field, they would roam the perimeter looking for a way out. If they found a low spot in the fence, they would climb over and run down the road. Most often, the avenue of their escape was a weak place in the fence. Finding it, they would push on that section until they got through. I have many memories chasing a hundred head of cattle down the road. The remedy for this problem took patient observation and planning, but eventually we were able to put a stop to the runaway cattle. Every time the cows escaped, my sister and I would look for the place they went over, examine it carefully, and decide on the best way to reinforce it. Just mending our fences wasn't sufficient; we had to make them stronger than they were before. More than that even, if we wanted to stop chasing cows altogether, we needed to be proactive. Eventually we started to check for weak spots in the fences and repair them *before* the cattle were let into the field.

It is clear how this applies to addicts of any kind. It is common for them to push boundaries and limits, and there will always be a need to help them define and maintain limits. When we focus this lens on the less obvious application for the wives of addicts, though, we begin to understand the need we have to likewise evaluate personal limits. Wives of addicts are often the ones to have their boundaries pushed through. As boundaries are continually disregarded and breached, it can become difficult to recognize where our own personal boundaries are and where our healthy limits should be. As you interact with your spouse, pay attention to the things that make you feel violated or undervalued. These instances will give you insight as to where you need to strengthen and reinforce your boundaries. Because each of us has different needs, our own boundaries will vary. I suggest you begin by identifying potential boundaries by exploring the importance of limits surrounding respectful communication; intimacy; valuing your own opinions; and embracing your gifts, talents, and interests.

As discussed in a previous section, a firm foundation of respectful communication should be a priority in your relationship. If hurtful things are said in conversation, communicate with your spouse clearly to make him aware of the things that hurt. You do not have to tolerate personal attacks. Respect within communication is not a luxury. It is a requirement. And you are worth it.

During difficult times, it is common for wives to abandon their own opinions to avoid tension with their husbands. Your opinions and needs are important. While successful communication entails give-and-take, do not continually abandon your opinions to avoid conflict or criticism. This is not healthy for you. Communicate your needs and opinions and require that they be respected. Use calm statements to share your thoughts.

Intimate situations can become warped when dealing with an addiction to pornography. Do not do anything that makes you feel less valuable. It is common for women to ignore boundaries particularly during intimacy. Generally there are two reasons for this: they believe it will fulfill the need to feel wanted; or they feel it is the only way to satisfy their spouse. Whatever the reason, it is not right. It is not good for you, and it is not good for your relationship. Ideally, intimate relationships are meant to bring husband and wife closer together. Agreeing to or allowing things that make you uncomfortable will only bring resentment and emptiness. You must find, communicate, and defend your physical boundaries if you want develop a fulfilling sexual relationship with your spouse.

Addictions are stressful things to deal with, for both the addict and the spouse. In the case of the addict, it is common for this stress to result in chronic criticism of the things and people around them. Frequently this criticism falls upon the wife's character traits and interests. If you find this to be the case, know that you are a valuable woman with great gifts, talents, and interests. The things that make you a unique individual are of great worth. You should not let these things fall away simply because your spouse appears not to value them. Your personal boundaries should include having your interests and gifts respected. As you search to define personal boundaries, you will likely become reacquainted with who you are and who you can become.

When you identify or define such boundaries, I encourage you to record them in your journal. This will allow you to refer to them often. As with the cattle and the weak-fence-made-strong, identify and convey your boundaries now, before they are pushed through again. By expressing your limits, you allow your spouse the opportunity to respect them. But he cannot respect rules you have not made him aware of.

If you find yourself repeatedly abandoning your boundaries, you may be struggling with codependency. In a broad sense, *codependency* is a term used to identify situations in which people habitually abandon their opinions, desires, and limitations as a means to avoid conflict with others. For the struggling wife, codependency can become a compulsive behavior.

The cycles and symptoms of codependency are vast, and I will not touch upon them here. Like any compulsion, they can encompass every facet of life. For me, I often found myself planning my entire days around what I thought my husband wanted. In doing so, I hoped to avoid criticism and conflict. Eventually I felt that I had lost sight of the healthy and happy person I once was. As I identified boundaries in the areas listed previously, I began to regain some of my previous strength.

More important, however, just as your husband can overcome his addiction, you too can overcome codependency. Breaking my own codependent cycles was a crucial part of my healing. The process was slow because it is hard to break bad habits. I visited with a counselor who helped me identify some of my codependent triggers. I also prayed for strength to stand up for my needs and made small goals to do the things I needed to do to feel whole again. Recognizing, defining, maintaining, and perhaps even defending your boundaries is an important way to initiate healing.

Refocus:

- Identify your boundaries.

- Communicate your limits.

- Have the courage to defend your boundaries.

- Research codependency, as necessary, and take the proper steps to reverse its effects.

Dealing with Abuse

Pornography addiction is selfish by nature. Selfishness often causes the addict to disregard the needs and feelings of others. Similarly, as the addict attempts to protect his secrets from those around him, defensive and aggressive behavior can increase. In their frantic efforts to conceal their activities, they may be unaware just how harsh and critical they have been or are being toward those closest to them. I want to reiterate that this often-unconscious effort to push people away has nothing to do with so-called flaws in wife or family but is a tool used to further separate the addict from those who might discover the addiction.

Sadly, the longer this addiction remains untreated, the more likely the addict is to mistreat others. Emotional, verbal, physical, and sexual mistreatment of family members, especially wives, is common and, in many cases, falls within the spectrum of abuse. Believing he has managed to contain the natural consequences of his addictive behavior so that no one else suffers the consequences, he may not recognize his maltreatment of others as destructive.

Manipulation of others is a common by-product of addiction. Frequently, manipulation comes into play when a loved one expresses concern about the attitude or conduct of the addict. Quickly the tables can be turned by the addict to point out the character flaws and faults of the spouse. Examples of imperfections are often cited as "proof" that the spouse is not qualified to express concerns. For me, these episodes had harsh consequences and were destroying me from the inside out. I realize now that my husband did not always recognize the damage he was causing me. He was bound so tightly by his addiction that he was, at times, blind to the effect his chastisement and manipulation were having on me.

Although all forms and degrees of abuse are excruciating and painful, it is important to recognize that your husband is not just a monster full of spite and hatred. He too is a victim of the disease of pornography. It has also been destroying him from the inside out. Abusive behavior by either party is in no way excusable, but this perspective allows us to see that it is a result of their struggle, rather than evidence of their true feelings for their family. This presents a dilemma for us as wives, as the hurt of cruel words and actions runs deeply. Many husbands feel that they are protecting their wives from pain by maintaining distance. If you feel you are being mistreated in any way or to any degree, find an opportunity to share your feelings with your spouse.

As we identify his behavior as a means to protect his secrets or as the result of his participation in pornography, we gain insights into his struggle and its destructive effects. But we should never submit ourselves or families to unsafe treatment. I must take an opportunity to speak to women and families who may be struggling with extreme or dangerous types of abuse. The path you are traveling will be particularly difficult, but healing can and will still come as you seek it. If you feel that you are in danger, seek help now. Quickly identify a support system that can be aware of your situation and offer you help as needed. In these instances, counseling can be a valuable tool because it allows an unbiased professional to observe and coach you on your interactions as a couple.

Throughout the process, do not allow negativity to permeate your own attitude. Remaining positive throughout your trials will be a great strength to you. Maintaining a humble and kind attitude will serve you well as you continue onward in your life and marriage. Personal cycles of pride and selfishness are hard to reverse. Do not tolerate or allow personal attacks of any kind, but be cautious not to become critical or unkind yourself.

Refocus:

- Do not tolerate abuse.

- Find a safe support person to be aware of your situation.

- Seek professional counseling to help you deal with and process effects of abuse.

Watch the Tide: Avoiding Emotional Entanglements

As a teenager, I had the opportunity to go with my grandfather on his traditional crabbing trip in the Pacific Northwest. He had a tiny boat with a weak motor. We had spent a great afternoon on the water, catching few crabs but enjoying each other's company, when we realized that the tide had pulled our little boat into the dangerous current of the outgoing tide. We started up the motor to return to the shore. It sputtered and strained, but it simply did not have enough power to escape the strong current. Our situation was quickly becoming dangerous. We had to call for help. We realized that the safety of everyone in the boat was far more valuable than the cost of embarrassment we might suffer in calling for help. Help came, and we were towed to safety.

Throughout your process, you will likely be aware of temptations you may not have dealt with before. Be on your guard! Watch for the subtle pull of the tide, especially during this time when you are not at full strength emotionally.

Because of the way my husband sometimes treated me, I felt that he did not love me. His participation in pornography left me feeling unattractive. His criticism left me feeling empty, unlovable, and powerless. Everywhere I went, I began to notice other men and wonder if any of them found me attractive or could ever really love me. This is a common experience among women who are hurting. If you have felt this way before, or if you feel this way now, be careful. These feelings are not wrong, but it is dangerous to entertain them, and certainly wrong if you act on them—no matter how justified you may feel. You do not have to be pulled away by the tide. At this point in your process, I believe that Satan will do all that is within his power to entice you to make mistakes similar to those made by your husband and by so doing lead you into dangerous waters much like the ones in which your husband struggles.

The methods of his enticement are vast. We live in a sea of technology. There are now more ways than ever to drift into currents that have power to pull harder than our motors have power to escape. Emails, texting, online chatting, video chatting, and social networking are just some of the many tools of communication that keep us connected to those we love. But they should be used wisely. Do not use them to connect with any member of the opposite sex unless your spouse is a part of the communication. Ever so subtly, contact of any kind with a member of the opposite sex has the potential to turn flirtatious and familiar. This will only serve to add more obstacles between you and your spouse and on the path toward healing.

I have met with women who responded to their hurt in this way, by seeking the love and validation of other men. The process was subtle. Slowly, these men became their confidants. When they were excited about something, their first thought was to tell these men. When they were sad, they again sought comfort by sharing with them their sorrows. Slowly all of the joys, sorrows, and even the mundane experiences that should be shared between husband and wife were confided in the "one friend that understands." For some, the correspondence happened from a distance, through texts or emails, but even in written word alone an emotional and inappropriate bond began to form. This does not necessarily mean the relationships became physical. For some it did; for others it did not. But in all cases, the correspondence served to pull the wife further away from her husband and into the heart, mind, and sometimes arms of another man. The degree to which we seek and find comfort will vary, but we must be watchful, always aware of the subtle shifts in our emotions and needs.

Maybe you have not experienced these temptations. Maybe you have and were able, like me, to push them aside without any significant consequence. Or maybe, to some degree, you have already given in. If you find you have been pulled out to sea in this manner, it is not too late to turn the boat around. Don't sit quietly and let the waters pull you farther out. No matter the degree of the relationship you have established, end it now and call for help! Talk to your husband. If he were to relapse or even just feel temptation, you would expect and even demand that he tell you. You too must adhere to this principle. It is hard. It will take honesty and courage, and your disclosure may very well, for a time, deepen the rift between the two of you. But this too can be repaired. No matter how far out you have drifted, you can be rescued.

Refocus:

- Exercise caution when sharing feelings with members of the opposite sex.

- Do not become emotionally reliant on a member of the opposite sex.

- Do not let your affection wander to another.

34

SEVEN STEPS OF GRIEVING

*"Do you know what hurts so very much? It's love. Love is
the strongest force in the world, and when it is blocked that
means pain. There are two things we can do when this happens.
We can kill that love so that it stops hurting. But then of course
part of us dies, too. Or we can ask God to open up another
route for that love to travel."[1]*

TWO YEARS AGO, A FAMILY FRIEND LOST HER HUS-
band in a sudden and tragic accident. He kissed her good-bye before
he left for work that morning, fully expecting to see her later for dinner.
He did not return. An unforeseen accident at work took his life. When
appropriate, we stepped in to offer support and comfort in any way we
could. But from afar we continued to watch her struggle to come to terms
with what this loss meant for not only her young family, but also herself
as a suddenly-single mother of four.

As this beautiful, young mother struggled to recover after the death
of her husband, I watched her travel the path of grieving.

As a distant observer, I came to an astonishing realization: the grieving process she was going through was profoundly similar to the one I had
gone through after finding out about my husband's pornography addiction. And why should it not be? She was mourning the loss of her husband

and their future together, while I was grieving the loss of everything I thought I knew about my husband and our relationship. Understanding the grieving process allowed me to identify my struggles and move toward resolution. I believe it can help you too.

Throughout the remaining sections of this book, I will allude to these steps—sometimes directly, but more often indirectly—as they relate to what I have been through and what you now are going through. The points I will make, though, are by no means comprehensive. Lack of professional experience and limited space in this book aside, I believe the real value to be gleaned from these steps will come as you seek to understand and apply them in accordance with your unique situation and personality. Before doing so, though, I want to provide an overview of the process as a whole. Refer to these steps as often as needed in order to determine where in this process you are and, more important, to look back on where you *were* and to rejoice in how far you have come. You have already come a long way. Take strength from that truth and let it propel you forward toward the ultimate step upon which acceptance is gained.

Shock/Denial: Shock is often a self-defense mechanism. It provides emotional protection and can help you from feeling overwhelmed. It is often accompanied by feelings of disbelief. "This cannot be." Often, the person in shock has a hard time performing simple tasks or making decisions. Time is often idled or "bumbled" away. It is common to not feel anything at all or to feel a sense of "numbness." These feelings easily morph into denial. The person in denial refuses to believe what has happened to them. Things can be bad enough that they believe it is all part of a bad dream. "This is not real. I must have misunderstood." There is no predetermined time in which this process is traversed.

Pain/Guilt: Subtly, denial gives way to reality. The numbness begins to wear off and the horror of what has happened settles deep. This can be a chaotic and frightening time. Intense feelings of guilt are natural by-products of this pain. Women blame themselves, thinking in error that the loss or betrayal is their fault. Subconsciously, the body and mind want to again feel the numbness experienced in the previous stage. It is in this phase that many people seek an escape. As hard as it will be, it is vital that you let the emotional pain you feel run its course. Do not hide it (from yourself and others), ignore it, avoid it, or try to escape it by taking a shortcut. Drugs, alcohol, food, shopping, another man, *et cetera*—these are all things that falsely promise a reprieve from the pain you feel, but that will never deliver. Be aware of these terrible vices.

Anger/Bargaining: Pain and guilt quickly lead to anger. In this stage, it is common to take "Why me?" and look for others on whom to place the blame. This is a dangerous phase in which hurtful things can be said and relationships damaged. Fueled by intense despair, it is then common to begin bargaining with others or with God as the means of reversing the situation or compensating the loss. "If you do *this,* I promise I will do *this"* or "If you bring *this* back, I promise I will never do *this* again."

Depression/Sorrow: In this stage, the person accepts the loss or betrayal but feels unable and unwilling to cope with it any longer. It can be a time of passive behavior, self-isolation, and extreme depression. It can also be a time of reflection, through which you think back on the good times in your past (especially with your spouse). These memories often only serve to accentuate the depression, rather than uplift and inspire hope. This natural and vital phase can be the most difficult to deal with. It often takes the stage when enough time has passed that those around you (and perhaps even yourself) being to think you should be or are feeling better. To "suddenly" show signs of depression may confuse and even infuriate them, especially if they are not aware of this process or if they have already moved past it. No matter how well meaning their intentions are, do not let their reasoning pressure you to hide your feelings from yourself or others. Tell them you need encouragement and understanding. Depression can take a long time to work through, but if not addressed in the right way, it can consume and destroy you and those around you. The more people you involve during this stage, the better. In some cases, professional help and medicinal assistance (only when prescribed by a doctor) may be required.

Testing/Reconstruction: This stage is about escaping your sorrow, but in a healthy and positive way. The overall depression begins to lift. As it does, your mind will clear, and you will begin to analyze life realistically and calmly, looking for and testing out potential solutions to the problems you face and the grief you may still feel on occasion. Some solutions will work and others will not, but because of them, you will begin to reconstruct your life, your emotional stability and trust, and—we hope—your marriage. This can be a empowering time in which you recognize the power that is yours to take control of the situation and determine the outcome. Hope and ultimate acceptance, you will sense, are just around the corner.

Acceptance/Hope: In this phase, you will learn to properly deal with and accept wholeheartedly the reality of your situation. You find joy in the here and now, and you will be able to confidently plan for the future and even look forward to it. It is important to remember, though, that just because you will have accepted your situation, does not mean you will necessarily be instantly happy, nor does it mean you will be without memory of the past. There may yet be days when you recall the past. These recollections may stir up some degree of sorrow or pain, but such feelings will be fleeting. You will be able to push them aside and move on—forward—enjoying life as you did before, surrounded by the people you love and who love you too.

35

MOURNING A LOSS

"Take my yoke upon you, and learn of me;
for I am meek and lowly in heart: and ye shall find rest
unto your souls." (Matthew 11:29)

Moving Past Denial

Denial is the first step in the process of grieving. Even before my husband confided in me about his addiction, I had a strong feeling that pornography was at the heart of the tension within our marriage. I simply wasn't willing to believe it. The image of a pornography addict did not fit with the person I believed him to be. When his past finally came to light, and I began to understand the depths and darkness of pornography addiction, I was barely able to carry on. Frankly, I did not want to carry on. When we feel such pain how do we carry on?

Several years ago, I was on a walk with some dear friends of ours. Their little girl was complaining to her dad. Finally he looked into her face and said in jest, "Well, sweetie, life is hard, and then you die." She looked right at him and said, "No, Daddy, life is hard, and then you live. You live anyway!"

With this in mind, I encourage you to live anyway. You can do it! You can move away from the aching heart you now feel to a place where you want to jump for joy, and if you are both willing to work for it, you can move to that place together.

Refocus:

- Realize that you are dealing with very hard things.

- There is nothing wrong with taking time to process your situation.

- Don't give up on yourself.

Dealing with Anger

A friend gave me a large cast-iron skillet when she was cleaning out her kitchen. It was so heavy that it took both hands for me to lift it. It was a bear to clean because I chronically overcook things, but I used it every day. Following the discovery of my husband's addiction, my heart, my body, my head—everything ached. I was so angry at him for all of the lies that I wanted him to feel the same kind of pain he had caused me. At this point, I did not comprehend the significant pain he too was feeling. The best idea I could come up with was to whack him over the head with my skillet. That would hurt him in a different way, but I figured it would do the trick.

These feelings and thoughts are obviously wrong and will land you in jail if acted upon. I share them simply to illustrate their natural place in the grieving process. By dealing with your own similar feelings, it is my hope you will be able to propel yourself beyond anger. Let me repeat: I do not promote anger or violence in any manner! Please do not open a chapter of physical abuse or intimidation in your lives. No good can come of it.

Letting my angry feelings stew was not good for me. I do not like confrontation, and it was really hard for me to explain to my husband the ugly feelings I felt inside. If we were ever able to repair our marriage, I didn't want him to remember the cruel words and feelings I struggled with. Having found solace for himself in writing, he suggested I freewrite all of the "ugliness" out of my system. I was skeptical, but I was really desperate. So I made time to write. Out came pages and pages of hurt and anger. I wept as I wrote. When I was done, I promptly tore the pages out of my notebook and destroyed them. Through this process, it was as if the hurt and anger were transferred from body to page then destroyed. I do not mean to imply that these feelings were gone forever. This process simply allowed me to safely confront my anger. I continued this purging ritual a couple times a week for a few weeks. It was excellent therapy for me.

Even then, I still struggled with significant anger and hatred, especially toward the pornography industry in general. I hated the men who profited financially by selling pornography. I hated the women who posed for it. I worried every time we watched movies, television shows, and commercials. I filtered catalogs and advertisements that came in the mail. There were few places I could go without being reminded of his past. Bookstores were off-limits because I knew they carried inappropriate magazines; the mall too because of their many sensual window displays. Beaches and swimming pools were especially trying. Everywhere I went, women dressed in revealing clothing angered me. I wanted to yell and scream and cry and tell them, "my husband is a recovering pornography addict, and your outfit could destroy his recovery."

On these occasions, it was common to experience anger to the point of feeling sick. I recall one afternoon in particular when a perfectly pleasant day was ruined by the extremely offensive advertising for a local nightclub. I wanted to throw up. Ugly and even violent feelings then consumed me. I wanted to tell them how *they* had ruined my life, even though my husband had never been there. I immediately recognized the danger of my situation and left the vicinity as fast as I could. If I had instead done something out of anger, there could have been no predicting the consequences. One thing is for certain, though, any action promoted by feelings of anger will only do more harm, thus hindering healing and recovery. As you work through your own angry feelings, be cautious. These emotions are natural, but they must be controlled. Write them down, talk them out, and if you ever sense your anger rising to the point of irrational behavior, move on as fast as you can.

Refocus:

- Recognize your anger as natural.

- Do not feel guilty because of your anger.

- Talk out and write down your feelings.

- Find other safe ways to deal with your anger.

- Move on quickly from dangerous situations.

On Revenge

In the movies, revenge is often glorified. In real life, it is devastating. Vindictive feelings will most likely present themselves in your mind, but be careful how much room you give them. Do not look for ways to get revenge or even entertain such thoughts if you think of them. Everything you do to get back at your husband will have a significant negative impact on your own life and your long-term relationship. Yes, the actions of your spouse have had a significant negative effect, but we need to focus on progressing toward healing and not revenge.

I have visited with women who, in their anger, have reached out to anyone who would love them. Do not let your pain or anger drive you to make mistakes similar to those that have already been made in your family. Again, the only thing that will bring is more pain! I had the opportunity to discuss this with one particular woman who had responded to her husband's unfaithfulness by having an affair. Her own unfaithfulness brought more misery and pain to her life and their relationship than originally existed. Although they have managed to mend their relationship and continue to improve their marriage, she is reminded daily of the devastating effects of her poor choices.

Be on you guard. Thoughts of revenge can come at any time and in any form. Personally, I have always had an easy time keeping myself sexually pure. However, I too struggled with this type of temptation. Shortly after my husband had a devastating relapse, he went on a trip. I was angry and hurt because of his mistakes. I clearly remember feeling tempted to find someone, anyone, with whom to have a sexual relationship. I wanted him to see how it felt to be betrayed. Thankfully, my sister happened to be staying with me during that week. I was able to dismiss the thought and move on. I know of other women who turned to subtle and not-so-subtle forms of pornography. Don't be frustrated with yourself if you feel similar temptations, which can be common. But do not pursue them. Protect yourself from these temptations by calling a good friend and admitting your weakness and talking to your husband about your feelings. Actions done in haste with the intent to retaliate will only drive away the peace you seek.

Refocus:

- Do not justify making poor choices because of those of your husband.

- Remember that any poor choice you make will bring you more pain.

- Honestly communicate feelings, temptations, and weaknesses to a trusted friend as needed and to your spouse.

Insecurities

We all have them. More than a sign of weakness, however, I believe they are a sign of trauma. The insecurities an addict's wife can suffer are many. It is common to feel insecure about yourself, your relationship, and your environment. Wondering if he was really where he said he was; waking up in the night and finding him gone, feeling sick with worry that he is looking at pornography somewhere; concerned that the whole problem is our fault because you are not attractive enough; worry that you can never meet his expectations after all that he has been through—these are just some of the many insecurities a woman might feel. Because my husband worked from home, I usually knew where he was. I was often afraid to leave him home alone, though. Occasionally I'd return home from an outing with the kids and find him gone. I'd panic. Even when I knew where he was, what he was doing, and when he'd be back, I'd still panic. That's how much anxiety had a hold on me. Most of the time, my insecurities culminated at night. I was afraid to fall asleep because in my dreams, I was haunted by my husband's mistakes and the emotional toll they had on me. Each night was different but always heartbreaking.

Please understand that your husband's addiction has little to do with you. This reality was hard for me to come to terms with, especially when I was pregnant or recovering from having a baby and didn't feel attractive or physically healthy. My initial perspective was that the problem was all about me. But this is just not so. His problems are not nor will they ever be because of you. When a pornography addict is being driven by his addiction, he will turn to pornography no matter what.

Regardless of the feelings of insecurity you have experienced, please know that you are not alone. Considering what you are going through, these feelings are natural. The best medicine for them is to talk with your spouse. Communicate your needs and concerns. If something in your relationship continually bothers you, try to find a solution together. Try to identify your own triggers. In identifying and addressing situations that make you uncomfortable or anxious, you are empowering yourself to find ways to deal with them.

Discussing your insecurities allows your spouse to support you through this trial and gives him a chance to address your concerns. You may find that the situation you are worried about isn't actually a temptation for him. Ask for his help in finding remedies for your fears. If your husband is working to overcome his addiction, he likely has a wide range of mental control techniques that he is using to maintain a wholesome focus. You may find that there is value for yourself in some of the methods he is using.

Throughout this process, many times it will be appropriate and advisable to visit with a counselor. These trained professionals can offer insights and suggestions that will empower and enable you to view your situation from a different point of view. This new viewpoint will make way for self-discovery in a safe and encouraging atmosphere. Counselors also have a multitude of techniques and tools to help you cope with the pain and suffering you are enduring. There is no shame in seeking the help of a professional. In my experience, professional counseling was both helpful and healing, giving me the strength, courage, and insight I needed to continue working through our struggles.

Ultimately, the greatest relief I found as I dealt with my insecurities came from the growth we saw in our relationship after much time and effort.

Refocus:

- Realize the addiction likely has nothing to do with you.

- Share your concerns with your husband.

- Identify your triggers, and discuss possible solutions with your spouse.

- Seek professional help as needed.

- Don't give up!

Intimacy in Marriage

It is common for wives of pornography addicts to feel their husbands have had sexual experiences or even affairs, albeit virtual ones, with thousands of women. You are not alone in these feelings. It is important for husbands to understand clearly the feelings of their wives in regards to this. The emotional infidelity of a pornography addict is a real struggle for his wife, and is compounded if the husband refuses to see it as such. Because the sexual experience for most women tends to be emotionally based first and physically based second, sexual trust, once broken, drastically affects a woman's willingness and even ability to be intimate with her spouse. As your relationship is rebuilt, and as your husband continues to resist temptation, it will be natural to once again desire a sexual relationship with your husband. However, don't be surprised if you find yourself unable to enjoy these intimate moments. This commonly occurs because of the memories of addiction as well as the sorrow and stress caused by it.

After learning of my husband's addiction, I felt broken—emotionally and sexually. I longed for an enriching sexual relationship with my husband, but because of the type of his addiction and the depth of my pain, I began to dread intimacy. I tried to create a physical relationship with my husband anyway. I hoped that frequent intercourse would keep him from seeking pornography. At the same time, I needed reassurance that he was attracted to me, and I hoped that intimacy would help me to feel wanted by him. However, it was hard for me to mentally separate our sexual relationship from his addictive behaviors. When we were intimate, I would often relive in detail some of the mistakes he had admitted to me. As a result, our sexual relationship was rarely emotionally fulfilling. Unfortunately, in the beginning, the emotional toll of sexual intimacy was usually greater than any comfort or reassurance gained by it.

Looking back, I now realize my line of reasoning was not entirely correct or emotionally healthy. My husband participated in pornography because he was addicted to it; it had nothing to do with the frequency of intimacy or how attractive he found me. As time passed, I learned the importance of patience and communication as it relates to rebuilding a healthy sexual relationship.

Over a year into his recovery process, my husband went through a significant period of relapse. At that time, instead of forcing myself to be intimate, I told him I needed time to recover emotionally before I could even think about sexual intercourse again. Communicating these feelings allowed him to understand how much his actions had affected me. It also gave him the opportunity to show respect for me by giving me the space I needed to heal. Whether or not you are ready to be intimate again with your husband, share your thoughts and feelings with him. Open and honest communication can not only save you both from further hurt and heartache, but will make intimacy more meaningful when the time comes to rebuild this important component of your relationship.

I don't think I need to go into any more detail than that, but I do want to make a couple suggestions that can help. Sex is a God-given gift to humankind with a two-fold purpose. First, it is meant to bind husband and wife together, giving them an opportunity to create a tender and trusting relationship. Second, it is the means by which children are brought into the world. This procreative responsibility can further bind husband and wife together. Realizing the importance of this matter in the eyes of God, I began to pray daily that I would be able to conquer my apprehension and hurt in regards to my intimate relationship with my husband. I did eventually find the relief I sought. I was also able to think of other ways to move past my struggles.

Among these, the following three ways were most helpful:

Discuss Your Concerns with Your Spouse: Many women have found some relief after discussing their concerns with their husbands. Pray for opportunities to share your feelings with your spouse. Pray for the wisdom to address these issues with kindness. Husbands should also exhibit an increase of sensitivity and concern when confided in. In no manner should either of you criticize or make light of the other's feelings regarding your sexual concerns.

Learn to Control Your Thoughts: Just like my husband had to control his thoughts, so I had to learn to control mine. I learned to identify certain triggers that often caused my emotional pain during intimacy. I had to train my brain to block these thoughts and images. Often during intimacy, I had to use all my strength to focus on the moment and not let negativity consume my thoughts.

Get Help: Because of the sensitive nature of this topic, support should be sought. As noted, your husband should be a part of this process as far as it is necessary, but because your concerns directly involve him, you may need to find help elsewhere. Friends and family always stand by to help, but there are few reasons, if any, to relate to them the details of your sexual relationship with your husband. If you do turn to them, be careful that you do not give too much information or that the information you give does not further damage your marital relationship. In most cases, though, depending on the degree of your needs, family and friends will be of little authoritative help. If you need help beyond a listening ear, consider seeking the experience of a professional counselor or ecclesiastical leader. They are equipped with the tools and perspective necessary to help you. With the added guidance of a counselor, you may be able to move more quickly through this phase and onto a healthier relationship.

Refocus:

- Share your concerns with your husband.

- Learn to control your thoughts

- Get help from a counselor or therapist as needed.

- Do not force intimacy.

Focus on What You Can Control

It is common to feel completely helpless while a loved one is struggling with addiction. Although there is truth in the feeling that we are victims of this addiction, it is important to recognize that our husbands have also been victimized by the quickly spreading pandemic of pornography. Please remember that you are a strong woman. You will have a great influence on the people around you. More important, because of your strength, you can positively affect the course of your own life.

As was the case with defining boundaries, in looking for ways to gain control of your life, begin small. Recognize that one of the main things you can control is how you treat others, including your husband. Compassion, it seems, is somewhat of a lost virtue, but it is vital to healing.

You will most likely encounter people who may mean well but come across critical. They cannot comprehend the depth of your struggles. This is the case for many reasons but mostly because you are not at liberty or it is not wise to discuss in detail the exact cause of your pain. In these cases, it will be important that you learn to contain feelings of frustration and instead show compassion. I remember one such occasion. In the thick of our struggles, I often cried wherever I happened to be. At my morning workout one day, my emotions boiled over. I started crying out of the blue. A couple of the older women there came to me to offer support. I offered only the explanation that my husband and I were having some struggles in our marriage. One of these women happened to know my husband. She thought I was overreacting and being unfair. After sharing some stories about men she knew who had been unfaithful to their wives, she said, "Well, he hasn't done anything like that, so it can't possibly be as bad as you think." I was hurt by her nonchalance, and it was hard for me not to voice my disappointment in her. My impulse was to tell her everything my husband had done as the means of proving to her that it was, as it seemed to me, every bit as bad. I am grateful that in that moment, when I was tempted to retaliate, I found the strength I needed to be kind to her and to be respectful of my husband's personal struggle. She was just trying to help in the only was she knew how. It is within your control to continue to be civil to the people who try to understand but cannot. Do not add to your burdens by developing resentment for them.

Withholding judgment and criticism of your husband is also within your control. This is particularly important when speaking to others. Maybe the one thing you can control is whether you say something unkind about him to another person. This is something that was difficult for me to learn. The hurt I felt went deep. I felt like anytime I opened my mouth to talk about my marriage or my life in general at the time, I could only think of negative things to say about my husband. Sometimes I gave voice to those thoughts, only to immediately realize my error and wish I had not. These instances only served to increase the rift that already existed between us. Other times, it made public what should have remained private. Being in control of tempers and emotional reactions is empowering. Again, it is within your control to be kind to your husband, even when you hurt. I know sometimes you might feel his privacy is not or should not be a priority, but it is still important to tread carefully. You don't want other people to remember what you are trying to forget.

Another thing you can control now is making daily religious studies or meditation a priority. These can help bring a greater sense of control into your life. Seeking answers through prayer, searching the scriptures, and taking time to focus on the good in your life can make clear your perspective, allowing you to see the steps you need to take to find peace now. Some days I was so overwhelmed and so mad at God that the last thing I wanted to do was study his word and communicate through prayer. So I didn't. Other days I did and, quite frankly, felt no relief. Eventually, though, I realized that returning to my daily habit of prayer and study was a key to inviting a greater daily sense of peace.

You can also control how honest you are. Realize that being honest in all that you do and say will increase your power to effectively face your struggles. Total honesty keeps us free from the bondage of deceit.

To get through this intense phase of recovery, you will also have to realize that some things you cannot control. If your husband continues to struggle with pornography, please realize that he is making his own choices, and no amount of pressure or persuasion will change him long term. Change is something he has to decide to do for himself. Let go of the responsibility for him. If you are trying to control his behavior, give the burden back to him. You have enough pain to carry.

Don't give up on him, though. I know it can be tempting to walk away from your spouse and leave the pain of his addiction behind you once and for all. After I was made aware of my husband's relapse, I felt strongly that I needed to ask him to leave our home. I did not demand he stay away forever, but I had no definite time frame for when I would allow him to return. Scariest of all to me, because his choices up until that moment made me feel as if he didn't care about our family or the rules we had established, I did not know if he would even choose to come back. In the darkness of that night, I was resigned to the fact that he was responsible for his own choices and I would move on without him as necessary, but as the sun rose the next morning, I realized that if he wanted to change, I wanted to help him. I prayed that he would have the desire and strength to overcome his addictive behaviors. For myself, I prayed for equal strength to carry on while he made those changes. In hindsight, I see now how badly he did want to change, and I am grateful for the strength we received that helped us change together.

I encourage you to continue to pray and hope for your husband's recovery. Above all, don't give up on him if he is willing change, and don't give up on yourself. Keep moving forward. Focus on what you can control and let peace begin to enter in.

Refocus:

- Continue to be kind to others.

- Let go of the responsibility of the addiction. That burden is not yours to carry.

- Commit to being completely honest.

Finding Support

Loneliness was a terrible burden for me for the first couple years. I felt like I was totally alone. My husband's parents were always supportive of me and made sure to be available when needed, but I tried not to rely on them too often because I wanted them to be completely free to support and love their son without my process interfering. Eventually I realized that if I wanted to survive, though, I needed to find a place where I could feel understood. I needed an understanding and supportive group with whom to sort out and examine my feelings and struggles. I needed to find someone who would say, "I have been there, and it was hard, but you can do it!" Finding a support group ended up being extremely important to the progress I made towards healing. Find somewhere to feel the validation you need.

I had never been to a support group of any kind before and, honestly, I was nervous about it. As I listened to the women there, I grew to love and respect all of them. The insights and perspectives of those farther along in their process definitely encouraged me to continue trying to improve my marriage and improve myself. The group functioned on a twelve-week cycle. During the first twelve weeks, I took a lot of notes. All of the notes, however, highlighted principles I wanted my husband to hear. The second time around, I again took notes. But this time all of the notes I took were about ways *I* could improve myself. It was wonderful to see the growth in myself as I progressed from blaming my husband to focusing on areas of self-improvement.

Unfortunately, not all of us may have access to a support group. Looking for a support group online may be a valid option, but I do want to caution you that I have come across many online groups that are overly angry and bitter. Many preach divorce as an only option. Support groups that are negative in tone can be more destructive than helpful. Be careful not to fuel feelings of man-hating. No good will come from that. An ideal support group should always include people who will respect you and your relationship. The people within these groups should also be encouraging and help you stay positive. Support and understanding are vital; carefully choose where you seek it. If you have a trusted religious leader, he or she may be able to locate a group of individuals who are also trying to rebuild rather than eliminate relationships. Remember, our goal is to progress toward healing.

Refocus:

- Recognize the need for understanding and support.

- Participate in a positive support group that will encourage you along your path to healing.

Coping with Depression

Depression was a real battle for me. Suddenly, my life was not what I thought it had always been. At random times, my husband's confessions would flood into my mind and heart. As a result, I often felt emotionally and even physically ill for the rest of the day. It got so bad that many times I could not even get out of bed two or three days a week. I would cry all day, and I had no desire to be active. On the other days, I was at least able to take care of my kids by myself and meet their needs, but I still felt "blah." I wanted to be happy, but I did not know how anymore. I was also angry with myself because I felt like I wasn't coping well or managing to carry on like a normal person should. I was so tired of feeling the pain in my chest that I simply stopped feeling anything at all. I was numb. This, of course, was not healthy.

Recognizing I was in dangerous territory, I went to a doctor about my depression. He asked me to describe the current challenges in my life. After I shared a bit about what we were going through, he looked at me and said, "You don't need antidepressants. Your life is just really rotten!" Some people may think that this is harsh or unprofessional, but to me it was validating!

If your depression is significant, please talk to your husband and your doctor about it. In talking to your doctor, be sure to be honest about the struggles causing your feelings. Only then will he or she be able to discern what medical needs you have, if any. Please know that antidepressants, when used with wisdom, are one of the blessings of modern medicine. They can be genuinely beneficial if you and your doctor agree that they are the correct approach to managing your depression. If a decision is reached that medication is needed to treat your depression, understand that it does not mean something is wrong with you. You are not broken. Your burdens are real and they are weighty. There is no shame in needing extra help to appropriately deal with them. Do be careful not to rely on prescribed medicine. Antidepressants can become a crutch. Your use of them can turn into an addiction of its own. Talk to your doctor and spouse about your concerns, and consider setting a time frame for their use. They are simply a temporary tool that, when used correctly, can help you get back on your feet.

Refocus:

- Depression is common under your circumstances.

- Communicate your feelings and concerns to your husband and doctor.

- If medication is prescribed, do not feel guilt or shame.

- Consider setting a time frame for their use.

Self-Medication

On the days that were particularly painful or stressful, I often found myself doing things to try and compensate. Specifically, I often went shopping for things we didn't necessarily need. On other occasions, I would stop by the ice cream shop to get a treat. When burdens are heavy, it is natural and easy to seek out temporary distractions from the pain. Without realizing it, we can imperceptibly develop our own compulsive behaviors. While eating and shopping are not wrong, constantly doing them as a means to combat stress can have negative long-term results. It took conscious effort to avoid developing any lasting habits. When I felt stressed or sad, I instead learned to direct my focus to something positive.

Redirection of focus is important. It will afford you the time you need to grieve and empower you to continue living through the pain. When my husband and I were dating, one day we were both feeling "blah." We decided to come up with a list of silly things to do to improve our moods. Among other things, we rolled down hills, built boats out of leaves and sticks and floated them in a pond, and listened to really old rock music. It worked! This has since become known in our family as a "Blah Day Emergency Kit."

This experience served me well years later as I was trying to overcome my chronic depression. I made a so-called emergency escape route for bad days to come. I included things such as arranging flowers to give to a friend, exercising, and listening to cheerful music. Memorizing positive songs was also valuable. On a bad day, by looking at my list, I could quickly recognize opportunities to look beyond my pain. Make your own lists of positive things you can do to distract you from sorrow. Post your list somewhere obvious like the fridge, a kitchen cabinet, next to your computer screen, or on the bathroom mirror.

Journal writing proved to be a powerful tool for me too. After several months of struggling to find ways to cope with my pain, I made a rule that at the end of every day I had to record something good that happened that day. In the beginning, it sometimes took a long time to recall a positive occurrence for the day. As the weeks went by, however, it became much easier to pinpoint the small miracles or blessings in my life. Occasionally the entries read: "Today the kids did not fight very much." Other times the positive vibe for the day was: "I started to tell him it was all his fault, but then I decided not to, and I said, I am hurting because . . ." Eventually, though, entries such as the following became the norm: "Today was a beautiful day. The sun was shining. It was so warm. The kids and I had a wonderful time playing outside."

Along with searching for the good in each day, many other things can help you manage your pain. You can create a happy moment for the day. You don't have to wait for it. Service to others is a fantastic way to bring joy into your own life. When I was feeling overwhelmed, I would call one of our church leaders and ask if anyone in particular in the congregation needed help. Focusing my energy on the needs and hardships of others brought me greater strength, as I was able to see a difference in their lives because of my efforts and kindness.

Refocus:

- Identify ways to serve others.

- Occupy your time with positive activities.

- Plan positive activities to do when you feel sad.

- Listen to good music.

Resistance Training and Stamina: Your Burden Is Heavy, Keep on Moving

Recently my family has made many sacrifices so that I could improve my health. I have been going to the gym six days every week. I am rapidly remembering how much I love to exercise! Quickly I have been reminded of the value of both resistance training and cardiovascular exercises. Resistance training entails increasing the weight you move, carry, or lift. This pushes the muscles to their limit, thereby increasing their capacity.

The more I lift, the slower I find myself moving. This is not a bad thing at all. Even though I slow down with greater resistance, the benefit, over time, is that my overall cardio performance can be improved because I am stronger. My stamina is also increased because I have been accustomed to more resistance over an extended period of time.

Clearly, during some periods in our lives, the load we carry is heavy. This is one of those times. Your burdens are real and they are heavy. Many times I was so overwhelmed by my husband's addiction that I missed appointments, neglected responsibilities at church, and forgot to send my kindergartner to school. Sometimes I even forgot to mail in our bills or balance the checkbook. Often I felt guilty for my inability to function the way I was used to. As my stress increased, I also began to fill every second of every day with activity. Unconsciously I created a schedule that left little time to think about my marriage. The breakneck pace the kids and I kept was wearing us all out physically and emotionally. I was not facing or dealing with my pain; I was trying to outrun it. Please recognize that with the increased load you now bear, you will move more slowly. This is not bad. In fact, I encourage you to slow down. Lower your expectations for yourself for a time. Begin by identifying things in your life that are not needful and let go of them.

Remember, high resistance increases strength. Eventually, when the weight of life decreases, you will be surprised at how strong you have become. You can do it! Your pace may slow, but you can continue on in spite of the burden you bear!

Additionally, I would like to counsel you to accept help when it is offered. Dealing with this addiction can be taxing. If a friend notices that you seem withdrawn or worn out and offers to bring dinner, take the kids, or go for a walk with you, accept their offer! Let others serve you. Please ask for help when you need it. When you allow others to help, it will save your own strength so that you will be able to bear well the portion of your burdens that cannot be shared.

Refocus:

- Simplify your life.

- Recognize the need to slow down.

- Allow others to serve and love you.

36

MOVING FORWARD

*"Let us not burden our remembrances with
a heaviness that's gone."*[1]

The Gift of Time: Be Patient with Yourself

For at least a year after I learned of my husband's addiction, I cried every day. I became frustrated with myself for taking so long to move on and get over it. After much soul searching, I realized that my impatience was only compounding my struggles, making it difficult to feel like I would find healing. I also came to the conclusion that if God knew my pains, and if God was patient with me, then I needed to offer myself these same considerations.

Please be patient with yourself. Remember, the grieving process takes time. Time to heal. Time to learn to trust. Time to learn to love again. You should not for any reason feel guilty if you still hurt inside or if you are still struggling to trust your spouse. Do not allow anyone else to make you feel guilty either. If he had passed away, you would not question the amount of time needed to recover and heal. Give yourself the gift of time now.

I cannot tell you how much time it will take for you personally to heal, but that doesn't really matter. Take all the time you need. Keep moving forward. If you find the path toward healing is longer than you hoped or expected, do not become discouraged. Great distances take time to travel. Deep wounds take time to heal. But they can be healed. Remember, God is patient with you and you should be too.

Refocus:

- Recognize that this process takes time.

- Be patient with yourself.

Acceptance: How and When Does Progress Come?

Springtime on a farm in the Pacific Northwest can be soggy, to say the least. I remember a time when I had been out in the field working all morning with my grandfather, dad, and sisters. We decided to take a break and began to cross the pasture to get back to the barn. The pasture, however, was quite muddy (I like to think that it was only mud), and, with every step I took, I sank deeper into the sludge. If I wanted to take a step, I had to grip the tops of my boots, one at a time, and pull as hard as I could until the muck released my foot. Pretty soon, though, the mud became so deep that it reached the top of my boots. At this point, I tried and I tried to get free, but no amount of pulling would help. My energy and strength had been sapped. I was stuck. To make it worse, any movement at all caused mud to spill into my boots. I couldn't do anything except call for help. My grandfather worked his way out to me (luckily his boots were taller than mine). With all his might, he dragged me out of the muck.

For a year or two after I found out about my husband's addiction, I was figuratively stuck. I had managed to accept the reality of it, to some degree, but I could not pull myself free from the immense sadness I still felt. This isn't to say I had been paralyzed by the sorrow I felt, as had been the case early on; rather, I was consumed by a consistent aching in my heart and mind. Through it all, I struggled to understand why I was unable to free myself from the pain I felt. I eventually came to the realization that I wasn't making progress because I had chosen to stop. For instance, I refused to do many things I had previously valued and enjoyed. I didn't want to go on a family vacation *until* I was over the hurt or I didn't want to "waste" money on frequent date nights with my husband *until* the pain was gone. We discussed earlier the need to control certain things in our lives. These were things I could have controlled, and, by controlling them, I would have been able to continue forward, at least in some measure.

Having said this, it is important that you do not confuse slow progress with no movement at all. Remember, the weight of this burden will naturally slow the pace of progress, but progress does not have to stop altogether. Keep moving forward. And if you get stuck up to your boot tops, then call for help; or take them off and keep going.

I determined to do what had previously brought me joy. In the beginning it was hard. I simply could not feel happy. But eventually this changed. Looking back, I recall many small instances when we were in the midst of doing something as a family and I was able to step back, notice, and admit that I was actually enjoying myself. This was so encouraging to me!

I encourage you to pick one thing to do this week that will bring you joy and then do it! Try not to be frustrated if you feel like you are unable to enjoy it at first. Some of the paths we travel in life are longer and steeper than others, but we will never reach our destination if we stop putting one foot in front of the other. I promise if you keep at it, you will begin again to enjoy life.

When these signs of progress present themselves, I further encourage you to write them down in a journal. Then look back on them as needed. By reviewing them, you will be able to clearly identify how much progress you have actually made. In these moments of realization, the seeds of future progress will be planted. And yes, you are making progress. Keep on going!

Refocus:

- Make a list of things that bring you joy.

- Keep a journal to allow you to track small signs of progress.

- Keep moving!

- Do something today that you enjoy.

Building Trust

"Will I ever be able to trust my husband again?" "How do we rebuild the trust we used to have?" Because every situation is different, these can be difficult questions to answer with any level of consistency. However, based on experience, I feel there are three main stages during which trust can be rebuilt.

First, I had to learn to trust that he was telling me all of the different ways he had been involved with pornography. In the beginning, it seemed like there was some new confession every day. This was frustrating, and I was certain he was purposefully withholding information from me. Eventually, though, I realized that this sporadic pattern was the natural result of him trying to recall a lifetime of mistakes in a short amount of time. Surely he would not be able to remember them all at once. Think of it as a door. Each confession simply opened the door to another wing of his past, in which he would often discover the existence of more doors. Over time, the more often he shared with me the details of his past, the faster I began to trust that he was trying to tell me everything.

While I know your husband is the one who has to regain your trust, I think it is important to realize that, to some extent, he too is trying to learn to trust you. Your reaction and attitude will go a long way to helping him determine whether or not he can trust you with even more of his struggles. But instead of a door this time, think of a set of stairs. Each time he shares something and does not feel hated for sharing it, it is a step up that will allow yet other steps in the near future.

The second phase of trust I encountered was similar. I wanted to trust that he would never make another mistake, but here I had to learn to trust that if he did relapse, he would tell me. This level of trust was only reached as we continued to communicate constantly and exhibit empathy toward one another. The safer he felt sharing his temptations with me, the more easily he shared; and the more often he shared them, the more confident I became that he was, indeed, sharing with me all of the temptations he had experienced, both those he was able to overcome and those he had given in to. This is so important. The sharing of the secret is what keeps it from growing larger.

As we continued to rebuild our relationship, we were able to reach a third phase of trust. In this phase I did not and do not worry as much about his daily activities. In my mind, this is the final phase. There is no phase where you simply never worry because, to me, it is wise for all of us, regardless our pasts, to show concern for those we love. Thus far, my husband and I have been able to strengthen and fortify our relationship through constant positive and honest communication. I have learned to trust that he will not intentionally seek out any manner of pornography. But I am also experienced enough to admit that in this day and age, when pornography is virtually everywhere, it may only be a matter of time before he sees something that entices him, whether he wanted to or not. For this reason, I am free to ask him at any time whether or not he has felt temptation or given in to it in any degree. This freedom to ask questions without fear of retaliation is vital to rebuilding trust. Additionally, I have learned to trust that he, of his own accord, will come to me and share his feelings or any moments of personal weakness. This has proven true on many occasions. Several times he has happened upon something only to tell me later that day. To my joy, these episodes are equally frustrating for him. As this process continues daily, my concerns are continually put to rest.

Be cautious not to do anything that will undermine the trust you seek. It is common, at first, for many women to snoop around, trying to find something bad their husbands looked at in order to prove they were right to distrust. This was certainly true for me in the beginning. I spent hours searching through computer folders and Internet histories. I even recall a time I secretly read parts of his journal. Do not add to your natural suspicions by doing these types of things. They will only build upon your sense of doubt and instill within your husband a distrust for you. You need him to trust you too. You need to know what he is going through. Instead of playing the role of a private investigator, talk to your husband; explain to him that it would help you feel more comfortable and confident if you could take some time together to go through his computer and phone histories and verify that there is nothing to be concerned about there.

"Are you ever going to trust me?" This is a common question you will no doubt field from your husband at some point. While it sounds cliché, "I trust you; I just don't trust pornography" might be the best way to respond. It is important for both you and your husband to realize that to trust doesn't mean that you won't sometimes wonder if he has stumbled. It also doesn't mean that you should just stand back and let him enter situations that might prove tempting because you are sure he will not give in. Common sense should never be abandoned. Safeguards should always be respected. Some situations just aren't safe for anyone, let alone a recovering pornography addict. In these situations, we need to watch out for the other person, not because we do not trust, but because we love them and want them to stay safe. Depending on your spouse's particular struggles, these potentially dangerous situations might include being home alone, social networking, or watching TV late at night. As you discuss these things with your husband, ask him if he is able to pinpoint any specific areas of past weakness. With this information, you will be better equipped to help him in time of need.

Although your own personal needs inevitably vary from those of others, remember that trust is built as you communicate honestly with your spouse. Also, remember to communicate openly about concerns, always making sure to do so in a nonthreatening manner. As you do, be sure to appreciate the times your husband responds to your questions without offense. Avoid anything that increases your sense of suspicion. Continue to use common sense and caution to protect the progress you have made. Recognize incremental progress and reevaluate what it means to trust, as needed. And as always, write down your experiences and thoughts. Then, when you feel to do so, look back on them and be amazed at the progress you have made and the amount of trust that has already been restored.

Refocus:

- Recognize that trust takes time to build.

- Identify and discuss things that help you to feel safe in your relationship.

- Again, track and record small signs of progress in your own recovery.

Supporting Your Spouse

In the early stages of recovery and healing, it is common for wives to confuse supporting their husbands with enabling them. Support is all about encouraging growth and progress. Enablement, on the other hand, stunts growth. A supportive wife must be willing to address concerns and act on intuition for the welfare of her husband. Sometimes this will require her to do hard things. Some of the most supportive women I know were also women who, at one time or another, kicked their husband out of the house. Compare this to the enabling wife who often facilitates bad behavior by keeping silent or withholding consequences. The line, however, is not always so clear. In the midst of your struggles, it can be hard to determine whether or not you are helping or hurting your husband's progress. So how can you know when he needs support and what support to give? Pay attention to your thoughts and feelings.

There was a time my husband began pursuing a new hobby. For reasons I could not explain, I did not feel good about it. Still, I wanted to be supportive of his talents and interests because it was important to him. So against my better judgment, I did not voice my concerns. Eventually, this seemingly innocent hobby led to a major relapse. Although I was not to blame for his poor decisions, had I acted on my feelings of concern, I might have spared our family the pain that followed.

From this experience, I learned again that supporting my husband did not mean allowing him to do whatever he wanted. Rather, it meant encouraging him to make good choices and rejoicing with him when he did. We can look to the Lord as the prime example of this. He does not support wrongdoing. But he will always sustain and direct us when we pursue the correct course.

Along the way, I realized one way I could support my husband was to celebrate his victories. Initially it was difficult to recognize his efforts because I was overwhelmed by the fact that our marriage was not what I thought it should have been. Over time, though, I began to recognize the work he was putting into becoming free from his past. This certainly deserved some kind of acknowledgment. My husband, however, is not comfortable with verbal congratulations or public recognition. So I began to look for other ways by which I could let him know I was proud of his efforts and excited for his progress. Little notes in which I expressed my appreciation went a long way. You may not feel like celebrating anything at first, but as you keep pressing forward and try hard to see where your husband has made progress, I promise you will eventually feel the joy of victory—yours and his.

Refocus:

- Recognize his efforts to change.

- Be grateful when he communicates about his struggles.

- Pay attention to your thoughts and feelings

- Identify signs of his recovery.

- Help him avoid dangerous situations.

Marriage Takes Two People

Throughout this book, we have tried to teach principles and offer suggestions by which to start rebuilding your marriage. We feel confident that these are some of the most important tools you and your husband will need and that if you use them together, you will succeed.

On that note, however, the truth is that if both husband and wife are not willing to work together for this common cause, the rebuilding process will fail. I recognize that many women out there have husbands who do not feel the need to change and, in fact, boldly refuse to do so. In these cases, no matter how bad you want to help him, no matter how bad you want to salvage your marriage, there is little you will be able to do by yourself to change his heart. That is a decision that only he can make.

If this describes your situation, my heart goes out to you. Do not allow yourself to feel guilty. This is not your fault. I do not want to encourage or discourage divorce. That is a decision that only you can make. But I do want to alleviate your concerns if you are now considering this option. Pray about it, talk it over with a family member or a close friend if you need to, carefully discuss it with your husband, and then make your decision. Let God guide your thoughts and feelings. If you come to the firm conclusion that separation or divorce is the best decision to make for the ultimate safety and happiness of all involved (especially for you and any children you may have) then hold your head up high and don't look back with doubt or guilt.

Your husband may have given up on himself, but don't you dare give up on yourself. God has not given up on you and, for what it's worth, neither have I. There is still hope. And betters days are in store for you, I promise. Personal healing does not depend on the choices of your husband or on the outcome of your marriage. It is available to all no matter what.

I recently had the opportunity to visit with three women about their decision to divorce. One had divorced decades ago, the other within the past ten years, and the last only recently. Despite their different circumstances and personalities, their stories were much the same. They each desperately wanted their marriage to work. They did everything they could to help their spouse recover from his addiction. They felt strongly it was the right thing to do, and for this reason alone, they stuck by their husband for years, hoping and waiting for his heart to change. But it never did. In some cases, things only got worse. In the end, after significant prayer and introspection, they each came to the conclusion that it was now time to seek divorce. They felt certain they had given their respective husbands every opportunity to change. They also felt an overwhelming sense of comfort, as if God was speaking to them, confirming in mind and heart the rightness of their decision. "Things will be okay," he seemed to say. "I have accepted the sacrifice you made by staying with your husband these many years. I will take care of him. Now is the time for you to move on with your life."

And so it is for all of us. No matter the situation you are in, no matter the decision you have made regarding your marriage, now is the time to move on, on to the victory, on to the day of promised peace.

As always, I encourage you to write down your thoughts, feelings, and experiences, especially those surrounding your decision to stay with or divorce your husband. In the days, months, and perhaps even years to come no doubt will you have moments when you question whether you did the right thing. If you feel this way, you will be able to look back on what you wrote and be reminded that you did, in fact, do the right thing for yourself, your family, and your husband.

To end, I want to share an anecdote. A couple of years ago, my oldest sat down to play before bedtime. He was, however, so intent on building a perfect scene using his train set, blocks, and other toys, that he spent his entire playtime building and not playing. With this mind, I say at last, make sure you do not focus so much time and effort on rebuilding that you forget to spend time enjoying what you've built.

Refocus:

- Recognize your marriage can be repaired if you are both committed to seeking healing.

- Let go of responsibility for his choices.

- Record your feelings and convictions for later reference.

- Create a safe environment for yourself and your family.

- Your healing does not depend on the choices of your husband.

- Take time to enjoy the life you are rebuilding.

37

HOPE AND HEALING

"The Master of Life's been good to me. He has given me strength to face past illnesses, and victory in the face of defeat. He has given me life and joy where others saw oblivion. He has given new purposes to live for. New services to render and old wounds to heal. Life and love go on. Let the music play."[1]

GROWING UP ON A FARM, I ONCE HAD A HORSE NAMED Hope. Tragically, one day my horse started bucking wildly then keeled over on the spot—dead. Distraught by the sudden loss of a beloved pet, one of my younger sisters, who was three years old at the time, was inconsolable. "Hope is dead," she cried that entire day. "Hope is dead."

I'm here to tell you, hope is not dead. There is always something to hope for. Above all, there is hope in healing. Look forward to it. It will take consistent, conscious effort, but as you do all you can to get through the days ahead, to do what you are supposed to, and to love and accept love from family and friends, little by little, step-by-step, things will become easier and the horizon will once again appear as bright as the noonday sun. Though dark clouds now cover the skyline, cling to this one silver lining of hope. Diligence and consistent effort will see you through. Bear all things; believe all things; hope all things; endure all things and don't you stop! (1 Corinthians 13:7). You keep moving forward—because you can!

Love Your Spouse: He, Too, Is in Pain

How can you love your spouse even when his actions hurt you? This is something that I struggled with off and on for several years. True to the grieving process, I was at first so angry with him that loving him was the last thing on my mind. Eventually, though, I reached a point where I was no longer angry with him. Instead I began to struggle with feelings of indifference toward him. This was hard for me because, at that point, I wanted to love my husband. But because of the pain I had felt previously, it seemed as if I no longer had the capacity to love. I longed for something different, something better. After several months of praying to understand how to love my husband again, I was blessed with a truly tender experience that opened my eyes and heart.

Sitting in our church services one Sunday, I happened to look over at my husband. In an instant, I saw him in a new light—as he was, not as he had been. In that same moment, I saw clearly the many ways he had been serving me. Through these acts of service, he was trying to show me he cared and was attempting to lift the burdens he brought into my life. In my mind, I saw afternoons when he took the boys to the park. I saw early mornings when he got up with the baby so I could sleep in. I saw days at a time that he postponed his work responsibilities so he could listen to me talk about my sorrow. More astonishing to me was that in that same moment I suddenly recognized how badly he too had been hurting through our entire process.

Yes, I was devastated, in pain, and brokenhearted over his choices. But he carried an additional burden I had not previously been aware of. In addition to the pains of addiction, he also felt the burden of being responsible for the pain he had caused me. It weighed on him heavily. From that moment on, I tried to realize that I was not the only one that needed to be loved and reassured. He too needed to feel these things.

Refocus:

- Identify and appreciate the ways your spouse is trying to help carry your burdens.

- Realize that your spouse hurts and also needs to feel loved.

The Choice to Forgive: My Personal Experience

Forgiveness is a process, but it is also a choice. It is, perhaps, the hardest choice of all though. This is especially true when the offense hits so close to home and heart, as is the case with pornography addiction. Most likely you will struggle to come to peace with three main groups: the sinner, the sin, and the maker of the sin. There is no shame in admitting frustration or even initial hatred toward these things. It is natural. But such emotions must not continue indefinitely. If such feelings are allowed to linger, they will in time fester into virulent thoughts and ultimately actions, all of which have the power to destroy not only your own inner peace and happiness but also that of your spouse, children, friends, and other loved ones.

Personally, I felt like I had to deal with all of my anger, depression, and hurt before I was even able to consider forgiving my husband. Two years came and went. My husband's recovery was going well, and our relationship was growing. But I still wasn't at peace. I often felt sadness and confusion. "How much time," I wondered, "will it take to relieve my suffering?" I realized then that I would never be at peace until I could somehow get rid of these feelings. I had to choose to forgive him.

Unsure of how to forgive something as difficult as the betrayal I felt, I explored of the principle of forgiveness. I diligently studied teachings on the subject. For me, many of these were found in the Bible. I observed the forgiving examples of Christ and others. I also prayed daily that my mind would be opened and my heart softened so that I could understand and accept the principles I had studied. I then began to seek the strength to forgive my husband. Specifically, I prayed to God for the strength I lacked. After one particular period of prayer and pondering, a brief image came into my mind. I saw myself wrapping up all of my pain and sorrow into a package and leaving it at the feet of the Savior. He had already felt all of these things in the Garden of Gethsemane, I realized. He had already paid the price for them. And because he had already paid for them, they didn't belong to me. My sorrow, my pain, my frustration— they were his, and by laying them at his feet, I was simply returning what he had purchased with his blood. From that moment on, forgiveness had nothing to do with my husband; rather, it had everything to do embracing the atonement of Christ. By this, I would be able to free myself from the pains I felt.

With this perspective, the need to forgive my husband and give up my hurt feelings became urgent. I made it my first priority. I shared all of my feelings and thoughts with him. I then concluded by telling him that I had forgiven him of everything. This part was hard for me, and I almost stopped short. But as I pressed forward, I received the strength I needed to say the words and to make the commitment that I would never look back.

To not look back meant that I would no longer bring up my husband's past mistakes. I needed to let him focus on the life he was now living, not the life he had lived. Likewise, I had to focus on the life that was ours to live going into the future, and not the life we had left behind.

In that moment, my struggle to forgive and move on came to an end, and peace slowly began to fill my soul. To this day, the past no longer causes me pain. Yes, I have regrets, as does he. But this is not about regretting the past; it is about moving forward with hope.

Refocus:

- Realize that it may take time before you are ready to consider forgiving your husband.

- When the time is right, though, make the choice to forgive.

- Ask God to bless you with a forgiving heart.

- Lay your hurt at the Savior's feet and leave it there.

- Share your thoughts with your husband and tell him you forgive him.

- Don't look back; move forward.

Forgiveness: The Gift

Forgiveness is often associated with religion. But the need for it touches all. On the heels of sharing my personal experience before, I have heard people say to some extent: "that's wonderful for you, but what about for someone like me who doesn't believe in Jesus Christ? I can't just hand my anger and hurt over to him like you did." My answer: then don't give it to Christ, but do give it up. For*give*ness, as the root of the word implies, is a gift we can and must give to those in need of it.

So how do you give up your hurt and forgive your husband? Well, theoretically speaking, no one can give away what he or she has not first received. Because of this, the better question might be: "How do I receive of it then, or how do I develop a forgiving heart, so that I can give it when and where it is needed?"

The wording of this question also touches upon the answer. How do we *receive* forgiveness? Have we not already received forgiveness in some manner? While the sins of our husbands may seem infinitely worse than any misdeeds we have ever committed, a key to properly forgiving lies in our realization that we have also been the recipients of forgiveness at some point in our lives. It is no secret that I believe that because Jesus Christ loves us, he suffered for our sins and willingly forgives us each and every time we repent of and forsake our errant ways. But all religion aside, certainly many people in your life, as in mine, have been offended or hurt by our words or actions. Have we not before been in need of their forgiveness? Or, perhaps, you are now still in need of their forgiveness. I recall with gratitude the times when someone's decision to forgive me and overlook my mistakes made a lasting difference in my life. In such cases, forgiveness, when freely given, made healing possible. Our relationship was able to move on in spite of the hurt that once seemed impenetrable. When I take the time to recall the charitable decisions these people made on my behalf, it is much easier to return the favor to the people waiting to receive the forgiveness I alone can give.

I have also found it easier to forgive when I have taken the time to consider what *might have been*, and by that, I mean employing the imagination to figuratively step into the shoes of your husband. There is value in realizing and then admitting that we do not completely comprehend the situations, upbringings, and influences that have affected the choices made by our husbands. If they had been brought up as us, they might well have been just as strong; and had we been brought up as they or endured the bombardment of certain situations, we might have likewise bowed before similar temptations. In this sense, your ability and willingness to envision different scenarios can open the gateway through which anger leaves and empathy enters. Percy Bysshe Shelley wrote, "A man, to be greatly good must imagine intensely and comprehensively; he must put himself in the place of another and many others; the pains and pleasures of his species must become his own. The great instrument of moral good is the imagination."[2] Making a conscious effort to imagine our husbands in a different set of circumstances or to imagine ourselves growing up in the situations in which they did, can help us foster the empathy necessary to separate the man from the sin. Empathy, in all cases, is a pertinent precursor to forgiveness. It allows us to see people as they were, as they really are, and as they may yet become.

Corrie ten Boom speaks to this point. A Dutch watchmaker, she risked her life to help Jews escape the Nazis during World War II. When she was caught and thrown into a concentration camp, it appeared all was lost. But she survived. Her account is one of faith, love, healing, and forgiveness. Said she: "Even as the angry vengeful thoughts boiled through me, I saw the sin of them. Jesus Christ had died for this man; was I going to ask for more? Lord Jesus, I prayed, forgive me and help me to forgive him. . . . Jesus, I cannot forgive him. Give me your forgiveness. . . . And so I discovered that it is not on our forgiveness any more than on our goodness that the world's healing hinges, but on His. When He tells us to love our enemies, He gives along with the command, the love itself."[3]

So how do you give forgiveness? The same way you love. You just do it. "Do not waste time bothering whether you 'love' your neighbor; act as if you did. As soon as we do this we find one of the great secrets. When you are behaving as if you loved someone you will presently come to love him."[4] The same can and should be said of forgiveness. Act as if you have forgiven them and eventually you will come to forgive them. As you do, the final stages of healing for which you have this long while waited and prayed, will be realized.

Refocus:

- Think of the times in your life when you needed forgiveness. Think of the people who willingly forgave you, and even those who did not.

- Imagine yourself in your husband's shoes. Imagine him growing up under a different set of circumstances. Does this help you see him as he is and can be and not as he did?

- Begin to think, speak, and act as if you have forgiven him.

Spiritual Healing: My Personal Feelings

Religion has always played a significant role in my life and it certainly played a significant role in the recovery and healing process for my husband and me. When I felt most alone and sad, and when it seemed there was no recourse, it was my faith in Jesus Christ that lifted me and carried me. I would be ungrateful if I did not now speak to you about the many ways in which God and Jesus Christ buoyed me up during this hardship. First of all, I feel compelled to assure you that they are real. In the midst of an agonizing struggle such as this, I know that can be hard to remember or even believe. But God does exist, and he knows you. You are his child. Jesus Christ knows you too, for in the Garden of Gethsemane he suffered the pains of all humankind, including the sorrow and heartbreak you and your husband feel. It is because of this suffering, though, that he knows how to comfort you. Turn to him.

When I was first made aware of my husband's addictions, I was angry with God. Little could comfort me. I felt that my heart and my marriage had been shattered and were beyond repair. This, however, was not the case for me, and it does not have to be the case for you. For with the Lord, nothing is impossible. He overcame suffering; he can comfort you in your trials. He healed the sick; he can heal your heartache. He forgave sins; he can help you forgive the sins of others too. He created the worlds and all that are in them and on them; he can help you rebuild your world. He conquered death and took up life anew; he can breathe life into your life and into your marriage.

Why do people suffer, especially when they have done no wrong? I don't know, really. But I do know that in my suffering, I came to know God better. The excruciating hurt that I felt forced me to my knees where I called out for him to help me. And he did. You too can get the help you need; in Christ, the great physician, you can find the peace and healing you seek. But you must ask for it.

I realized early that I was not strong enough to make it on my own. When I humbled myself and sought God's help through prayer, he began, by degrees, to lift my burdens and heal my wounds. I was further strengthened so that I could bear my trials more easily. I feel now that I have made a full recovery. At the beginning, I thought I knew what healing was. I thought it would come into my life and remove from my mind and heart all memories of pain and suffering. I know now that this is not true. In my mind, I can remember the struggle; I can recall the hurt. But in my heart, peace resides. Is my heart the same as it was before? No. It is stronger. Its capacity to love has increased. In this I have found purpose. I wish I had never had to go through such an experience. But I am grateful for the person I have become and for the people I can help and have been able to help because of it.

In accordance with my faith, Christ came into the world to bind up the broken hearts and to lift up the heads that hang down. I believe he does so still. Invite him into your life. Find ways to draw near to him. Plead for his healing power. It is my promise that he will soothe and mend your broken heart and increase its capacity to love as he loves, which love has the power to heal all things.

Refocus:

- Humble yourself and stop trying to heal on your own.

- Seek healing and comfort through prayer.

- Consider studying and/or writing down your feelings about the Savior and his power to heal the brokenhearted.

Principles of Healing

A friend of ours is a physical therapist. He once explained to me the process by which physical wounds heal and the necessity of swelling and bruising during that process. When an injury occurs, fluids immediately rush to the area and surround it. The increase of these fluids causes swelling and unsightly bruises, but there is a greater purpose behind this occurrence. In addition to forming a protective cushion, these fluids also bring to the wounded area elements and minerals vital to healing. Over time, the excess of red blood cells are washed away and the swelling subsides. This is a natural process that depends on the severity of the wounds and the depth of internal bruising. If the swelling and bruising seem to last longer than they should, though, that may indicate that blockages have formed, thus preventing the excess fluids from leaving. While it is not within our power to magically make bruises disappear, we can do certain things to assist in the healing process. Applying ice right after the injury occurs has the power to prevent excessive swelling. Days later, gently massaging the bruised area or applying heat can encourage blood flow and relieve pain. In all cases, rest and the prevention of reinjury are essential. In time, moderate exercise can then be reintroduced. This is important so the muscles surrounding the injured area can regain the strength lost to injury and time.

So it is with healing in our own lives and relationships. Denial, anger, hurt, insecurity—these are natural things to feel in such a case as yours.

Yes, they may appear to be ugly, but they are a normal and a necessary part of the grieving process. Find comfort in this and let them run their course. That having been said, be careful not to continually aggravate these feelings, thus preventing the healing you desire and need. This will only enlarge the wound and increase pain. Unfortunately, it can be very difficult to realize when we are pushing too hard. In the same token, you might ask "How do I know when the emotional swelling should begin to dissipate?" "Can I do things now to alleviate the pain and increase the rate of healing?"

Time must play its part, but yes, there are things you can do. It is a personal process and will take constant effort and, to some degree, experimentation for you to discover what best helps relieve the pain and sorrow you feel. I encourage you to write down your thoughts and feelings, as well as the specific things you try and how they have helped or not helped. For me, at first, I didn't have the strength to do anything. Rest, in this case, helped prepare me for the process to come. From there, communication—with my Father in Heaven, with my husband, and with counselors—helped me deal with the pain and swelling. After a significant amount of time had passed, I was then ready to try "moderate exercise." This took the form of positive activities. I began again to do things that I had previously found joy in doing. My husband and I also began to make going on dates a priority. The joy experienced during these activities increased as we continued to do them.

If your husband has a desire to change, you have a beautiful opportunity to create a new future together. Embrace this new beginning. If you feel you are ready to expel the pain and exercise your relationship, then take time now to decide with your husband what you will do to bring a moment of joy into your relationship. Remember, as with all things along this path to recovery and healing, you may feel a need to start small. That's fine; the key is to start!

If your husband does not have the desire to change, my heart goes out to you. But you too can experience healing. The swelling may take longer to go down, but your heart can be mended. As you notice the intensity of your pain decreasing, fill the space with good things. The past cannot be altered, but your future is completely up to you. There is life after addiction and it can be wonderful!

Refocus:

- Recognize the grieving process for what it is.

- Take the time you need to rest from your emotional wounds

- Find ways to "massage" the wounds and alleviate the pain

- When ready, fill your life with joyful experiences.

38

THE END IS JUST THE BEGINNING:

A Final Word from Husband and Wife

"What we call the beginning is often the end. And to make an end is to make a beginning. The end is where we start from."[1]

IN THE BEGINNING, I WROTE THIS BOOK FOR MYSELF and for my family. It was the means to an end. I wanted to understand by way of reflection the "ins and outs" of my experience with pornography, compulsive behaviors, and recovery. More than that, though, I needed to come to terms with what I had gone through. As I did, it became clear to me that I needed to make this available to others. "I can help people," I told myself. "And if I don't do something with all of my experiences and with all of the things I've learned, then that period of my life is nothing more than a painful, secretive sixteen-year waste of time." We began passing out digital copies as requested. It did not take long for word of mouth to coax people out of their shells of secrecy in the hopes of finding comfort and guidance in our story. We have been privileged to play a small part, I think, in the recovery and healing of some men and some women. I don't know how many. I don't keep track. But even if this book has helped just one person, then writing it has been worth it to us. In them, in you, we have found purpose and comfort in suffering. We are all in this together, I often say. And we are.

In the beginning, as we set out to overhaul the book I had initially written for family, it was simply our hope and prayer that we would be able to convey what needed to be conveyed without forcing content. Not long ago, near the tail end of filling the dishwasher, I came across a few remaining unwashed dishes. Not one to let dishes sit overnight, and too lazy to take the old-fashioned approach and wash them by hand, I decided to find a way to cram them into the dishwasher. The silverware, tiny plates, and plastic cups found space easy enough. In the end, though, I came to one last dish, the glass mug. I pulled out the top rack and began easing it into place. "Don't force it," warned my wife, who had just come around the corner, "or it will break." "*Naah*," I replied confidently. "It won't break." Mere seconds later, I heard a sharp crack and watched the handle fall to the floor. We keep that broken mug on the shelf in our bedroom to remind us to be patient and not force life into the space we think it best fits. To you, we say the same thing: do not force life. Loosen your expectations. Broaden your understanding. Be humble. Be patient. Listen to each other. Help each other. And let recovery and healing happen. In the end, as you do, you will again realize the peace and love you seek.

In the beginning, there was love. "For God so loved the world that he gave his only begotten Son, that whosoever believeth in him should not perish, but have everlasting life" (John 3:16). I realize not all of you may believe as we do, but that does not mean love does not have the power to change lives. It does. We believe love, in the end, will still be there. It is out of love—love for one another and love for you—that we shared these experiences. It is our hope that, in some form or another, they have been and will continue to be a help to you as you begin this journey and as you see it to its ultimate conclusion.

In the beginning, this book ended with an entire section called "After the Conflict is Over." But we decided to cut it and disseminate the chapters elsewhere. We felt this was necessary for a number of reasons. Above all, we concluded that it was not for us to assign a definite end to this struggle. The reality is both of you, husband and wife, will spend the rest of your lives recovering and rebuilding trust. I say this not to fill your hearts with worry but to remind you that to be healthy and happy all relationships take consistent effort—from beginning to end. "Once an addict, always an addict"—personally, I do not subscribe to this philosophy. I believe hearts can change. They can become new and stronger than they once were. This does not mean you, with your restored hearts, will not come across things that tempt you because you will. We live in a world of temptation, and regardless of whether someone was once addicted or not, we must learn to conquer these temptations as they come. And this does not mean that when you do trust each other again, you will not need to continue building upon that trust. Trust, like love, needs room to grow; in fact, it is intended to grow infinitely; and it is only with the benefit of hindsight that we ever see the degree to which these feelings at the outset of our journey pale in comparison to the love and trust we feel now at the end, which is only a new beginning. The end, "the after the conflict is over" section of your life, as cliché as it may sound, is yours to write. Write it well, letter by letter, word by word.

"In the beginning was the Word, and the Word was with God, and the Word was God" (John 1:1). I find it amazing that God, the great creative genius behind the universe in which we are a small part, uses language as a metaphor for himself, deity, *Alpha* and *Omega*, the beginning and the end. There is power in the written and spoken word, and it is our hope and prayer that you have felt, at least in part, the power of the words we chose to share with you. Yes, they came as a result of our experiences, our discussions, and the incessant pecking of our fingers across the keyboard, but in the end, regardless any mistakes there may be, they are not our words. We felt inspired to write them. The message and principles are true. They can set you free. We are grateful to have been but a tool in the hands of an Author greater than ourselves.

In the beginning, I started by mentioning my grandfathers, both veterans of World War II, men who sustained injuries in war and life and healed from them, men who loved and were loved, men who were sacrificed for, and men who sacrificed for others. I am honored to carry their names. In name and deed, their legacy is mine to carry on. It is one of victory. My paternal grandpa used to say, "I always hit what I aim at." I used to think he was boasting, but I have since begun to comprehend the true principle behind this statement. No matter what we think we are aiming at, we always end up down the path toward which we were pointed all along. Apply this to your lives, to recovery, to healing, to the peace of mind and happiness toward which you strive. As you analyze your lives and make any and all changes necessary for ultimate recovery and healing to take place, we promise your aim will be true. The conflict will end. When we put our heartfelt desires at the forefront of our lives, we begin to work and sacrifice with purpose, and everything we do becomes the means to an end, certain and sure—a legacy of victory! May healing and recovery and happiness be for you that end.

A FINAL NOTE TO PARENTS AND LEADERS

"Beseech you, sir, be merry. You have cause,
So have we all, of joy, for our escape
Is much beyond our loss."[87]

NOT LONG AGO, I SAT IN FRONT OF A GROUP OF TEEN-agers to talk about pornography. They did not know it yet. After talking to the group generally, I dismissed the boys. I asked the girls if they thought pornography was a problem among the boys they associated with, including friends, brothers, and even dads. They all nodded their heads. I asked them if they saw pornography at school. They told me they stumbled upon it almost daily. "But it is not just printed images and magazines anymore," they clarified. "Kids everywhere are accessing it all around us—on laptops and desktops, on phones, tablet computers, e-readers, music devices, gaming devices"—the list goes on and on. In today's technological world, information and entertainment have never been so accessible. As a result, pornography, among other dangerous influences, is just as accessible. The girls and I then talked at some length about the need to watch out for and help the men in our lives avoid the inroads of pornography addiction. Among options discussed, participating in good entertainment, walking away from inappropriate situations, and dressing and acting appropriately were foremost mentioned. We went on to discuss this vice of pornography as it applies to women (it is not just a man's problem). Several sexually and emotionally charged books, television shows, movies, and popular songs were mentioned. "Be strong,"

I encouraged them. "Stand up for each other. Watch out for each other, and do not hesitate to speak up if you see a friend or a family member participating in something that offends you or may hurt them. It will make all the difference."

I then dismissed them, and the boys entered the room. Without wasting any time, I asked each of them to raise their hand if they had looked at pornography. Though hesitant at first, every boy in that room raised his hand, including me. This was a shock for many of them. But I was not embarrassed. I wanted them to know I understood the temptations surrounding them. "Look around," I said, "We are all in this together. You, you, me—we all raised our hands. That means this is a struggle common to us all, common to your brothers, to your friends, and to your fathers. But the point," I reiterated, "is not the struggle we have in common, but the common opportunity to help each other. Together, once and for all, we can end the conflict—starting right now."

As parents and leaders, it is our responsibility to help our children as they make their way across the pornography battlefront. If we are not aware of it already, we need to wake up to its real presence in the lives of our children. This is not to say they are looking at pornography, but it is to say they are surrounded by it. We all are—which means we are going to have to work together to avoid or get rid of its influence.

Pornography, masturbation—these subjects have been and continue to be taboo. They are the proverbial "elephant in the room" that very few people want to address or feel comfortable addressing. But this cannot be. We must start talking with our children about these things now. And by now, I mean now, today, as in after you are done with this chapter. Plan a time to talk to them about it, make it a matter of prayer if you have to, and then do it. "Son [Daughter], do you have a second? This is a bit awkward, but there's something that's been on my mind lately, a concern really, and I'd like to talk to you about it."

Now, I understand this can be an embarrassing thing to talk about—for both parent and child. But frankly, the world is not embarrassed. It is full of "teachers" eager to inform, entice, or mold your children as they see fit. If you do not talk to them about the common sexual temptations among us all, someone or something else will: television, the Internet, movies, friends, and so on.

So, parents, leaders—please talk *with* your children. Not *to* but *with* them. Discussions about pornography and masturbation need to be just that: dialogue wherein both sides speak and, perhaps most important, listen.

Too often I see parents, teachers, and ecclesiastical leaders going on and on about how bad and dangerous it is to look at pornography. *Evil, plague, disease, disgusting, perverted*—these are just some of the words that are commonly used to describe pornography and those who view it. I am not arguing the truthfulness of these descriptions—pornography, I believe, *is* the plague of our time—but I am saying that we need to be more cautious and more considerate when addressing our feelings on the subject. The reality is that most kids have already been exposed to pornography. They don't need to be lectured; they need to be understood.

In my lifetime, I've heard a lot of people talk to youth groups about pornography. "Shun it." "Don't look at it." "It will ruin your life." When I was a teenager struggling to overcome my addiction, though, these public soapbox sermons rarely inspired me to change. Instead, they left me feeling ashamed and discouraged. I did not need to be told pornography was bad or, indirectly, that I was bad. I knew it was wrong. I knew it was hurting me. And because of that what I really wanted, what I truly needed was for someone to stop talking and listen, and then to admit that they, at least in part, knew what I was going through and that there was a way to overcome it. This is important to remember. We want our children to feel comfortable coming to us and not afraid that we won't understand or that we will be angry with them.

For this to happen, though, we must be honest, caring, and considerate of their feelings. We also must be willing to sacrifice personal pride for the sake of parent-child unity. What do I mean by this? When you are talking with them, do not be afraid or ashamed to admit your own weaknesses and, when appropriate, some of the mistakes you made when you were their age. "My parents don't understand me" is a phrase so commonly uttered and felt by children that it is almost cliché. Do parents really not understand their kids? No, of course not. We understand them *and* what they are going through. "We have been there before," we often vaguely offer. Well, if we have been *there* and we have experience that might help our children, why then do we remain silent about our personal past struggles? Often, as adults, we feel like we have to be perfect or at least *appear* perfect. This, we mistakenly think, will give us the credibility we need to be revered, heard, and obeyed by our children. However, quite often the opposite is true. By purposefully omitting the "ugly" in our lives, we are, in fact, building a dishonest relationship with them. In the long run, this may only serve to alienate them and prevent them from coming to us. Think about it. We listen to and learn from those with whom we share a connection, correct? Well, our children are no different. If they do not feel connected, they will not relate to us; and if they do not relate to us, why would they come to us for help?

Imagine, on the other hand, a boy going to his father about a problem with pornography, only to hear his dad admit that it too had been a struggle for him in his youth and that it still takes effort to look away from inappropriate pictures. "And, son, if you are in a situation like that now, or if you ever find yourself battling temptations or habits you know to be wrong, I want you to know that I love you, I'm in your corner, and I stand ever ready to help. And maybe you can help me too." All of a sudden, instead of sharing a problem he thinks his dad will never understand, the son realizes that this problem is not just *his*, but everyone's, and there is a way to overcome it.

When you do this, I submit your credibility and your relationship with your children will be strengthened, not weakened. In turn, they will come to you more often, listen to you more often, and even obey your advice more often. Why? Because they will know you are honest and understanding, and that you are, in essence, just like them, and they, like you, and we are all in this together.

"Will you tell your children?" I am often asked. Yes, when the time is right. I feel it is my responsibility. But when I do have this discussion, I will not focus on the details, the pain, or the bondage of addiction; rather, by disclosing my past to them, I want them to know that no matter what, from the sins that enslave, there is a way to escape. Together, no matter the struggle, we can end the conflict now.

NOTES

Front Matter

1. Fyodor Dostoevsky, *Crime and Punishment* (New York: Bantam Books, 1981), 505.

Authors' Notes

1. William Drummond, preface to *Academical Questions*, vol. 1 (London: W. Bulmer, and Co., 1805), xv.

Introduction

1. William A. Donne.

2. Stephen E. Ambrose, *Americans at War* (New York: Berkley, 1997), 65.

3. Lincoln to J.M. Cutts, 26 October 1863, in *The Whit and Wisdom of Abraham Lincoln: A Book of Quotations*, ed. Bob Blaisdell (New York: Dover Publications, 2005), 7.

Preface: Road Map to Recovery

1. John Bunyan, *Pilgrim's Progress* (New York: Oxford University Press, 2008), 11.

2. James Allen, *As a Man Thinketh* (Avon, MA: Adams Media, 2002), 113.

Chapter 1: Defining Addiction

1. Leo Tolstoy, *War and Peace* (New York: Oxford University Press, 1998), 675.

2. Dictionary.com, s.v. "addiction," accessed January 8, 2013, http://dictionary.reference.com.

3. Jeffrey R. Holland, "Remember Lot's Wife" (speech, Brigham Young University, Provo, UT, January 13, 2009).

4. Ralph Waldo Emerson, *The Essential Writings of Ralph Waldo Emerson*, ed. Brooks Atkinson (New York: Modern Library, 2000). 135.

Chapter 2: Self-Reliance & Self-Mastery

1. *King John*, ed. Sylvan Barnet (New York: Signet Classics, 2004), 5.2.79. References are to act, scene, and line.

2. Henry David Thoreau, *Civil Disobedience: Solitude and Life without Principle* (New York: Prometheus Books, 1998), 15.

3. Martin Luther King Jr., *The Autobiography of Martin Luther King, Jr.* (New York: Warner Books, 1998), 14.

4. James Allen, *As a Man Thinketh* (Avon, MA: Adams Media, 2012), 16.

5. Ibid., 55.

6. John Newton, *Out of the Depths*, ed. Dennis R. Hillman (Grand Rapids, MI: Kregel Publications, 2003), 154.

Chapter 3: On Defining Pornography

1. Mahatma Gandhi, *The Essential Gandhi: An Anthology of His Writings on His Life, Work, and Ideas*, 2nd ed., ed. Louis Fischer (New York: Vintage, 2002), 163.

2. Paul Gerwtiz, "On 'I Know It When I See It,'" *The Yale Law Journal* 105, no. 4 (1996): 1023–47, http://www.jstor.org/stable/797245.

3. Wilford M. McClay, "Remembering Santayana," *The Wilson Quarterly* 25, no. 3 (2001): 48.

4. Howard J. Curzer, *Aristotle and the Virtues* (New York: Oxford University Press, 2012), 43.

Chapter 4: Is Pornography Adulterous?

1. John Newton, *Out of the Depths*, ed. Dennis R. Hillman (Grand Rapids, MI: Kregel Publications, 2003), 151.

Chapter 5: Where Do You Draw the Line?

1. Leo Tolstoy, *War and Peace* (New York: Oxford University Press, 1998), 462–63.

2. *Random House Webster's College Dictionary*, 2nd ed., s.v., "Pornography."

3. Friedrich Nietzsche, *The Portable Nietzsche*, ed., trans. Walter Kaufmann (New York: Penguin Group, 1982), 153.

4. C.S. Lewis, *The Screwtape Letters* (New York: Harper Collins, 2001), 60–61.

5. George Gordon Byron, "Child Harold's Pilgrimage," in *Lord Byron: The Major Works*, ed. Jerome J. McGann (New York: Oxford University Press, 2008), 110.

6. Mahatma Gandhi, *The Essential Gandhi: An Anthology of His Writings on His Life, Work, and Ideas*, 2nd ed., ed. Louis Fischer (New York: Vintage, 2002), 163.

Chapter 6: On Masturbation

1. Alan Jay Lerner and Frederick Loewe, *Camelot*, 1960.

2. Information from various sources.

3. "Talking with Your Children about Moral Purity," *Ensign*, Dec. 1986, 57.

4. Billy Graham, "What the Bible Says about Sex," *Reader's Digest*, May 1970, 118.

Chapter 7: On the Role of Curiosity

1. William Blake, "Proverbs of Hell," in *The Complete Poetry and Prose of William Blake*, ed. David V. Erdman (New York: Anchor Books, 1988), 36.

2. Mary Shelley, *Frankenstein*, ed. Stephen A. Scipione (Boston: Bedford/St. Martin's, 2000), 97.

Chapter 8: The Real Cause of Addiction

1. C.S. Lewis, *The Screwtape Letters* (New York: Harper Collins, 2001), 44.

2. "Samuel Johnson," in *The Norton Anthology of English Literature*, 8th ed., ed. Stephen Greenblatt (New York: W.W. Norton, 2006), 2064.

3. C.S. Lewis, *The Screwtape Letters* (New York: Harper Collins, 2001), 43.

Chapter 9: On Love and Reversing the Trend

1. Mitch Albom, *Tuesdays with Morrie* (New York: Broadway Books, 1997), 52.

2. Leo Tolstoy, *War and Peace* (New York: Oxford University Press, 1998), 1132.

3. Ester Rasband, *Confronting the Myth of Self-Esteem: Twelve Keys to Finding Peace* (Salt Lake City: Bookcraft, 1998), 4.

Chapter 10: On Our Initial Reaction

1. Mahatma Gandhi, *The Essential Gandhi*, 2nd ed., ed. Louis Fischer (New York: Vintage, 2002), 173.

2. Daniel Defoe, *Robinson Crusoe* (United States: Stellar Classics, 2012), 29.

Chapter 11: On Communication

1. William Blake, "The Poison Tree," in *The Complete Poetry and Prose of William Blake*, ed. David V. Erdman (New York: Anchor Books, 1988), 28.

2. Mahatma Gandhi, *The Essential Gandhi*, 2nd ed., ed. Louis Fischer (New York: Vintage, 2002), 173.

Chapter 12: When Desire Is Lacking

1. James Allen, *As a Man Thinketh* (Avon, MA: Adams Media, 2012), 113.

2. Stephen R. Covey, *The 7 Habits of Highly Effective Families* (New York: Golden Books, 1997), 35.

Chapter 13: On Marriage and Divorce

1.   William Wordsworth, "Ode ('There Was a Time')," in *William Wordsworth: Major Works*, ed. Stephen Charles Gill (New York: Oxford University Press, 2008), 302.

2.   Leonardo da Vinci, *Leonardo da Vinci: Notebooks*, comp. Irma A. Richter (New York: Oxford University Press, 2008), 308.

Chapter 15: On Evil and Hate

1.   Joseph Campbell, *The Power of Myth* (United States: Anchor Books, 1991), 199.

2.   John Newton, *Out of the Depths*, rev. Dennis R. Hillman (Grand Rapids, MI: Kregel Publications, 2003), 152.

3.   Paul Laurence Dunbar, "We Wear the Mask," in *Selected Poems*, ed. Paul Negri and Glenn Mott (United States: Dover Publications, 1997), 17–18.

Chapter 16: Threshold of Victory

1.   Abraham Lincoln, in *The Whit and Wisdom of Abraham Lincoln: A Book of Quotations*, ed. Bob Braisdell (New York: Dover Publications, 2005), 82.

2.   Paul H. Dunn, unknown source information.

3.   *Chariots of Fire,* directed by Hugh Hudson (1981; Burbank, CA: Warner Home Video, 2011), DVD.

Chapter 17: How Long Will It Take?

1.   Mother Teresa, *Where There Is Love, There Is God: A Path to Closer Union with God and Greater Love for Others* (New York: Doubleday Religion, 2010), 191.

2.   Leo Tolstoy, *War and Peace* (New York: Oxford University Press, 1998), 1149.

Chapter 18: Building a Foundation

1.   Robert Louis Stevenson, *The Amateur Emigrant* (New York: Carroll & Graf, 2002).

Chapter 20: Tell the Whole Truth

1. John Bunyan, *Pilgrim's Progress* (New York: Oxford University Press, 2008), 93.

2. Mark Twain, *Mark Twain at Your Fingertips: A Book of Quotations*, ed. Caroline Thomas Harnsberger (New York: Dover Publications, 2009), 484.

Chapter 21: It's the Little Things That Count

1. Charles Dickens, *A Christmas Carol* (United Kingdom: CRW Publishing Limited, 2004), 106.

2. Leo Tolstoy, *War and Peace* (New York: Oxford University Press, 1998), 1055.

Chapter 23: U-Turn Sacrifices

1. Sir Thomas Browne, *Religio Medici and Urne-burial,* ed. Stephen Greenblatt and Ramie Targoff (New York, NY: New York Review of Books, 2012), 82.

2. Mahatma Gandhi, *The Essential Gandhi,* ed. Louis Fischer (New York: Vintage, 2002), 155.

Chapter 24: Filling the Voids

1. Leo Tolstoy, *War and Peace* (New York: Oxford University Press, 1998), 1150.

2. Simon and Garfunkel, "The Boxer," on *Bridge Over Troubled Water* (1969; Sony Music, 2001), CD.

3. Ester Rasband, *Confronting the Myth of Self-Esteem: Twelve Keys to Finding Peace* (Salt Lake City: Bookcraft, 1998), 30.

4. Ronald L. Eisenberg, *Essential Figures in the Talmud* (United Kingdom: Jason Aronson, 2013), 89.

Chapter 25: Control Your Surroundings

1. Johann Wolfgang von Goethe, quoted in Stephen Covey, *Principle-Centered Leadership* (New York: Fireside, 1992), 59.

Chapter 26: Ever Watchful

1. James Allen, *As a Man Thinketh* (Avon, MA: Adams Media, 2012), 100.

Chapter 27: Building for Championships

1. Henry B. Eyring, "Always," *Ensign*, Oct. 1999, 9.

2. Allen, *As a Man Thinketh*, 76.

Chapter 28: Protecting Your Victory: An Analogy

1. Richard Price, quoted in Steve Pincus, *1688: The First Modern Revolution* (United States: Yale University Press, 2009), 21-22.

2. Lynn H. Nicholas, The Rape of Europa: The Fate of Europe's Treasures in the Third Reich and Second World War. (New York: Vintage Books, 1995), 54.

Chapter 29: Is the Conflict Over?

1. Olaudah Equiano, *The Interesting Narrative of the Life of Olaudah Equiano, or Gustavus Vassa, the African,* ed. Shelly Eversley (New York: Modern Library, 2004), 135.

Chapter 30: Purpose in Suffering

1. Dieter F. Uchtdorf, "Two Principles of Any Economy," *Ensign*, Nov. 2009, 58.

2. Leo Tolstoy, *War and Peace* (New York: Oxford University Press, 1998), 1050.

3. Mahatma Gandhi, *The Essential Gandhi,* ed. Louis Fischer (New York: Vintage Books, 2002), 154.

4. David Hackett Fischer, *Liberty and Freedom: A Visual History of America's Founding Ideas* (New York: Oxford University Press, 2005), 525.

Chapter 31: Preface to My Wife's Section

1. W. H. Auden, "In Memory of W. B. Yeats," in *W. H. Auden: Selected Poems*, second edition, ed. Edward Mendelson (New York: Vintage Books, 2007), 91.

2. Gandhi, *The Essential Gandhi*, 163.

Chapter 33: The Toll of Addiction

1. C. S. Lewis, *The Screwtape Letters* (New York: Harper Collins, 2001), 65.

Chapter 34: Seven Steps of Grieving

1. Casper ten Boom, quoted in Corrie ten Boom, *The Hiding Place* (Grand Rapid: Chosen Books, 2006), 60.

Chapter 36: Moving Forward

1. William Shakespeare, *The Tempest* (New York: Modern Library, 2006), 79 (Act 5, Scene 1, line 24–26). *

Chapter 37: Hope and Healing

1. Johnny Cash, quoted in Steve Turner, *The Man Called Cash: The Life, Love, and Faith of an American Legend* (Nashville: W Publishing Group, 2004), back cover.

2. Percy Bysshe Shelley, *A Defence of Poetry*, in *Percy Bysshe Shelley: Major Works* (New York: Oxford University Press, 2009), 682.

3. Corrie ten Boom, *The Hiding Place* (Grand Rapid: Chosen Books, 2006), 247.

4. C. S. Lewis, *Mere Christianity*, in *The Complete C.S. Lewis Signature Classics* (San Francisco: HarperCollins, 2002), 73.

Chapter 38: The End Is Just the Beginning

1. T. S. Eliot, "Little Gidding," in *Four Quartets* (Orlando: Harcourt, Inc., 1971), 58.

Final Notes

1. *The Tempest* Act II, Scene I, 1–8 (Gonzalo, the faithful servant)

ABOUT THE AUTHORS

WILLIAM A. AND MAE DONNE ARE THE PARENTS OF four children. Mae, a stay-at-home mom, has a passion for flowers, gardening, and nutrition. She homeschools their children. William is a business owner, writer, and public speaker. He has facilitated pornography addiction support groups and continues to act as an advisor to various groups promoting decency in the community. Both he and Mae have been able to speak with and help many individuals and couples—young and old—work through their own process of healing and recovery. With a bachelor's degree in English emphasizing creative writing, William believes in the power of the written word. In addition to writing creatively, he also spends his time teaching children and adults how to write. Both raised in Washington State, William and Mae currently reside in Idaho.

Learn more at www.ourvictories.com.